Age in the Workplace

The workforce across industrialized nations has become both older and more age-diverse, and this trend is expected to continue in the coming decades. These changes will have important implications for motivating and managing both individual employees and teams and because people are retiring later, it is important to address ways to sustain the wellbeing and productivity of workers.

With a specifically international focus, this volume addresses these critical issues from the individual and psychological perspectives. Based primarily in empirical research, it covers a wide range of topics related to the aging workforce, including the motivation of older workers – to work and to retire; what organizations can do to attract and retain the talent of older workers; how to improve relations and productivity among age-diverse teams; how to design jobs to support older and younger talent; and how to better understand why older workers may choose to return to work. This volume includes contributions from the top psychological researchers in the field of the aging workforce.

This book was originally published as a special issue of the *European Journal of Work and Organizational Psychology*.

Donald M. Truxillo is a Professor of Psychology at Portland State University in Portland, Oregon, USA and a fellow of the Society for Industrial and Organizational Psychology and the American Psychological Association. His research examines how to support workers across the worklife span through job redesign and reducing age stereotypes. His has published in leading organizational psychology journals.

Franco Fraccaroli is a Professor of Work and Organizational Psychology at Trento University, Italy. He is Past President of the European Association of Work and Organizational Psychology and Fellow of the Society for Industrial and Organizational Psychology. His research is devoted to the late career and transition to retirement and to psychosocial risks and quality of organizational life.

T0346807

Age in the Workplace
Challenges and Opportunities

Edited by
Donald M. Truxillo and Franco Fraccaroli

Routledge
Taylor & Francis Group

LONDON AND NEW YORK

First published 2015 by Routledge

2 Park Square, Milton Park, Abingdon, Oxfordshire OX14 4RN
711 Third Avenue, New York, NY 10017

Routledge is an imprint of the Taylor & Francis Group, an informa business

First issued in paperback 2018

British Library Cataloguing in Publication Data
A catalogue record for this book is available from the British Library

ISBN13: 978-1-138-78762-9 (hbk)
ISBN13: 978-1-138-37930-5 (pbk)

Typeset in Times New Roman
by Taylor & Francis Books

Publisher's Note
The publisher accepts responsibility for any inconsistencies that may have arisen during the conversion of this book from journal articles to book chapters, namely the possible inclusion of journal terminology.

Disclaimer
Every effort has been made to contact copyright holders for their permission to reprint material in this book. The publishers would be grateful to hear from any copyright holder who is not here acknowledged and will undertake to rectify any errors or omissions in future editions of this book

Contents

Citation Information

The chapters in this book were originally published in the European Journal of Work and Organizational Psychology, volume 22, issue 3 (June 2013). When citing this material, please use the original page numbering for each article, as follows:

Please direct any queries you may have about the citations to clsuk.permissions@cengage.com

Notes on Contributors

Phillip L. Ackerman, School of Psychology, Georgia Institute of Technology, Atlanta, GA, USA

P. Matthijs Bal, Department of Management and Organization, VU University Amsterdam, Amsterdam, The Netherlands

Margaret E. Beier, Department of Psychology, Rice University, Houston, TX, USA

Jemima Bidee, Department of Work & Organizational Psychology, Vrije Universiteit Brussel, Brussels, Belgium

Donatienne Desmette, Université catholique de Louvain, Belgium

Lisa M. Finkelstein, Department of Psychology, Northern Illinois University, DeKalb, IL, USA

Franco Fraccaroli, Department of Cognitive Science and Education, University of Trento, Trento, Italy

Caren B. Goldberg, Department of Management, Kogod School of Business, American University, Washington, DC, USA

H. Hoel, Manchester Business School, University of Manchester, Manchester, UK

L. Holdsworth, Manchester Business School, University of Manchester, Manchester, UK

Gert Huybrechts, Department of Applied Economics, Vrije Universiteit Brussel, Brussels, Belgium

Caroline Iweins, Université catholique de Louvain, Belgium

Marc Jegers, Department of Applied Economics, Vrije Universiteit Brussel, Brussels, Belgium

S. J. Johnson, Manchester Business School, University of Manchester, Manchester, UK

Ruth Kanfer, School of Psychology, Georgia Institute of Technology, Atlanta, GA, USA

Annet H. de Lange, Department of Work and Organizational Psychology, Radboud University Nijmegen, Nijmegen, The Netherlands

Susanne C. Liebermann, Institute of Work, Organizational and Social Psychology, Technical University Dresden, Dresden, Germany

Andreas Müller, Institute for Occupational Medicine and Social Medicine, Medical Faculty, University of Düsseldorf, Düsseldorf, Germany

Roland Pepermans, Department of Work & Organizational Psychology, Vrije Universiteit Brussel, Brussels, Belgium

Elissa L. Perry, Teachers College, Columbia University, New York, NY, USA

Amanda Shull, Department of Management, Kogod School of Business, American University, Washington, DC, USA

Florence Stinglhamber, Université catholique de Louvain, Belgium

Donald M. Truxillo, Department of Psychology, Portland State University, Portland, OR, USA

Beatrice I. J. M. Van der Heijden, Institute for Management Research, Radboud University Nijmegen, Nijmegen, The Netherlands, Open Universiteit, The Netherlands, University of Twente, Enschede, The Netherlands

Tim Vantilborgh, Department of Work & Organizational Psychology, Vrije Universiteit Brussel, Brussels, Belgium

Mo Wang, Department of Management, Warrington College of Business of Administration, University of Florida, Gainesville, USA

Jürgen Wegge, Institute of Work, Organizational and Social Psychology, Technical University Dresden, Dresden, Germany

Jurgen Willems, Department of Applied Economics, Vrije Universiteit Brussel, Brussels, Belgium

Xiang Yao, Department of Psychology, Peking University, Beijing, China

Vincent Yzerbyt, Université Catholique de Louvain, Belgium

Hannes Zacher, School of Psychology, University of Queensland, Brisbane, Australia

Sara Zaniboni, Department of Psychology and Cognitive Sciences, University of Trento, Rovereto, Italy

D. Zapf, Johann Wolfgang Goethe-University, Frankfurt, Germany

Yujie Zhan, School of Business and Economics, Wilfrid Laurier University, Waterloo, Ontario, Canada

Research themes on age and work: Introduction

Donald M. Truxillo[1] and Franco Fraccaroli[2]

[1]Department of Psychology, Portland State University, Portland, OR, USA
[2]Department of Cognitive Science and Education, University of Trento, Trento, Italy

The workforce is ageing in most industrialized countries, with people working longer and fewer younger workers entering the workforce. These trends can be attributed to a number of factors: increased lifespans and subsequent increases in the retirement age; lower birth rates; and high levels of youth unemployment, particularly in Europe. These trends have resulted in the development of a broad range of workplace challenges associated with age, such as larger numbers of older and younger people working together, organizations needing to find ways to motivate and accommodate workers across the work-life span, and the emergence of new forms of retirement such as bridge employment.

These changes have many implications for individuals, employers, governments, and societies, and they have become a focus of study in a number of academic disciplines such as economics, demography, and ergonomics. Recently, the number of age-related studies in the field of work and organizational psychology has also increased, resulting in several books, journal Special Issues, and conferences. Specifically, age has moved from being a statistical control variable in work and organizational psychology research to a central focus of study.

The development of this Special Issue originally grew from an EAWOP small group meeting on age in the workplace, expanding from there to an open call for journal articles. The results of the call were far beyond our expectations, with well over 50 formal submissions. Our goal in this editorial is to introduce the articles in this Special Issue, contextualizing them within the field of workplace ageing and giving a "bird's eye" view of the current research landscape. The articles in this Special Issue show the diversity of research that work and organizational (W/O) psychologists around the world are conducting on age and the ways in which W/O psychology can help address the challenges of an ageing and age-diverse workforce.

EXPLANATORY VARIABLES FOR CHRONOLOGICAL AGE

Chronological age is a useful variable for researchers—and useful for government and organizational decision-makers as well—because it can be easily measured. However, chronological age is in many ways simply a marker for other factors such as health, life stage, cognitive change, motivation, expectations, and generational status. There is a need to go beyond simple chronological age for a deeper understanding of what age means in the workplace and the explanatory variables underlying age. Bal, de Lange, Zacher, and Van der Heijden (this issue, 2013) do just this, digging deep into the chronological age construct to better understand the complexity of chronological age. Specifically, they look at the indirect effects of age to the extent that it represents a person's future time perspective (FTP), and how age and FTP interact with contract fulfilment to explain the employee's relationship with the organization in terms of normative and continuance commitment. Similarly, Liebermann, Wegge, and Müller (this issue, 2013) note the importance of considering younger workers specifically, and develop a variable they call *expectation of remaining in the same job until retirement* (ERSJR) using a demands–resources model. They also examine differences in blue-collar and white-collar workers and older and younger workers in terms of the determinants of ERSJR.

WHAT ARE THE DIFFERENT EXPECTATIONS, NEEDS, AND GOALS OF OLDER AND YOUNGER WORKERS?

A worker's place in the lifespan can be important for understanding his or her work motivation and what he or she wants from the job. This may be due to the physical and psychological changes that come with age as well as differences in what workers want from the work and nonwork realms. Work motivation remains central to understanding age-related differences in work behaviour and attitudes. Kanfer, Beier, and Ackerman (this issue, 2013) develop an integrative model of adult goals related to work and differentiate motivation *to work*, motivation *at work*, and motivation *to retire*. These authors also identify individual and contextual factors that may affect these goals and provide directions for future research. Vantilborgh et al. (this issue, 2013) illustrate that there may be differences in the way that older and younger persons view psychological contracts. In particular, these authors emphasize the importance of considering chronological age in order to understand the expectations of older and younger volunteers in terms of relative outcomes for the person versus the organization. Zaniboni, Truxillo, and Fraccaroli (under editor Vicente Gonzalez-Roma; this issue, 2013) used two time-lagged samples to show that older and younger workers may react differently to the same job characteristics. Interpreting their findings through the lenses of socioemotional selectivity theory and selection, optimization, and compensation theory, they found that younger workers experienced better outcomes (lower burnout and turnover intentions) with increased task variety, whereas older workers had better outcomes with increased skill variety.

ARE THERE DIFFERENCES IN SOME JOB-RELATED SKILLS AND COMPETENCIES?

Another question to consider is the strengths that people —of all ages—bring to the workplace in terms of skills and competencies. In this vein, Johnson, Holdsworth, Hoel, and Zapf (this issue, 2013) examined age differences in stress management strategies as a response to customer stressors among retail workers. Their findings suggest that older workers' use of emotional control and active coping generally had a more positive effect on emotional exhaustion and cynicism compared to younger employees. Specifically, the article shows that older workers may be more competent in managing coping strategies compared to younger workers, and that this may lead to a more positive customer experience.

HOW ARE OLDER AND YOUNGER WORKERS TREATED, AND HOW CAN WE REDUCE AGEISM AND GENERATIONAL CONFLICT?

Although the increasing age diversity of today's workforce provides opportunities for employers, it presents challenges as well. Research continues to examine how older and younger workers are perceived by each other and how to reduce stereotyping and conflict. Goldberg, Perry, Finkelstein, and Schull (this issue, 2013) take a highly practical approach to these issues by examining

which factors influence whether HR professionals target older workers in hiring. The authors identify positive organizational diversity climate and recruitment sources as factors affecting what HR professionals actually do regarding older and younger workers. Such studies on the phenomenon of age stereotyping then beg the question: What can organizations do to reduce ageism in the workplace and any generational conflict that may ensue? Iweins, Desmette, Yzerbyt, and Stinglhamber (this issue, 2013) answer this call by examining perceptions of older workers and ways to mitigate ageism at work. Across two studies, they find that intergenerational contact and an organizational multi-age perspective attenuated ageism and common stereotypes of older workers, and that procedural justice may be an explanatory factor in these effects.

RETIREMENT AND BRIDGE EMPLOYMENT

The nature of the final phases of the work-life span is evolving as workers live longer, remain healthier, and face economic challenges that require them to continue working beyond the statutory retirement age. One example is the emergence of bridge employment, or continuing work of some kind beyond retirement. Thus, understanding which workers will choose bridge employment and why they do so is a critical issue. In their article, Zhan, Wang, and Yao (this issue, 2013) differentiate "career" from "organizational" bridge employment as dependent variables, that is, bridge employment that occurs within the existing career, and bridge employment that involves working with the pre-retirement employer. Zhan et al. use the principle of compatibility and the theory of planned behaviour to show that organizational and career commitment predict career and organizational bridge employment, respectively, and that the effects of commitment are moderated by a key contextual factor, economic stress.

FUTURE RESEARCH DIRECTIONS

Each article in this Special Issue describes areas for future research. In addition, having reviewed these articles—as well as many others as a result of the call for articles—we offer a few directions for future research.

First, broadly, is research on what people of different ages want from work, what they expect from work, and what they need from work. What do older and younger people expect in terms of the relationship between their work and life spheres? How might jobs be redesigned at the micro and macro levels to best fit the needs of workers (e.g., Truxillo, Cadiz, Rineer, Zaniboni, & Fraccaroli, 2012), and how might workers craft their jobs as they age? An interesting question is how such factors might tie in with the idea of happiness and life satisfaction at different life stages (Diener & Suh, 1997). The answers to these questions are likely to be drawn from a wide range of theoretical perspectives such as motivation (e.g., Kanfer & Ackerman, 2004; Kooij, De Lange, Jansen, Kanfer, & Dikkers, 2011), adult lifespan theories (e.g., Baltes & Baltes, 1990; Carstensen, Isaacowitz, & Charles, 1999), career theory (e.g., Arthur, Hall, & Law, 1989), and models that consider the interplay of work and nonwork arenas. Comprehensive lines of research on topics such as age-related expectations of work and age-related motivation are needed (see Hertel et al., 2013).

Relatedly, much of the work thus far has been descriptive in nature, while more prescriptive research work on interventions and age is needed, such as on which HR practices benefit older and younger workers (see Kooij, Jansen, Dikkers, & de Lange, 2010). Accordingly, research is needed to provide very specific recommendations to HR professionals on how to deal with age, legally and fairly, across all HR functions, including recruitment, selection, compensation, and training.

With the increasing age diversity comes the issue of how older and younger workers are perceived by others and themselves. Specifically, what are the older worker stereotypes (Posthuma & Campion, 2009) and how might they be changing? How do older and younger workers perceive themselves—and how do they believe that others perceive them (e.g., Finkelstein, Ryan, & King, 2012). Given the demonstrated importance of age diversity climate to organizational health (Kunze, Boehm, & Bruch, 2011), how can organizations nurture a positive climate?

Research on age implies that older and younger workers differ in some essential ways: Meta-analytic research has shown that in fact there are some differences between older and younger workers on certain attitudes (Ng & Feldman, 2010) and performance dimensions (e.g., Ng & Feldman, 2008), although the stereotyped differences between the age groups are generally unsupported (Ng & Feldman, 2012). However, the explanatory mechanisms for any performance and attitude differences deserve deeper examination, including factors such as cohort, biology, career stage, and life stage. A deeper understanding of these explanatory variables (e.g., future time perspective; Zacher & Friese, 2009) could do much to enhance the performance and attitudes of older and younger workers.

Finally, improvements in health care have led to a longer lifespan, and thus the retirement age in many countries continues to drift upwards. Research that unpacks the different forms of retirement and partial retirement, their antecedents, and outcomes, can do much to benefit societies, governments, organizations, and individuals (e.g., Wang, 2007).

In conclusion, facing the issues related to the ageing workforce offers an exciting new focus for the field of work and organizational psychology, and it is imperative that we stay ahead of the curve to address this challenge. Furthermore, because of the complexities involved, we will need to be cognizant of the perspectives available from other disciplines that can help us in our work. But the consequences for workers, for employers, and for society are so significant that we must accept this challenge.

REFERENCES

Arthur, M. B., Hall, D. T., & Lawrence, B. S. (Eds.). (1989). *Handbook of career theory.* New York, NY: Cambridge University Press.

Bal, P. M., De Lange, A., Zacher, H., & van der Heijden, B. I. J. M. (2013). A lifespan perspective on psychological contracts and their relations with organizational commitment. *European Journal of Work and Organizational Psychology, 22,* 279–292.

Baltes, P. B., & Baltes, M. M. (1990). Psychological perspectives on successful aging: The model of selective optimization with compensation. In P. B. Baltes & M. M. Baltes (Eds.), *Successful aging: Perspectives from the behavioral sciences* (pp. 1–34). New York, NY: Cambridge University Press.

Carstensen, L. L., Isaacowitz, D. M., & Charles, S. T. (1999). Taking time seriously: A theory of socioemotional selectivity. *The American Psychologist, 54,* 165–181.

Diener, E., & Suh, M. E. (1997). Subjective well-being and age: An international analysis. *Annual Review of Gerontology and Geriatrics, 17,* 304–324.

Finkelstein, L. M., Ryan, K. M., & King, E. B. (2012). What do the young (old) people think of me? Content and accuracy of age-based metastereotypes. *European Journal of Work and Organizational Psychology.* doi:10.1080/1359432X.2012.673279

Goldberg, C., Perry, E., Finkelstein, L., & Schull, A. (2013). Antecedents and outcomes of targeting older applicants in recruitment. *European Journal of Work and Organizational Psychology, 22,* 265–278.

Hertel, G., Thielgen, M., Rauschenbach, C., Grube, A., Stamov-Roßnagel, C., & Krumm, S. (2013). Age differences in motivation and stress at work. In C. Schlick, E. Frieling, & J. Wegge (Eds.), *Age-differentiated work systems* (pp. 119–148). Berlin: Springer.

Iweins, C., Desmette, D., Yzerbyt, V., & Stinglhamber, F. (2013). Ageism at work: The impact of intergenerational contact and organizational multi-age perspective. *European Journal of Work and Organizational Psychology, 22,* 331–346.

Johnson, S., Holdsworth, L., Hoel, H., & Zapf, D. (2013). Customer stressors in service organisations: The impact of age on stress management and burnout. *European Journal of Work and Organizational Psychology, 22,* 318–330.

Kanfer, R., & Ackerman, P. L. (2004). Aging, work motivation, and adult development. *Academy of Management Review, 29,* 440–458.

Kanfer, R., Beier, M., & Ackerman, P. (2013). Goals and motivation related to work in later adulthood: An organizing framework. *European Journal of Work and Organizational Psychology, 22,* 253–264.

Kooij, D. T. A. M., De Lange, A. H., Jansen, P. G. W., Kanfer, R., & Dikkers, J. S. (2011). Age and work-related motives: Results of a meta-analysis. *Journal of Organizational Behavior, 32,* 197–225.

Kooij, D. T. A. M., Jansen, P. G. W., Dikkers, J. S., & De Lange, A. H. (2010). The influence of age on the associations between HR practices and both affective commitment and job satisfaction: A meta-analysis. *Journal of Organizational Behavior, 31,* 1111–1136.

Kunze, F., Boehm, S. A., & Bruch, H. (2011). Age diversity, age discrimination climate and performance consequences—a cross organizational study. *Journal of Organizational Behavior, 32,* 264–290.

Liebermann, S., Wegge, J., & Müller, A. (2013). Drivers of the expectation of remaining in the same job until retirement age: A Working Life Span Demands-Resources model. *European Journal of Work and Organizational Psychology, 22,* 347–361.

Ng, T. W. H., & Feldman, D. C. (2008). The relationship of age to ten dimensions of job performance. *Journal of Applied Psychology, 93,* 392–423.

Ng, T. W. H., & Feldman, D. C. (2010). The relationships of age with job attitudes: A meta-analysis. *Personnel Psychology, 63,* 677–718.

Ng, T. W. H., & Feldman, D. C. (2012). Evaluating six common stereotypes about older workers with meta-analytic data. *Personnel Psychology, 65,* 821–858.

Posthuma, R. A., & Campion, M. A. (2009). Age stereotypes in the workplace: Common stereotypes, moderators, and future research directions. *Journal of Management, 35,* 158–188.

Truxillo, D. M., Cadiz, D. A., Rineer, J. R., Zaniboni, S., & Fraccaroli, F. (2012). A lifespan perspective on job design: Fitting the job and the worker to promote job satisfaction, engagement, and performance. *Organizational Psychology Review, 2,* 340–360.

Vantilborgh, T., Bidee, J., Pepermans, R., Willems, J., Huybrechts, G., & Jegers, M. (2013). From "getting" to "giving": Exploring age-related differences in perceptions of and reactions to psychological contract balance. *European Journal of Work and Organizational Psychology, 22,* 293–305.

Wang, M. (2007). Profiling retirees in the retirement transition and adjustment process: Examining the longitudinal change patterns of retirees' psychological well-being. *Journal of Applied Psychology, 92,* 455–474.

Zacher, H., & Frese, M. (2009). Remaining time and opportunities at work: Relationships between age, work characteristics, and occupational future time perspective. *Psychology and Aging, 24,* 487–493.

Zaniboni, S., Truxillo, D., & Fraccaroli, F. (2013). Differential effects of task variety and skill variety on burnout and turnover intentions for older and younger workers. *European Journal of Work and Organizational Psychology, 22,* 306–317.

Zhan, Y., Wang, M., & Yao, X. (2013). Domain specific effects of commitment on bridge employment decisions: The moderating role of economic stress. *European Journal of Work and Organizational Psychology, 22,* 362–375.

Goals and motivation related to work in later adulthood: An organizing framework

Ruth Kanfer[1], Margaret E. Beier[2], and Phillip L. Ackerman[1]

[1]School of Psychology, Georgia Institute of Technology, Atlanta, GA, USA
[2]Department of Psychology, Rice University, Houston, TX, USA

Demographics of workforce aging in the developed world have spurred research on the determinants of older worker motivation to work, motivation to retire, and motivation at work. We propose an integrative framework of later adulthood goals related to work and the motivational determinants of these goals in order to better understand goal relations. We also discuss the common and unique effects of person and contextual determinants of later adulthood work-related goals and propose new directions for future research.

The changing nature of work, workers, and socio-economic conditions has spurred the emergence of a new sub-discipline in work motivation that focuses specifically on older workers, typically between the ages of 50 and 70. To date, most studies in this area have examined older worker motivation in specific contexts (e.g., pre-retirement) and for specific goals, such as job performance, skill learning, retirement, bridge retirement, and post-retirement employment (for reviews, see Czaja & Sharit, 2009; Shultz & Adams, 2007; Wang & Shultz, 2010). Results from these studies have greatly advanced knowledge and have proved useful for public policy makers and organizations.

However, studies on older worker motivation are difficult to aggregate, due in part to the variety of worker goals studied and the different points in the transition from work to non-work when these goals are studied. Further, researchers often use theories of work motivation that do not take account of older worker life circumstances or unique patterns of work-related goals associated with aging. In studies that use age-insensitive theories of work motivation, such as expectancy-value models, age-related influences are often only distinguishable in terms of the perceived attractiveness of different job rewards or job demands.

Such differences may occur in part as a consequence of age-related changes in: motives (Kooij, De Lange, Jansen, Kanfer, & Dikkers, 2011), job demands (Johnson, Mermin, & Resseger, 2011), social stereotyping by others (Bal, Reiss, Rudolph, & Baltes, 2011; Posthuma & Campion, 2009), non-work demands (Allen & Shockley, 2012; Baltes & Young, 2007), financial demands and opportunities associated with retirement (Humphrey, Costigan, Pickering, Stratford, & Barnes, 2003), worker experiences (Flynn, 2010), and retirement experiences (Taylor, Goldberg, Shore, & Lipka, 2008).

In this paper, we suggest that a comprehensive understanding of work motivation among older adults in the 21st century requires a holistic, worker-centred perspective that delineates the nature of older worker goals, their relationships over time, and the factors that influence motivation for goal accomplishments in later adulthood. For most of the 20th century, national workforce policies fostered the development of retirement age norms between the ages of 50 and 65 years, approximately a decade less than average male life expectancy. In that era, work motivation among people nearing normative retirement age was often assumed to be characterized by a decline in motivation at work, an increase in motivation to retire, and full withdrawal from the workforce following the retirement event. For many of these (mostly male) workers, leisure and coping with declining health were presumed to be the retiree's major activities after retirement.

Over the past few decades, however, there has been a radical change in the landscape. Adult life expectancies have steadily risen, so that many workers may now anticipate sufficient health for maintaining work capability two or more decades beyond traditional normative retirement age. Demographic trends and economic conditions have also changed with respect to older adult options, and evidence challenging many long-standing assumptions about older worker motivation continues to accumulate. Findings across the developed world indicate that older adult motivation and performance at work do not uniformly decline with calendar age (e.g., Gellert & Schalk, 2012; Zacher, Heusner, Schmitz, Zwierzanska, & Frese, 2010). Recent studies also show that for a growing number of workers, retirement and the end of work life are no longer closely linked (Pleau & Shauman, in press). Instead, people are working after retirement, often in arrangements that accommodate age-related and non-work-related changes in competencies, needs, and interests.

To date, research on older worker motivation has tended to focus mainly on relationships between calendar age and relatively specific outcomes, such as job satisfaction, workplace performance, or retirement. Reviews of these studies show a relatively small relationship between calendar age and job performance (Ng & Feldman, 2008), job attitudes (Ng & Feldman, 2010), and work motives (Kooij et al., 2011), at least through age 65. Such research has encouraged investigations that reframe older worker motivation less in terms of calendar age and more in terms of the psychological factors (e.g., work centrality, future time perspective), contextual factors (e.g., retirement age norms), and psycho-social factors (e.g., psychological contract breaches) that become salient in later adulthood. Consistent with this trend, a small but growing number of studies have examined determinants of older worker decisions to continue working past normative retirement age (Kim & Feldman, 1998; Pleau & Shauman, in press; Weckerle & Shultz, 1999). However, few studies have concurrently examined the relationships among goals and motivation at work, to work, and to retire as they affect one another or as they change over time.

Investigations of work-related goals and motivation at work have delineated several important person and situational determinants, such as health, finances, and work attitudes. Nonetheless, relatively little is known about the common and unique impacts of these factors across work-related goals. For example, although individuals often cite financial need, health

concerns, and the centrality of work in one's life as reasons for delaying retirement or continuing to work in later adulthood (Wang & Shultz, 2010), these factors are rarely evaluated in studies of older worker motivation *at* work. Further, although investigations of older worker motivation at work document the influence of work-unit age norms, social support, and negative age-stereotyping on older worker motivation and performance (Posthuma & Campion, 2009), there are few studies examining the functional equivalents of such factors (e.g., socio-cultural norms; age bias in hiring) in predicting retirement and post-retirement work goals and motivation.

In this paper we adopt a person-centered perspective similar to Warr (2001), Baltes, Rudolph, and Bal (2012), and Loretto and White (2006) in order to articulate the major work-related goals among older workers and to suggest potential relationships among these objectives in terms of common and unique determinants of work-related goals and motivation. Although the proposed framework represents a first step towards developing a comprehensive approach to older worker motivation, we suggest that this approach may stimulate fruitful new research directions and permit greater understanding of discontinuities, such as the high levels of motivation for early retirement followed by post-retirement employment that are increasingly observed among older workers.

AN ORGANIZING FRAMEWORK

Figure 1 presents our meta-level framework of the three broad work-related goals that are proposed to gain salience in later adulthood, their interrelations, and their major determinants. Several features of the framework warrant note. First, we emphasize work-related *goals* (i.e., at work, to work, and to retire), rather than specific work-related outcomes (job performance, retirement, and post-retirement work, respectively) in order to capture temporal relationships among salient motivational objectives for adults nearing or in the age-normative period of retirement (typically ages 50 through 65 in developed countries). For example, motivation to retire from one's current job is typically relevant prior to formal retirement. In contrast, motivation to work may wax and wane prior to and long after retirement.

Second, our framework assumes a variety of behavioral outcomes associated with each class of work-related goals. For example, motivation at work is typically indexed by the direction, intensity, and persistence of work role behaviors, such as time-on-task, organizational citizenship, and job performance (Kanfer, 2012). By contrast, retirement goals and motivation to retire may be indexed by the age at which retirement is first considered, intended retirement age, or level of retirement goal (e.g., full-time

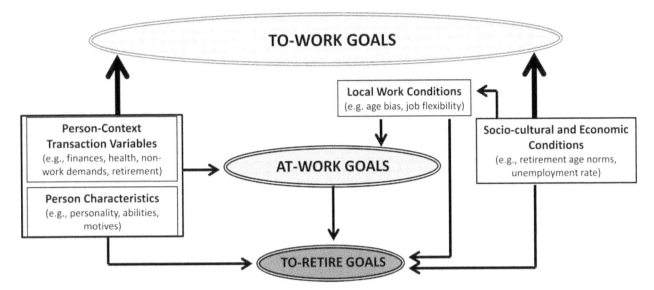

Figure 1. An organizing framework of work-related goals and their determinants in later adulthood.

retirement, part-time retirement). Indices of motivation to work have been assessed in two ways. In studies of retirement and post-retirement intentions, self-report measures assessing individual differences in work centrality and the perceived value of work for intrinsic and extrinsic outcomes are often used as proxies for motivation to work (e.g., Donaldson, Earl, & Muratore, 2010). Behavioral measures of motivation to work have also been used in research among unemployed individuals (pre- and post-retirement). Typical measures in this domain include employment outcome, measures of career exploration, and the intensity and effort devoted to job search activities (Kanfer, Wanberg, & Kantrowitz, 2002).

Third, we assume that each goal class involves a set of approach-oriented motivational processes through which individuals allocate personal resources in the form of effort, time, and capital toward motive/goal accomplishment. When more than one goal is active, such as when an individual who is motivated to retire also desires post-retirement employment, he/she must allocate resources across multiple goals. What distinguishes the three goals is the direction to which resources are allocated. *Motivation at work* pertains to cognitions, affect, and behaviors directed toward job accomplishments (either individual- or unit-level), and is often the primary focus of work motivation theorizing. *Motivation to work* pertains to cognitions, affect, and behaviors related to participation in an observable work arrangement. *Motivation to retire* pertains to exit from a current job, though the definition of retirement may vary. In general, motivation to retire refers to cognitions, affect, and behaviors directed towards exit from an existing work arrangement, career, or to total exit from the workforce (low motivation to work).

In the proposed framework we posit that patterns of motivational strength in and across the three goal classes are distinct but related, and may fluctuate over time and as a function of work experiences and personal circumstances. For example, an individual may be highly motivated at work yet adopt a retirement goal in order to obtain financial benefits offered by the organization for early retirement. In this instance, individuals may distribute attentional resources to both the work role and retirement planning. By contrast, individuals who are low in motivation at work and hold a strong retirement goal can be expected to devote fewer personal resources to the work role than individuals who maintain strong at-work goals. An interesting and practical question for future research pertains to how different goal profiles and changes prior to retirement relate to post-retirement employment and adjustment.

Fourth, the proposed relationships among work-related goals highlight the problems associated with studying determinants of retirement. As Shultz and Wang (2011) noted, the meaning and experience of retirement has substantially changed over the past two decades. Improved health and increased longevity, volatile economic conditions, changing socio-cultural norms, and insufficient worker financial resources to support non-work for longer life expectancies have reduced the previously close association between retirement and full exit from the workforce. In recognition of these new realities, we adopt Feldman's (1994) definition of retirement as "the exit from an organizational position or career path of considerable duration" (p. 287). It is also important to note that retirement is typically job-specific and is considered a singular life event. As such, a retirement goal may be accompanied by low motivation to work goals, which would likely result in complete exit from the workforce. Alternatively, a retirement goal may be accompanied by a high motivation to work goal, which would likely result in job search behavior. In our model, to-work goals represent independent, non-job-specific objectives that are posited to be determined by a different set of antecedents than retirement goals.

Fifth, we note findings by Beehr, Glazer, Nielson, and Farmer (2000) and Bidewell, Griffin, and Hesketh (2006) on retirement expectations as a function of time, to suggest that the retirement experience itself may induce co-variation in retirement and to-work goals. Consistent with the notion of retirement as a process that occurs over time, the goal of retiring from one's job is likely to become salient for many workers years prior to the retirement event. When individuals hold both at-work goals and retirement goals, they may be more likely to enter bridge employment positions that satisfy both goals. However, as the retirement event looms closer, motivation to retire may diminish and motivation to work may increase. Consistent with Wang (2007), the proposed framework also suggests that the retirement experience (as a person–context transaction influence) may promote the development of to-work goals, such as when people find that their pre-retirement expectations were unrealistic or that non-work is unsatisfying.

Summary

We propose a multi-dimensional model of motivation related to work among older adults organized around three goal classes: To-work goals, at-work goals, and to-retire goals. We posit that the salience and strength of each goal class has important implications for predicting patterns of work activity in later adulthood. In the following sections, we further describe work-related goal classes and their determinants.

WORK-RELATED GOALS IN LATER ADULTHOOD

To work

At the broadest level, to-work goals refer to purposive goals and motivation to enter into a formal or informal public work arrangement in which the individual allocates personal resources (e.g., time, attendance, mental and/or physical effort) in exchange for a portfolio of expected intrinsic (e.g., sense of competence) and/or extrinsic (e.g., pay, healthcare benefits) outcomes. We note however, that the strength of to-work goals does not typically determine allocations of effort at work, but rather indexes the individual's motivation to participate in such an exchange. Individuals engaged in an active job search, for example, may be committed and motivated to find employment, but not committed or motivated for performing many of the work activities of the job they eventually obtain. Among midlife and older adults, we conceptualize to-work goals as motivation for participation in the labour force beyond normative retirement age, in terms of full- or part-time employment, self-employment as a contractor or small business owner, and/or volunteer work.

Studies on older worker motivation to work have often focused on the reasons individuals give for working. Dendinger, Adams, and Jacobsen (2005) identified four reasons for working based on Mor-Barak's (1995) meanings of work: Social (to interact with others and obtain positive regard from others), personal (to obtain intrinsic and self-rewards), financial, and generative (to transmit knowledge to others). For many people, motivation to work involves a combination of reasons, and the respective roles of these reasons for establishing different work-related goals in later adulthood remains unclear.

Erikson's (1963) normative theory of adult development posits that motivation to work increases in importance from youth through midlife as a consequence of corresponding biological, educational, psychological, and societal forces. In early adulthood, these forces provide support for the development of new skills, high levels of job performance, and career interest as a means of attaining salient desired outcomes, such as sense of competence, social recognition, pay, and work identity. Although some young adults may deliberate whether or not to work, most must work in order to gain the financial resources to take care of themselves and to attain resources necessary to accomplishing non-work life goals (e.g., owning a home, providing for family members). Accordingly, the need to work frequently precludes the choice about whether to work in early adult life, and motivation to work among younger adults is only infrequently studied. When motivation to work is examined, it is often in the context of prolonged unemployment (e.g., Feather & O'Brien, 1986).

Although motivation to work may continue to be relatively strong through midlife for similar reasons (to obtain resources and maintain an established standard of living), lifespan theories of development and associated research by Heckhausen and Schultz (1995), Baltes and Baltes (1990), and others (Baltes et al., 2012; Furchgott, 1999) suggest that there are age-related changes in motivation to work during later adulthood. After decades of work experience, workers often possess a high level of work competence, a strong sense of self, and social networks that may, in turn, make it feasible to choose whether or not to work. In this environment of choice, findings from several studies show that individuals who perceive work as providing satisfaction of salient motives for personal development and generativity are more likely to engage in post-retirement employment. For instance, Schlosser, Zinni, and Armstrong-Stassen (2012) found that motivation to work (defined as intention to unretire) among retirees aged 50 to 70 was more likely among retirees with financial concerns, who missed aspects of their previous jobs, or who were interested in new skill learning.

To retire

Motivation to retire and motivation to work have often been viewed as different sides of the same coin. For 21st century workers, however, motivation to work and motivation to retire have distinctly different antecedents and meanings. As noted above, measures of retirement and retirement intentions typically assess the worker's exit from an existing work arrangement, rather than total work withdrawal. In countries that do not mandate retirement at a particular age, there has been a steady increase in the number of retirees who subsequently engage in post-retirement employment, suggesting that retirement goals refer to exit from the current job and not necessarily to exit from the workforce.

The definition of a retirement goal in terms of exit from a current job and/or career path, rather than the cessation of all work activity, suggests that these goals represent a unique case of turnover. Specifically, retirement refers to a life event that is often financially rewarded by the organization the worker is leaving, and encouraged by society. Retirement is often construed by the worker and the organization as the end of a career path. These unique features of retirement as a form of exit from a job often weigh heavily in the development of retirement goals and the motivation to retire.

Until recently, studies investigating the determinants of retirement intentions often failed to distinguish independently motivation to retire from one's current job and motivation to work (post-retirement). A burgeoning literature on the determinants of retirement decision-making indicates the importance of economic, psychological, and contextual variables for the motivation to retire voluntarily or accept bridge employment (see Topa, Moriano, Depolo, Alcover, & Morales, 2009; Wang & Shultz, 2010). However, far less is known about the relationship between retirement goals and to-work goals among pre-retirees.

At work

Most work motivation research focuses on the determinants and consequences of motivation in the context of performing one's work role. Theories of motivation designed to predict motivation for at-

work goals and their outcomes have emphasized the importance of person–situation interactions that occur over time (Kanfer, 2012). Formulations of motivation at work by Kanfer and Ackerman (2004) and Seo, Barrett, and Bartunek (2004) have emphasized the impact of age-related changes in abilities and affect on job self-efficacy and work attitudes. Research derived from selective optimization and compensation theory (SOC; Baltes & Baltes, 1990) has also focused on factors influencing work strategies and their effects on job performance and attitudes among older workers (Wiese, Freund, & Baltes, 2002; Zacher & Frese, 2011). Research from lifespan development theory (Carstensen, Isaacowitz, & Charles, 1999) emphasizes future time perspective (i.e., perceptions of time left at work) and work conditions (i.e., autonomy/job complexity) as they affect perceptions of opportunities at work (Zacher & Frese, 2009). Taken together, these findings indicate that at-work goals and corresponding motivation at work do not uniformly decline with calendar age, at least through age 65 or so, and that older worker goals and motivation at work are often associated with person characteristics and job demands.

Summary

The proposed framework articulates three goal classes related to work during later adulthood. We recommend that researchers attend to developing goal measures that will permit better understanding of goal inter-relations over time and the relationship of different goal profiles to work-related behaviors and retirement adjustment. For example, at-work goals and retirement goals are job-specific, though motivation at work is relevant for any work arrangement, including pre- and post-retirement work. In contrast, to-work goals are not job-specific and as such remain relevant, regardless of retirement status.

From the proposed framework we suggest several directions for future research. One promising area pertains to the relationship between motivation at work and motivation to work. We propose that to-work goals do not directly affect at-work goals, but are related in part through the common influence of person characteristics and person–context transaction antecedents. Traits such as achievement motivation, for example, may promote higher levels of motivation to work and at work. However, as shown in Figure 1, to-work goals are also influenced by socio-cultural and economic conditions, while at-work goals are most strongly influenced by local work conditions. Thus, we propose:

Proposition 1: To-work goals and motivation will be only weakly associated with at-work goals and motivation.

Findings in the employee turnover literature indicate that an individual's motivation to exit a job is negatively related to motivation at work. Older workers who are bored with their work role or who experience age-related changes that make their jobs difficult to accomplish can be expected to be less motivated at work and more likely to hold stronger retirement goals compared to workers who enjoy their jobs and maintain strong at-work goals. Thus, we propose that:

Proposition 2: At-work goals and motivation will exert a negative effect on retirement motivation and to-retire goals.

DETERMINANTS OF WORK-RELATED GOALS IN LATER ADULTHOOD

Researchers investigating determinants of work and retirement frequently organize predictor variables in terms of push (e.g., financial need, non-work demands) and pull (e.g., satisfaction of a generative motive, work centrality, to support sense of identity) factors (e.g., Beehr, 1986; Feldman, 1994). In our framework, determinants of goals and motivation related to retirement and for work are organized into three broad classes based on primary locus of origin: Within the person, the person–context transaction, and the broader external environment. Person characteristics refer to psychological characteristics and competencies that characterize adult development over the life course, such as abilities, personality, interests, and motives. Person–context transaction variables, such as financial need, health, non-work demands, and work centrality, refer to influences on work-related goals and motivation that develop over time as a consequence of the individual's life and career experiences. External determinants refer to features of the socio-cultural and macro-economic environment, such as retirement age norms and employment conditions, over which the individual often has little control, that, in turn, affect work-related goals and motivation through their effects on worker perceptions. In contrast to person–situation and push–pull organizations of older adult goal and motivational determinants, the proposed tripartite scheme allows for consideration of timescale and malleability differences associated with each antecedent class.

Person characteristics

Person characteristics refer to inter- and intra-individual differences in cognitive and non-ability attributes. Inter-individual differences in personality and motivational propensities, such as self-determination (Van den Berg, 2011), conscientiousness (Robinson, Demetre, & Corney, 2010), and affective commitment (Luchak, Pohler, & Gellatly, 2008) have been found to influence work/life transition decisions. In addition, a substantial literature indicates the existence of normative, age-related (intra-individual) changes in a wide variety of person attributes, and their relationships with work outcomes (see Kanfer & Ackerman, 2004). Although a review of these age-related changes is beyond the scope of this paper (see Ackerman, 1996; Charles & Carstensen, 2009; Salthouse, 2011; Specht, Egloff, & Schmukle, 2011), a summary of key findings is shown in Figure 2.

As shown in Figure 2, mean-level changes associated with age over the adult life course show different patterns by attribute. While some person characteristics, such as fluid intellectual abilities (novel problem solving and memory abilities) and motives related to extrinsic rewards, show gradual mean-level decline in later decades of life (Salthouse, 2011), other person characteristics such as crystallized intellectual abilities (abilities associated with the knowledge acquired through education and experience), job knowledge, conscientiousness, and emotion regulation show gradual mean-level increases, at least up to age 65–70 (see, e.g., Ebner, Freund, & Baltes,

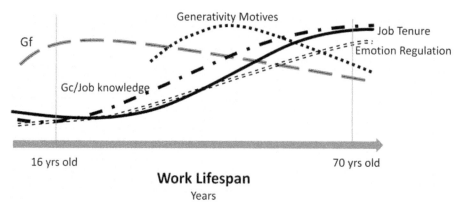

Figure 2. Age-related trends in person attributes over the work lifespan.

2006; Kooij et al., 2011; Urry & Gross, 2010). Furthermore, motives such as generativity do not emerge until midlife (Clark & Arnold, 2008; McAdams, de St. Aubin, & Logan, 1993). Although these findings do not typically distinguish inter-individual differences from cohort or cultural influences, they point to a qualitatively different, though not necessarily better or worse, portfolio of person attributes that characterize younger versus older workers.

Summary

Inter-individual differences in abilities and other traits have long been recognized as major determinants of at-work goals and motivation. Age-related changes in these characteristics may influence person–job fit, and organizational practices to modify the work role so as to improve person–job fit may mitigate age-related deterioration in person–job fit and associated declines in motivation at work. Consistent with previous findings, we posit:

Proposition 3: Person characteristics and local work conditions will interact in their influences on at-work goals and motivation.

Recent work investigating effects of inter-individual differences in select person characteristics, such as future time perspective, on older worker motivation further suggests that individual differences in traits and attitudes may exert influence on motivation to work beyond retirement. Thus, we propose:

Proposition 4: Person characteristics will exert a significant influence on older adult to-work goals and motivation.

Person–context transactions

In contrast to person characteristics, person–context transaction variables reflect the cumulative effects that an individual's life and work experiences with his/her environment have on work-related goals and motivation. Transaction variables that arise from life histories and occupational experiences include financial resources, health, non-work demands, and differences in perceived work centrality. Among older adults, the retirement transition can also be viewed as a transactional variable that affects motivation and to-work goals after retirement. Although transactional variables are influenced by unpredictable events, such as sudden changes in health due to an accident or the illness of a spouse, research suggests that these variables are also associated with relatively stable person characteristics that condition particular work and life experiences. For example, stable person

characteristics influence particular life and work experiences, which are in turn associated with later adulthood financial resources, health, work versus non-work demands, and work centrality.

Large-scale studies show that demographic and biographical person attributes such as education, occupation, and gender are associated with retirement age and patterns of workforce participation in later adulthood (Johnson et al., 2011). For example, Gower (1997) found that individuals with higher levels of education were more likely to have jobs characterized by low physical labor demands, which might lead to later retirement age goals. Similarly, a worker's occupation influences his/her financial resources, which might affect to-work goals (e.g., occupations high in job insecurity may influence perceptions of financial insecurity, which would increase motivation to work; Bildt & Michelsen, 2003).

Self-employment is an occupational variable often associated with financial insecurity, but there is evidence that goals may widely differ between self-employed individuals and employed workers. Templer, Armstrong-Stassen, and Cattaneo (2010) and Kanfer and Nguyen (2011) found that self-employed professional workers reported later age to retire goals and higher levels of motivation to continue work, compared to professional employees. It may be that the higher levels of control associated with self-employment diminish the motivational strength of retirement goals by increasing the motivational strength of at-work goals.

Indirect evidence for the importance of person–context transaction variables is also provided in findings that show that workers in physically demanding jobs or in poor health retire earlier and are more likely to exit the labour force compared to workers in less demanding jobs or in better health (Rice, Lang, Henley, & Melzer, 2011; Saure & Zoabi, 2012). Because these studies do not assess retirement, at-work, and to-work goals directly, the role of motivation in these findings remains unclear. However, the results raise important questions about the impact of occupational sector on motivation to work in later life. For example, do workers who retire early due to poor health or physical demands at work hold lower to-work goals post-retirement or do they exit the workforce due to an inability to craft a suitable work arrangement?

Research on job search among older workers also shows that person–context transaction variables, such as financial well-being, health, and non-work demands, play a role in motivation to retire and motivation to seek post-retirement work (Klehe, Koen, & De Pater, 2012; Templer et al., 2010). Studies on motivation related to work among retired and older unemployed persons are still relatively scarce, though several studies examine determinants of post-retirement work (Adams & Rau, 2004; Gobeski & Beehr, 2009; Griffin & Hesketh, 2008). The findings indicate that inadequate personal finances exert a positive influence on to-work goals, while non-work demands (e.g., caregiving) are negatively related to post-retirement employment motivation. Furthermore, descriptive studies of older adults who have experienced involuntary job lay-offs suggest that the motivational strength of to-work goals may diminish as a consequence of positive non-work experiences (e.g., hobby pursuit) and as a consequences of the difficulties associated with finding reemployment (e.g., low job search self-efficacy, emotionally distressing job search experiences).

Summary

Variables such as finances, health, and non-work demands that affect older worker motivation arise as a consequence of person–context transactions that occur over the life course. Research to date suggests that person attributes, such as education, gender, and career path influence transaction variables through the effects of these attributes on the job demands, rewards, and opportunities that older workers experience in different occupational sectors. These broad influences are hypothesized to have their primary effects on retirement goals and to-work goals, and are expected to play a lesser role in at-work goals and motivation. Thus, we propose:

Proposition 5: Person–context transaction variables, such as finances, health, and non-work demands, will be positively related to retirement goals and motivation, and goals and motivation to work.

Local work conditions

Studies have also examined the impact of work conditions, including job demands, workplace relations, supervisory support, age-diversity, age bias, and human resources practices on older worker retirement and work-related behaviors (e.g., Armstrong-Stassen, 2008; Finkelstein & Farrell, 2007; Kooij, Jansen, Dikkers, & De Lange, 2009). Research on the effects of age stereotypes held by organizations, supervisors, and co-workers and their effects on human resource management practices, work unit norms, and interpersonal treatment suggests that these factors can function as potent determinants of motivation at work and motivation to retire. Posthuma and Campion (2009) reviewed evidence for five stereotypes relevant to workplace aging: productivity, resistance to change, learning ability, tenure, and cost. They found evidence to refute the validity of the stereotypes, and ample evidence that these stereotypes exist and can be held by both younger and older employees. This internalization of age-related stereotypes can be expected to affect motivation at work negatively among older workers.

A more recent meta-analysis by Bal et al. (2011) extends the Posthuma and Campion (2009) findings by indicating the multidimensional and varied nature of perceptions held about older workers. That is, although many perceptions about older workers are negative (e.g., they are unlikely to be identified for advancement and training opportunities), there are also positive views about older workers (e.g., they are more reliable than younger workers). Potocnik, Tordera, and Peiro (2009) found that organizational pressures and group norms influenced retirement intentions. Similarly, Armstrong-Stassen and Schlosser (2010) found a positive relation between age-supportive HR practices and increased perceptions of older worker "belonging", which may lead to later retirement age intentions.

Recent findings by Weiss and Lang (2012) suggest yet another interesting impact of negative age stereotypes on motivation at work. They found that older workers seeking to maintain a positive self-concept psychologically distanced themselves from their chronological age group when negative age stereotypes were salient. The authors suggest that when negative age stereotypes are salient, the organization of work into age-diverse teams may *facilitate* rather than reduce motivation at work. Findings by Wegge, Roth, Neubach, Schmidt, and Kanfer (2008) provide additional evidence for the positive impact of age-diverse teams with respect to performance and well-being in complex, but not simple team task assignments.

A few studies have also examined the impact of organizational variables on retirement and post-retirement work motivation and intentions. Zappala, Depolo, Fraccaroli, Guglielmi, and Sarchielli (2008), Armstrong-Stassen and Ursel (2009), and Bal and Visser (2011) found that perceived organizational support for older workers had a positive impact on delaying retirement intentions. Potocnik et al. (2009) and Zaniboni, Sarchielli, and Fraccaroli (2010) found that different types of management practices influenced retirement intentions. Madvig and Shultz (2008) found that positive perceptions of the organization contributed to post-retirement work with the organization. Based on findings to date on the role of organizational policies and psychosocial variables on older worker at-work motivation and retirement goals, we posit:

Proposition 6: Local work conditions exert influence on both at-work and retirement goals and motivation.

Socio-cultural and macro-economic conditions

A growing body of research has highlighted the role that ubiquitous socio-cultural and macro-economic conditions, such as the labour market and cultural norms, play in older job search behavior (Kulik, 2000; Leppel & Clain, 1995). In contrast to both person characteristics and person–context transaction variables, socio-cultural and economic conditions represent external forces that impinge on broad segments of the workforce. For example, changes in the nature of work have highlighted the need for continuous skill learning over the work life. For older adults, the demand for job skill updating to maintain one's current job may promote the adoption of a retirement goal. At the same time, however, changes in employment opportunities across industry sectors may selectively promote to-work goals. As such, we propose:

> *Proposition 7:* Socio-cultural and macro-economic conditions have their primary impact on worker goals and motivation related to retirement and to work, but are less likely to impact at-work goals and motivation.

Summary

Socio-cultural factors and economic conditions importantly shape the milieu in which older workers develop and modify their goals to work and to retire. National laws governing retirement age and benefits, the type and availability of jobs, and cultural norms governing the role of older people are just a few examples of variables in this class of determinants that affect motivation to work and to retire. Although prior research has focused largely on the impact of these factors on motivation to retire, future research is needed to examine the extent and mechanisms by which these variables influence motivation to work after retirement.

CONCLUSIONS

We have proposed a person-centric framework that delineates three salient work goals in later adulthood: at-work goals, retirement goals, and to-work goals. We conceptualize retirement as a process that culminates with the retirement event in which an individual exits his/her current and often long-tenured position, and we distinguish to-retire goals from objectives to participate in the workforce, or to-work goals. We also proposed an expanded framework of proximal antecedents to these goal classes that distinguishes between person characteristics, variables associated with cumulative life and work experiences, and variables that characterize the socio-cultural and economic environment in which individuals function.

We proposed that the relative impact of these diverse factors on motivational goal strength among older adults differs by goal class. Consistent with prior findings, we noted that at-work goals and motivation are influenced by person attributes, the results of person–context transactions over the life course, and local work conditions. Broad socio-cultural and economic conditions are posited to exert only an indirect influence on at-work goals, through their effects on local work conditions. In contrast, socio-cultural and economic conditions are expected to exert direct influence on to-work and to-retire goals. We further suggested that older adult retirement goals are the most complexly determined goal class, requiring additional consideration of local work conditions and at-work goals and their satisfaction.

This framework highlights several directions for future research. Clearly, additional work is needed to develop valid measures of different work-related goals in later adulthood. Measures to assess strength and commitment to retirement goals should distinguish between retirement as an event, retirement as exit from the current job (turnover), and retirement in terms of workforce exit. New measures to assess to-work goals are also needed to investigate goal variability over time and the impact of different antecedents at different points in time. Measures should also be developed to evaluate the timescales associated with each goal and the anticipated outcomes of goal attainment and non-attainment.

Similarly, we suggest that there are important differences between psychological attributes that unfold primarily as a function of the life course, such as emotion regulation, and person–context transaction antecedents (e.g., health) that unfold as a function of the person's work and non-work experiences over the life course and reflect the "personal ecologies" (cf. Hobfoll, 2011) of the older worker. Although person characteristics such as education clearly play a role in subsequent person–context transactions, transaction variables such as health represent the cumulative outcomes of these transactions that act as the proximal determinants of goals related to retirement and for work. To examine this notion fully, future studies on older worker motivation will need to obtain more complete information about the individual's educational, life, and work histories.

From a practical perspective the proposed framework highlights the potential for mitigating early retirement through organizational practices that support older worker motivation at work and at-work goal satisfaction. The proposed framework also suggests that interventions to sustain motivation to work after retirement are likely to be most useful for individuals in occupations and careers that are characterized by low levels of continuous skill learning, low pay, or physically demanding work, and/or for individuals who are embedded in larger social systems that discourage workforce participation in later adulthood.

The proposed framework takes an initial step towards understanding motivation and work goals among older adults as they consider the meaning and attractiveness of their jobs, retirement, future work and non-work options, and how best to satisfy personal needs in their particular life circumstances. Consistent with growing calls for understanding older work-related goals and motivation beyond retirement, we hope that the proposed framework will stimulate new research on the dynamic relationship between to-work, at-work, and retirement goals, and the distinct roles that person characteristics, life and work histories, local work conditions, and system factors play in work motivation across the lifespan.

REFERENCES

Ackerman, P. L. (1996). A theory of adult intellectual development: Process, personality, interests, and knowledge. *Intelligence, 22,* 227–257.

Adams, G., & Rau, B. (2004). Job seeking among retirees seeking bridge employment. *Personnel Psychology, 57,* 719–744.

Allen, T. D., & Shockley, K. M. (2012). Older workers and work–family issues. In J. W. Hedge & W. C. Borman (Eds.), *The Oxford handbook of work and aging* (pp. 520–537). New York, NY: Oxford University Press.

Armstrong-Stassen, M. (2008). Organizational practices and the post-retirement employment experience of older workers. *Human Resource Management Journal, 18,* 36–53.

Armstrong-Stassen, M., & Schlosser, F. (2010). When hospitals provide HR practices tailored to older nurses, will older nurses stay? It may depend on their supervisor. *Human Resource Management Journal, 20,* 375–390.

Armstrong-Stassen, M., & Ursel, N. D. (2009). Perceived organizational support, career satisfaction, and the retention of older workers. *Journal of Occupational and Organizational Psychology, 82,* 201–220.

Bal, A. C., Reiss, A. E. B., Rudolph, C. W., & Baltes, B. B. (2011). Examining positive and negative perceptions of older workers: A meta-analysis. *Journals of Gerontology Series B: Psychological Sciences and Social Sciences, 66B,* 687–698.

Bal, P. M., & Visser, P. (2011). When are teachers motivated to work beyond retirement age? The importance of support, change of work role and money. *Educational Management Administration and Leadership, 39,* 590–602.

Baltes, B. B., Rudolph, C. W., & Bal, A. C. (2012). A review of aging theories and modern work perspectives. In J. W. Hedge & W. C. Borman (Eds.), *The Oxford handbook of work and aging* (pp. 117–136). New York, NY: Oxford University Press.

Baltes, B. B., & Young, L. M. (2007). Aging and work/family issues. In K. S. Shultz & G. A. Adams (Eds.), *Aging and work in the 21st century* (pp. 251–275). Mahwah, NJ: Lawrence Erlbaum Associates.

Baltes, P. B., & Baltes, M. M. (1990). Psychological perspectives on successful aging: The model of selective optimization with compensation. In P. B. Baltes & M. M. Baltes (Eds.), *Successful aging: Perspectives from the behavioral sciences* (pp. 1–34). New York, NY: Cambridge University Press.

Beehr, T. A. (1986). The process of retirement: A review and recommendations for future investigation. *Personnel Psychology, 39,* 31–55.

Beehr, T. A., Glazer, S., Nielson, N. L., & Farmer, S. J. (2000). Work and nonwork predictors of employees' retirement ages. *Journal of Vocational Behavior, 57,* 206–225.

Bidewell, J., Griffin, B., & Hesketh, B. (2006). Timing of retirement: Including a delay discounting perspective in retirement models. *Journal of Vocational Behavior, 68,* 368–387.

Bildt, C. & Michelsen, H. (2003). Occupational conditions exceed the importance of non-occupational conditions and ill health in explaining future unemployment among women and men. *Archives of Women's Mental Health, 6,* 115–126.

Carstensen, L. L., Isaacowitz, D. M., & Charles, S. T. (1999). Taking time seriously: A theory of socioemotional selectivity. *American Psychologist, 54,* 165–181.

Charles, S. T., & Carstensen, L. (2009). Social and emotional aging. *Annual Review of Psychology, 61,* 383–409.

Clark, M., & Arnold, J. (2008). The nature, prevalence and correlates of generativity among men in middle career. *Journal of Vocational Behavior, 73,* 473–484.

Czaja, S. J., & Sharit, J. (Eds.). (2009). *Aging and work: Issues and implications in a changing landscape.* Baltimore, MD: Johns Hopkins University Press.

Dendinger, V. M., Adams, G. A., & Jacobson, J. D. (2005). Reasons for working and their relationship to retirement attitudes, job satisfaction and occupational self-efficacy of bridge employees. *International Journal of Aging and Human Development, 61,* 21–35.

Donaldson, T., Earl, J. K., & Muratore, A. M. (2010). Extending the integrated model of retirement adjustment: Incorporating mastery and retirement planning. *Journal of Vocational Behavior, 77,* 279–289.

Ebner, N. C., Freund, A. M., & Baltes, P. B. (2006). Developmental changes in personal goal orientation from young to late adulthood: From striving for gains to maintenance and prevention of losses. *Psychology and Aging, 21,* 664–678.

Erikson, E. H. (1963). *Childhood and society.* New York, NY: W.W.Norton.

Feather, N. T., & O'Brien, G. E. (1986). A longitudinal study of the effects of employment and unemployment on school-leavers. *Journal of Occupational Psychology, 59,* 121–144.

Feldman, D. C. (1994). The decision to retire early: A review and conceptualization. *Academy of Management Review, 19,* 285–311.

Finkelstein, L. M. & Farrell, S. K. (2007). An expanded view of age bias in the workplace. In K. S. Shultz & G. A. Adams (Eds.), *Aging and work in the 21st century* (pp. 81–95). Mahwah, NJ: Lawrence Erlbaum Associates.

Flynn, M. (2010). Who would delay retirement? Typologies of older workers. *Personnel Review, 39,* 308–324.

Furchgott, E. (1999). *Aging and human motivation.* New York, NY: Kluwer Academic/Plenum.

Gellart, F. J., & Schalk, R. (2012). Age-related attitudes: The influence on relationships and performance at work. *Journal of Health Organization and Management, 26,* 98–117.

Gobeski, K. T., & Beehr, T. A. (2009). How retirees work: Predictors of different types of bridge employment. *Journal of Organizational Behavior, 30,* 401–425.

Gower, D. (1997). Measuring the age of retirement. *Statistics Canada,* Catalogue no. 75-001, 11–17.

Griffin, B., & Hesketh, B. (2008). Post-retirement work: The individual determinants of paid and volunteer work. *Journal of Occupational and Organizational Psychology, 81,* 101–121.

Heckhausen, J., & Schulz, R. (1995). A life-span theory of control. *Psychological Review, 102*, 284–304.

Hobfoll, S. E. (2011). Conservation of resource caravans and engaged settings. *Journal of Occupational and Organizational Psychology, 84*, 116–122.

Humphrey, A., Costigan, P., Pickering, K., Stratford, N., & Barnes, M. (2003). *Factors affecting the labour market participation of older workers*. Research report No. 200. London, UK: Department for Work and Pensions.

Johnson, R. W., Mermin, G. B. T., & Resseger, M. (2011). Job demands and work ability at older ages. *Journal of Aging and Social Policy, 23*, 101–118.

Kanfer, R. (2012). Work motivation: Theory, practice, and future directions. In S. W. J. Kozlowski (Ed.), *The Oxford handbook of industrial and organizational psychology* (pp. 455–495). Oxford, UK: Blackwell.

Kanfer, R., & Ackerman, P. L. (2004). Aging, adult development and work motivation. *Academy of Management Review, 29*, 440–458.

Kanfer, R., & Nguyen, J. (2011, April). *Retirement and workforce participation intentions in a down economy*. Paper presented at the 26th Annual Conference of the Society for Industrial and Organizational Psychology, Chicago, IL.

Kanfer, R., Wanberg, C., & Kantrowitz, T. M. (2001). Job search and employment: A personality–motivational analysis and meta-analytic review. *Journal of Applied Psychology, 86*, 837–855.

Kim, S., & Feldman, D. C. (1998). Healthy, wealthy, or wise: Predicting actual acceptances of early retirement incentives at three points in time. *Personnel Psychology, 51*, 623–642.

Klehe, U.-C., Koen, J., & De Pater, I. E. (2012). Ending the scrap heap? The experience of job loss and job search among older workers. In J. W. Hedge & W. C. Borman (Eds.), *The Oxford handbook of work and aging* (pp. 313–340). New York, NY: Oxford University Press.

Kooij, D. T. A. M., de Lange, A. H., Jansen, P. G. W., Kanfer, R., & Dikkers, J. S. E. (2011). Age and work-related motives: Results of a meta-analysis. *Journal of Organizational Behavior, 32*, 197–225.

Kooij, D. T. A. M., Jansen, P. G. W., Dikkers, J. S. E., & De Lange, A. H. (2009). The influence of age on the associations between HR practices and both affective commitment and job satisfaction: A meta-analysis. *Journal of Organizational Behavior, 31*, 1111–1136.

Kulik, L. (2000). Women face unemployment: A comparative analysis of age groups. *Journal of Career Development, 27*, 15–33.

Leppel, K., & Clain, S. H. (1995). The effect of increases in the level of unemployment on older workers. *Applied Economics, 27*, 901–907.

Loretto, W., & White, P. (2006). Work, more work and retirement: Older workers' perspectives. *Social Policy and Society, 5*, 495–506.

Luchak, A. A., Pohler, D. M., & Gellatly, I. R. (2008). When do committed employees retire? The effects of organizational commitment on retirement plans under a defined benefit pension plan. *Human Resource Management, 47*, 581–599.

Madvig, T. L., & Shultz, K. S. (2008). Modeling individuals' post-retirement behaviors toward their former organization. *Journal of Workplace Behavioral Health, 23*, 17–49.

McAdams, D. P., de St. Aubin, E., & Logan, R. L. (1993). Generativity among young, mid-life, and older adults. *Psychology and Aging, 8*, 221–230.

Mor-Barak, M. E. (1995). The meaning of work for older adults seeking employment: The generativity factor. *International Journal of Aging & Human Development, 41*, 325–344.

Ng, T. W. H., & Feldman, D. C. (2008). The relationship of age to ten dimensions of job performance. *Journal of Applied Psychology, 93*, 394–423.

Ng, T. W. H., & Feldman, D. C. (2010). The relationships of age with job attitudes: A meta-analysis. *Personnel Psychology, 63*, 677–718.

Pleau, R., & Shauman, K. (in press). Trends and correlates of post-retirement employment, 1977–2009. *Human Relations*. Advance online publication. Retrieved September 25, 2012. doi:10.1177/0018726712447003

Posthuma, R. A., & Campion, M. A. (2009). Age stereotypes in the workplace: Common stereotypes, moderators, and future research directions. *Journal of Management, 35*, 158–188.

Potocnik, K., Tordera, N., & Peiro, J. M. (2009). The role of human resource practices and group norms in the retirement process. *European Psychologist, 14*, 193–206.

Rice, N. E., Lang, I. A., Henley, W., & Melzer, D. (2011). Common health predictors of early retirement: Findings from the English Longitudinal Study of Aging. *Age and Ageing, 40*, 54–61.

Robinson, O. C., Demetre, J. D., & Corney, R. (2010). Personality and retirement: Exploring the links between the Big Five personality traits, reasons for retirement and the experience of being retired. *Personality and Individual Differences, 48*, 792–797.

Salthouse, T. (2011). Consequences of age-related cognitive declines. *Annual Review of Psychology, 63*, 201–226.

Saure, P., & Zoabi, H. (2012). Retirement age across countries: The role of occupations. *Swiss National Bank Working Papers, 6*, 1–54.

Schlosser, F., Zinni, D., & Armstrong-Stassen, M. (2012). Intention to unretire: HR and the boomerang effect. *Career Development International, 17*, 149–167.

Seo, M., Barrett, L. F., & Bartunek, J. M. (2004). The role of affective experience in work motivation. *Academy of Management Review, 29*, 423–439.

Shultz, K. S., & Adams, G. A. (2007). *Aging and work in the 21st century*. Mahwah, NJ: Lawrence Erlbaum Associates.

Shultz, K. S., & Wang, M. (2011). Psychological perspectives on the changing nature of retirement. *American Psychologist, 66*, 170–179.

Specht, J., Egloff, B., & Schmukle, S. C. (2011). Stability and change of personality across the life course: The impact of age and major life events on mean level and rank order stability of the Big Five. *Journal of Personality and Social Psychology, 101*, 862–882.

Taylor, M. A., Goldberg, C., Shore, L. M., & Lipka, P. (2008). The effects of retirement expectations and social support on post-retirement adjustment: A longitudinal analysis. *Journal of Managerial Psychology, 23*, 458–470.

Templer, A., Armstrong-Stassen, M., & Cattaneo, J. (2010). Antecedents of older workers' motives for continuing to work. *Career Development International, 15*, 479–500.

Topa, G., Moriano, J. A., Depolo, M., Alcover, C.-M., & Morales, J. F. (2009). Antecedents and consequences of retirement planning and decision-making: A meta-analysis and model. *Journal of Vocational Behavior, 75*, 38–55.

Urry, H. L., & Gross, J. J. (2010). Emotion regulation in older age. *Current Directions in Psychological Science, 19*, 352–357.

Van den Berg, P. T. (2011). Characteristics of the work environment related to older employees' willingness to continue working: Intrinsic motivation as a mediator. *Psychological Reports, 109*, 174–186.

Wang, M. (2007). Profiling retirees in the retirement transition and adjustment process: Examining the longitudinal change patterns of retirees' psychological well-being. *Journal of Applied Psychology, 92*, 455–474.

Wang, M., & Shultz, K. S. (2010). Employee retirement: A review and recommendation for future investigation. *Journal of Management, 36*, 172–206.

15

Warr, P. (2001). Age and work behaviour: Physical attributes, cognitive abilities, knowledge, personality traits and motives. In C. L. Cooper & I. T. Robertson (Eds.), *International review of industrial and organizational psychology* (Vol. 16, pp. 1–36). New York, NY: Wiley.

Weckerle, J. R., & Shultz, K. S. (1999). Influences on the bridge employment decision making among older USA workers. *Journal of Occupational and Organizational Psychology, 72,* 317–330.

Wegge, J., Roth, C., Neubach, B., Schmidt, K., & Kanfer, R. (2008). Age and gender diversity as determinants of performance and health in a public organization: The role of task complexity and group size. *Journal of Applied Psychology, 93,* 1301–1313.

Weiss, D., & Lang, F. R. (2012). "They" are old but "I" feel younger: Age-group dissociation as a self-protective strategy in old age. *Psychology and Aging, 27,* 153–163.

Wiese, B. S., Freund, A. M., & Baltes, P. B. (2002). Subjective career success and emotional well-being: Longitudinal predictive power of selection, optimization, and compensating. *Journal of Vocational Behavior, 60,* 321–335.

Zacher, H., & Frese, M. (2009). Remaining time and opportunities at work: Relationships between age, work characteristics and occupational future time perspective. *Psychology and Aging, 24,* 487–493.

Zacher, J., & Frese, M. (2011). Maintaining a focus on opportunities at work: The interplay between age, job complexity, and the use of selection, optimization, and compensation strategies. *Journal of Organizational Behavior, 32,* 291–318.

Zacher, H., Heusner, S., Schmitz, M., Zwierzanska, M., & Frese, M. (2010). Focus on opportunities as a mediator of the relationships between age, job complexity, and work performance. *Journal of Vocational Behavior, 76,* 374–386.

Zaniboni, S., Sarchielli, G., & Fraccaroli, F. (2010). How are psychosocial factors related to retirement intentions? *International Journal of Manpower, 31,* 271–285.

Zappala, S., Depolo, M., Fraccaroli, F., Guglielmi, D., & Sarchielli, G. (2008). Postponing job retirement? Psychosocial influences on the preference for early or late retirement. *Career Development International, 13,* 150–167.

Antecedents and outcomes of targeting older applicants in recruitment

Caren B. Goldberg[1], Elissa L. Perry[2], Lisa M. Finkelstein[3], and Amanda Shull[2]

[1]Department of Management, Kogod School of Business, American University, Washington, DC, USA
[2]Teachers College, Columbia University, New York, NY, USA
[3]Department of Psychology, Northern Illinois University, DeKalb, IL, USA

Inspired by Rynes and Barber's and Avery and McKay's theoretical work, we examined factors that influence organizations' decision to target older applicants and the influence of this decision on other recruiting strategies. Our study of two samples of HR professionals provides mixed support for these theoretical frameworks. Incumbent age and an organizational climate that rewards diversity were related to targeting older workers, whereas an ageist climate and labour market tightness were not. Further, the decision to target older applicants was related to the number of recruitment sources used and, in one sample, an emphasis on work environment benefits. However, this decision was not related to an emphasis on financial stability benefits or to recruiter age.

A sizeable number of Baby Boomers are expected to retire over the next several years, but many older workers are needing or choosing to continue working into their retirement years (AARP, 2005). Even with this trend towards an ageing workforce, a recent survey indicated that 28% of global executives thought that they needed to improve their age diversity efforts (Zimmy, 2011). Consequently, many employers will be recruiting from an increasingly older applicant pool that probably has different experience and skill configurations than younger applicant pools. A focus on older applicants seems wise, given the ageing of the working population and the experience older workers may bring to the table. As Shalla (2010) noted, however, despite rhetoric regarding changing attitudes and behaviours towards the hiring of older workers, researchers need to investigate the veracity of such changes. As organizations move towards recruiting older applicants, an understanding of the factors associated with organizational decisions to target older applicants is critical.

Although researchers have begun to explore the effectiveness of different recruitment strategies in attracting older applicants (Doverspike, Taylor, Shultz, & McKay, 2000; Fyock, 2005), we know very little about the factors that influence an employer's decision to target older workers and the implications of this decision for specific types of organizational recruitment activities (Hedge, Borman, & Lammlein, 2006). Moreover, relatively little work has been done exploring the role of age in recruitment in general (Perry & Parlamis, 2005) or the particularities of recruiting experienced individuals (Rynes, Orlitzky, & Bretz, 1997). Given that the pursuit of older applicants is likely to become an increasingly important aspect of organizational recruitment, additional research in this area is needed (Rynes & Barber, 1990). Rynes and Barber (1990) are among the few authors who have expressly theorized about recruitment from an organizational, rather than an applicant's, perspective. For that reason, we use parts of their framework as the basis for our empirical model, and we identify various theories that help us make propositions about some components of their framework. For background purposes, Figure 1 depicts Rynes and Barber's entire framework; the highlighted elements are those tested in the current study.

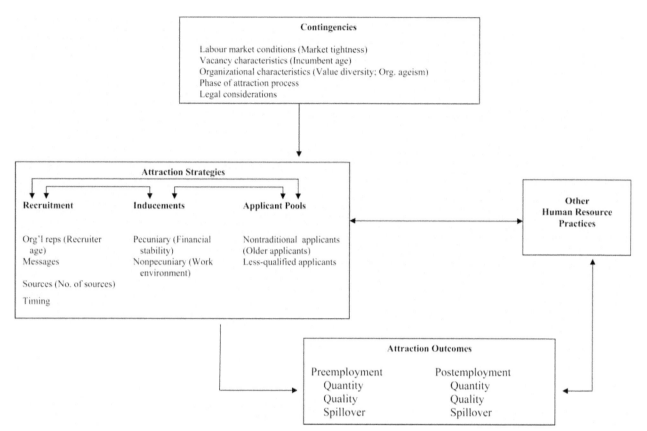

Figure 1. Rynes and Barber's (1990) model of the attraction process (highlighted variables examined in the current study).

Rynes and Barber (1990) describe nontraditional applicants as those who are less marketable than traditional applicants due to real or perceived productivity differences. Similar to other researchers (Doverspike et al., 2000), we refer to older workers as nontraditional, because they are often perceived less positively (e.g., less effective, less trainable, less potential for development) than younger applicants (Perry & Parlamis, 2005; Posthuma & Campion, 2009) and thus as less marketable. More specifically, we use the term "older" to refer to individuals who are older than the norm for a given job-type. This approach is consistent with an abundance of literature (Perry, 1994; Perry & Finkelstein, 1999) indicating that the notion of "older" is job specific. For example, a 40-year-old model may be quite old, whereas a 40-year-old senior finance officer may be quite young.

Rynes and Barber's (1990) framework suggests that characteristics of the labour market, vacancy, and organization, which they refer to as "contingencies", are likely to influence the extent to which employers target nontraditional workers in recruitment. An Organizational Impression Management (OIM) framework (Avery & McKay, 2006; Elsbach, Sutton, & Principe, 1998) suggests that organizations will take

purposeful actions to recruit nontraditional applicants. In the current study, we rely on these two theoretical frameworks to guide our investigation of the factors that influence older worker recruitment, and assess whether and how targeted recruitment influences the use of other recruitment strategies. In so doing we fill two important voids in the literature. First, although there is an abundance of studies examining attraction from the applicant's perspective, there is a dearth of empirical studies of attraction from the *organization's* perspective (Rynes et al., 1997). Second, we contribute to the very limited number of studies that examine the factors that influence employers' decisions to target older workers (Hedge et al., 2006). The few studies that exist have focused on specific subsets of older workers, such as retirees (Hirshorn & Hoyer, 1994; Rau & Adams, 2005).

In light of the limited research and theory development that has been done, we do not propose that the contingencies are related (directly or indirectly) to the targeted recruitment strategies. Rather, we are interested in determining whether the decision to target older works is associated with attraction strategies proposed by prior research and theory (Avery & McKay, 2006; Rynes & Barber, 1990).

PREDICTORS OF TARGETED OLDER WORKER RECRUITMENT

Rynes and Barber (1990) suggest that contingency variables (e.g., labour market conditions, vacancy characteristics, organizational characteristics, phase of attraction process, and legal considerations) influence the targeting of nontraditional applicant pools. We excluded phase of attraction (i.e., the stage of the recruiting process such as submitting applications, undergoing multiple interviews) because we were most interested in the overall recruitment strategy employed across stages. Further, given the lack of theory regarding the precise nature of how legal considerations might affect targeted recruitment (Rynes & Barber, 1990, p. 301), we also excluded this contingency variable.

Labour market conditions

Becker's theory of labour market discrimination (1957) holds that discrimination is a "taste or preference", but that organizations may only have the discretion to indulge this preference in a loose labour market. As labour markets are specific to jobs and/or industries, market conditions at the job and industry levels have variability and can influence recruitment strategies used, regardless of general economic conditions.

The demography literature has used similar reasoning to explain discrimination, in general, as well as age discrimination, in particular. For example, Fields, Goodman, and Blum (2005) found that the difficulty an organization had procuring and maintaining an adequate supply of human resources was positively related to the subsequent representation of Black employees. Shore and Goldberg (2005) used similar logic to develop a model of discrimination against older workers. They posited that tight labour markets increase opportunities for older workers by increasing their value both inside (through retention efforts) and outside (through recruitment efforts) the organization.

Becker's theory is also consistent with the work of recruitment researchers (Rynes & Barber, 1990) who contend that labour market conditions are apt to influence the use of more costly and risky attraction strategies. In particular, they proposed that the greater the discrepancy between supply and demand and the longer the expected duration of the labour shortage, the more likely organizations will be to use riskier recruiting strategies such as the use of nontraditional applicant pools. Therefore, we propose that:

Hypothesis 1: The tightness of the labour market will be positively related to the decision to target older applicants.

Vacancy characteristics

In the current study, we explore the vacancy characteristic, incumbent composition. Both Schema Theory (Fiske & Taylor, 1991) and Attraction–Selection–Attrition (ASA; Schneider, 1987) theory suggest that employment decisions are based on a matching process, in which raters compare information they have about a worker to information they have about a job (Goldberg, Finkelstein, Perry, & Konrad, 2004; Perry, 1994, 1997). The greater the match between these two pieces of information, the more likely the individual will be perceived as a good fit for the job.

Schema Theory (Fiske & Taylor, 1991) suggests that people have mental representations of people (e.g., applicants) and things (e.g., jobs). Perry (1994, 1997) found that decision makers make assessments of fit based on whether applicants possessed demographic characteristics (age) that are consistent with their existing stereotype for a given job (old- vs. young-typed). For example, Perry (1994) and Perry and Bourhis (1998) found that applicants whose age matched the prototypical age associated with a given job were evaluated more favourably than applicants whose age was less consistent with the job prototype. These findings are consistent with ASA theory (Schneider, 1987), which suggests that organizations attract individuals who are similar to existing organizational members. To the extent that jobs are populated by older workers, organizations are likely to see older applicants as appropriate candidates for those jobs. Ironically, organizations that have fewer older workers are less likely to reap the potential of targeting older workers and the benefits of tapping an underutilized applicant pool. We hypothesize that organizations are more likely to target older applicants in recruitment when the job is predominantly held by older incumbents.[1]

Hypothesis 2: The typical age of incumbents will be positively related to the decision to target older applicants.

Organizational characteristics

Rynes and Barber (1990) suggested that an organization's culture and values would likely influence its recruiting strategies including the extent to which it would recruit nontraditional applicants. Empirical

---

[1]As noted in the Methods section, because high-level jobs typically require more experience (which indicates an older average incumbent age), we control for the amount of vocational preparation required for the job in our analyses. Thus, the effect of incumbent age on the decision to target older workers controls for the skill and experience level associated with the given job.

evidence suggests that organizations that value diversity are likely to be perceived as particularly attractive to nontraditional applicants (Martins & Parsons, 2007; Slaughter, Sinar, & Bachiochi, 2002). Further, Rau and Adams (2005) demonstrated that firms' commitment to equal opportunity had a significant positive influence on retirees' attraction to organizations. Consistent with the OIM perspective that nontraditional recruitment results from deliberate organizational efforts (Avery & McKay, 2006), a sincere commitment to diversity, in general, and towards older workers, in particular, is apt to be associated with targeted older worker recruitment.

Valuing diversity reflects the importance ascribed to seeking and rewarding the achievement of diversity and inclusion goals, as evidenced by HR practices. For example, Gilbert and Ivancevich (2000) and Loudin (2000) suggested that rewarding those who help meet diversity-related goals is critical to fostering an organization that welcomes diversity. Such organizations are more likely to have a strong climate of inclusion and therefore to target nontraditional applicants, including older applicants across a variety of jobs.

Organizational ageism refers to the extent to which members of an organization espouse beliefs that are consistent with negative stereotypes about older workers (e.g., older workers are seen as "dead wood"). Organizational ageism may influence HR decisions through subtle or overt cues that negative stereotypes about older workers are accepted. For example, Perry and Finkelstein (1999) suggested that organizations that espouse values that are negatively associated with older workers are more likely to experience age discrimination. Consistent with this view, in a study of personnel managers and directors in the UK, Taylor and Walker (1998) found that employers seeking to recruit a greater number of older people were more likely to report positive attitudes about older workers (e.g., beliefs that older people want to train and have a lot of mileage left in them). Therefore, we hypothesize that:

Hypothesis 3a: Valuing diversity will be positively related to the decision to target older applicants.
Hypothesis 3b: Organizational ageism will be negatively related to the decision to target older applicants.

OUTCOMES OF TARGETED OLDER WORKER RECRUITMENT

The OIM perspective holds that, to be effective, the decision to target nontraditional applicants should be

followed by purposeful actions that are apt to favourably influence the target group's perception of the organization (Avery & McKay, 2006; Elsbach et al., 1998). Indeed, research on older worker attraction indicates that organizations that seek to attract older workers engage in other recruitment strategies that have been shown to be effective at attracting older applicants (Rau & Adams, 2005). However, we have little understanding about whether and how the decision to target older workers influences organizations' recruitment activities. Thus, we examine the impact of a targeted older applicant recruiting strategy on recruitment practices (choice of organizational representatives and recruitment sources used) and inducements and benefits offered.

Organizational representatives

Signalling theory suggests that to cope with the uncertainty of job choice decisions, applicants use the limited information available as signals of what the organization is really like (Highhouse, Stierwalt, Bachiochi, Elder, & Fisher, 1999). Recruiter characteristics are often used by applicants to make inferences about organizational and job characteristics and influence perceptions of person–organization fit (Rynes & Cable, 2003), which, in turn, can predict job choice intentions (Cable & Judge, 1996). Breaugh and Starke (2000) observed that recruiter demographics (e.g., female, minority recruiters) may signal to an applicant that an employer values diversity and make the job more attractive to certain candidates.

The ASA framework (Schneider, 1987) provides further support for selecting recruiting representatives that appear similar to the target population. One premise of ASA is that individuals are attracted to organizations with people that fit with their personality and values (Schneider, 1987). Applicants make a judgement about what an organization is like and whether they will be similar to the people in them based on their first contact, the recruiter.

Empirical support for applicant–recruiter similarity effects has been inconsistent (Kulik & Roberson, 2008; Rynes & Cable, 2003; Young, Place, Rinehart, Jury, & Baits, 1997). Moreover, there has been very little research specifically exploring the impact of recruiter–applicant age similarity on applicant attraction (Cable & Judge, 1996; Goldberg, 2003; Maurer, Howe, & Lee, 1992; Taylor & Bergmann, 1987). However, given the strong theoretical rationale suggesting that targeted older worker recruitment should be associated with the use of older organizational representatives, we hypothesize that:

Hypothesis 4: The decision to target older applicants will be positively related to the age of organizational representatives used in the recruitment process.

Number of recruitment sources

The applicant attraction literature indicates that recruitment sources differ in the types of applicants they produce (Rynes & Cable, 2003). Only a few studies have specifically examined reliance on different recruitment sources as a function of age. For example, Kirnan, Farley, and Geisinger (1989) found that applicants aged 40 and over tended to use self-initiated sources (e.g., walk-ins, write-ins) more than did their younger counterparts. Other researchers (Vecchio, 1995) have found that applicants hired through certain types of referrals (e.g., acquaintances) were older than those hired through other types (e.g., relatives and friends). Finally, some have suggested that specific activities such as job fairs targeting older applicants and locations (e.g., libraries) may be useful in producing older applicants (Doverspike et al., 2000; Sullivan & Duplaga, 1997; Taylor, Shultz, & Doverspike, 2005).

Although these studies suggest that these particular sources are likely to attract older workers, this literature provides little theoretical guidance regarding the specific sources. Avery and McKay (2006) noted that relying on recruitment sources that are targeted to particular groups of applicants is an effective means of ingratiating the organization with that group. Further, Nakai, Chang, Snell, and Fluckinger's (2011) study indicates that three distinct profiles of older job seekers exists; thus, a one-size-fits-all set of recruitment sources is likely inadequate. Consequently, employers that make the decision to target older applicants should cast a wider net, using recruiting sources beyond those that they use to attract traditional applicants, resulting in the use of a larger number of recruitment sources. Therefore, we hypothesize that:

Hypothesis 5: The decision to target older applicants will be positively related to the number of recruitment sources used.

Choice of inducements and benefits

Signalling Theory has primarily been used to explain the role of recruiters in the applicant attraction process, but it is likely that applicants attend to other cues as signals of whether they will be valued organizational members; as such, targeted recruitment should be related to the types of inducements and benefits offered (Rynes & Barber, 1990). One means of signalling to older candidates that they would be valued is to emphasize aspects of work most appealing to them (Doverspike et al., 2000). A study

by the Conference Board (Parkinson, 2002) found that over two-thirds of older workers indicated that financial security was a determinant of how long they intended to stay in the workforce. Concerns about social security and the changing structure of pensions make retirement planning and contributions very attractive benefits to older workers (Pitt-Catsouphes & Smyer, 2005). Additionally, the Employee Benefits Research Institute (2010) indicated that 43% of workers who planned to work in retirement reported that retaining health benefits was an important consideration in their decision. Older workers continue working past the traditional retirement age for nonfinancial reasons, as well. For example, several researchers have suggested a number of work environment benefits that are perceived as attractive to older workers, such as opportunities for mentoring (e.g., Fandray, 2000), social relationships (Fyock, 2005; Taylor et al., 2005), and satisfying work (Pitt-Catsouphes & Smyer, 2005). Consistent with these ideas, a GAO study (United States Government Accountability Office, 2005) found that employers indicated that using older workers as mentors is a key feature necessary to recruit and retain older workers. We therefore hypothesize that organizations that target older workers should be more likely to emphasize work environment benefits that are likely to be of particular interest to them (e.g., professional growth, varied work tasks, satisfying/meaningful work, friendly work environment, and opportunities to mentor others).

Hypothesis 6: The decision to target older applicants will be positively related to emphasizing (a) financial stability and (b) work environment benefits that are perceived as attractive to older applicants.

METHOD

Sample and procedure

Respondents were 374 HR professionals employed in small to medium-sized organizations who attended a training programme provided by the Council on Education in Management (CEM), an organization that provides HR and employment law training to human resource and other business professionals throughout the USA. Respondents' average age was 43.33 years ($SD = 10.49$). The majority (81.8%) were female. The racial breakdown was as follows: Caucasian = 74.9%, Asian = 1.6%, Native American = 6.0%, African-American = 9.5%, Hispanic = 4.4%, other = 3.5%. Average organizational tenure was 8.46 years ($SD = 7.90$).

We collected data from two samples drawn from the same population. Our first sample ($n = 130$)

completed paper and pencil surveys that were distributed at the conclusion of a legal update seminar. A total of 756 (response rate = 17.2%) individuals participated in the 8-hour seminars, which were held at multiple locations throughout the USA. At the conclusion of the seminar, the trainer distributed the survey along with a cover letter from the first author, then collected the completed questionnaires and sent them to the Vice-President of CEM, who sent them to the first author.

Our second sample was drawn from the same population of HR professionals who had attended a CEM training programme, but rather than complete paper surveys, they completed Web-based surveys. We defined our sampling frame for the second sample using a two-stage process. In Stage 1, the first author wrote an article on recruiting, which appeared in *HR Watch*, an electronic practitioner newsletter published by CEM. CEM provided us with a list of the email addresses of individuals who had clicked to that particular article ($n = 501$). In the second stage, we sent an email to those individuals, requesting that they follow a link to a survey on recruitment practices at their organization. Of the 501 individuals who had clicked on the article, 244 completed the survey, yielding a response rate of 48.7% for the Web survey.

Measures

The introduction to the survey instructed respondents to think about and describe a job for which they had recently recruited and answer a series of questions about this job. All of the items not specified in the following text are presented in the Appendix. Unless otherwise noted, responses were measured using a 7-point (1 = "strongly disagree", 7 = "strongly agree") scale. Some measures required different response formats, and we mixed the order of predictor and outcome items throughout the survey; these design choices were made to help eliminate some of the threat of common method bias associated with the cross-sectional methodology that we employed (Conway & Lance, 2010; Podsakoff, MacKenzie, Lee, & Podsakoff, 2003; Tourangeau, Rips, & Rasinski, 2000).

Labour market tightness. We used Fields, Chan, Akhtar, and Blum's (2006) measure of difficulty attracting labour. However, to include other aspects of the labour market that recruitment researchers (Rynes & Barber, 1990) regard as important, and to allow for a more encompassing and reliable measure of labour market conditions for the job, we added additional items to reflect the length of time needed to fill the position, the size of the applicant pool, and the perceived labour shortage that existed in the labour market for the job. An exploratory factor analysis

indicated that these items loaded (.71–.89) on a single factor, which explained 67% of the combined variance.

Typical age of incumbents. Several researchers have demonstrated that perceptual measures of age context provide more meaningful assessments than do actual chronological measures (Cleveland, Shore, & Murphy, 1997; Riordan & Wayne, 2008). Therefore, we asked respondents to indicate their perception of the typical age of job holders in an open-ended format. The average incumbent age reported was 37.42 years ($SD = 6.96$).

Organizational climate variables. We used the managing diversity factor of Hegarty and Dalton's (1995) Organizational Diversity Inventory as the basis for our valuing diversity measure. However, as two of the items ("My organization has sponsored classes, workshops, and/or seminars on managing the diverse work force" and "My company accommodates the needs of disabled persons") are more focused on what organizations *do*, as opposed to what they *value*, we replaced these items with the following: "Recruiting a diverse work force is a high priority in my organization" and "Managers' efforts at recruiting a diverse workforce are rewarded".

We also created a six-item organizational ageism measure that taps negative ageist stereotypes in the age stereotypes at work literature (e.g., Posthuma & Campion, 2009; Rosen & Jerdee, 1976), at the organizational level.

Both climate measures ask respondents for their perceptions of their organization's views (not their own), which should minimize social desirability restriction of range. Because we expected the two climate measures to represent related but distinct constructs, we provide confirmatory factor analysis results in the Results section.

Decision to target older applicants. Because of the straightforward, behavioural nature of this construct, we used a single-item measure. We asked respondents to indicate the title of a job for which they had recently recruited, and provided the following stem: "To what extent did you use each of the following strategies to fill the position you identified...?" To make age less salient, we embedded the remainder of the question, "targeted older workers", in a series of items aimed at assessing the extent to which they relied on other targeted recruitment strategies (e.g., female workers, minority workers, workers with disabilities). Responses ranged from 1 ("not at all") to 7 ("a very large extent").

Age of organizational representative. For the paper survey, we asked respondents to estimate the age of the recruiter (open-ended). The item was worded in a similar fashion for the Web survey; however, because of constraints imposed by our data collection site, respondents were asked to select from ten, 5-year ranges (e.g., 26–30, 31–35).[2] Where respondents indicated that multiple recruiters were used, we calculated the average age.

Number of recruitment sources used. Respondents indicated whether they used each of 15 recruitment sources (plus an open-ended "other" source) to fill the position they indicated. Responses to each item were coded as "no" (0) or "yes" (1). These were then summed to yield the total number of recruitment sources used.

Inducements and benefits emphasized. We asked respondents to indicate the extent (1 = "not at all", 7 = "a very large extent") to which each of eight benefits that previous researchers (Doverspike et al., 2000; Fandray, 2000; Fyock, 2005; Kindelan, 1998; Pitt-Catsouphes & Smyer, 2005; Taylor et al., 2005) have indicated are valued by older workers, was emphasized in recruiting for the position they indicated. As these items ostensibly represent two distinct sets of benefits (financial stability and work environment), we show the results of a confirmatory factor analysis in the Results section.

Control variables. Because salary competitiveness plays an important role in recruitment (Clugston, Howell, & Dorfman, 2000), we asked respondents to indicate on a 5-point scale (1 = "well below market", 5 = "well above market"), how competitive the total compensation package was for the job they indicated.

Next, as employer reputation influences applicant attraction (Cable & Turban, 2003; Rindova, Williamson, Petkova, & Sever, 2005; Turban & Cable, 2003), we included a two-item measure of organizational reputation adapted from Williams and Bauer (1994).

Additionally, organizational size is likely to influence the means by which organizations attract applicants. Thus, we asked respondents to indicate the number of employees employed by their organization (1 = "less than 100", 8 = "more than 20,000").

Finally, because recruitment strategies differ based on the level of the position being filled and because organizations are more likely to target older applicants for higher level jobs (Perry & Finkelstein, 1999), we included job level as a control variable. *O*Net* provides a measure of the amount of time required by a typical worker to learn the techniques, information, and skills needed for average performance on a job,

specific vocational preparation (SVP). Values range from 1 ("short demonstration only") to 9 ("over 10 years").

In addition, we also control for data collection method. Observations that were collected via paper surveys were coded as 0; observations that were collected via Web surveys were coded as 1.

RESULTS

Preliminary analyses

Confirmatory factor analyses were performed for (a) the climate measures, and (b) the benefit measures. Both of these analyses showed satisfactory fit to the expected two-factor structures (see Table 1 for details).

As we were working with single-source survey data, we not only attempted to prevent common method bias at the data collection stage (as described previously), but also conducted some diagnostics to look for indicators of this potential. A factor analysis of all[3] of the predictors, outcomes, and control variables in our study yielded nine factors with eigenvalues greater than one, with the first factor accounting for 15.59% of the shared variance. Thus, our data do not appear to represent a "general" factor. Further, as suggested by Lindell and Whitney (2001), for each of the hypothesized relationships that had a significant bivariate correlation, we partialled out the effects of the correlation between the criterion

TABLE 1
Confirmatory factor analysis results for climate and benefits measures

	Two-factor measurement model	*Null model*
Climate measures		
Chi square	48.25**	220.00**
Degrees of freedom	26	27
Chi-square difference	171.75**	
CFI	.97	.72
TLI	.96	.64
RMSEA	.05	.15
SRMR	.04	.11
Benefits measures		
Chi square	34.76*	145.09**
Degrees of freedom	19	20
Chi-square difference	110.33**	
CFI	.96	.79
TLI	.96	.71
RMSEA	.05	.15
SRMR	.04	.09

$n = 374$. *$p < .05$; **$p < .01$.

---

[2]We tested the hypotheses proposing effects of the decision to target older workers on other recruitment strategies for each sample separately. Therefore, these measures were not combined across the samples.

---

[3]Note that recruiter age was omitted from this analysis, because we were forced to scale it differently for the paper and Web versions of the survey.

variable and the variable with which it had the lowest correlation. In each case, the significant hypothesized correlation remained significant, after controlling for the correlation between the marker variable and the criterion. Additionally, Table 2 shows a diverse pattern of relationships with several nonsignificant correlations, which would not be the case if common method bias were present.

Finally, because our data were collected via two distinct modes, we performed t-tests to compare the means of the two samples on our variables of interest prior to testing our primary hypotheses. Results indicated that there were significant mean differences between the two samples on two of our outcomes (number of sources used [7.86 for Web vs. 7.11 for paper; $p < .01$] and emphasis on older work environment benefits [4.29 for Web vs. 3.53 for paper; $p < .01$]). Therefore, we provide the results for each sample separately for our analyses linking the decision to target older workers with other targeted recruitment strategies. As there were no significant mean differences between the groups on the variables of interest in our model predicting the decision to target older workers, we combine the samples and control for data source (Web vs. paper) for that analysis.

Tests of the hypotheses

Our first three hypotheses were tested in a single hierarchical regression equation in which the five control variables were entered in the first step, followed by the predictors in a second step. As shown in Table 3, the control variables, as a set, accounted for 2% of the variance in the decision to target older applicants. The second step, which included our predictor variables, accounted for a significant amount of additional variance (6%). However, we found mixed support for our hypotheses. H2 and H3b were supported: Average incumbent age and a climate that values diversity were significantly and positively related to the decision to target older workers. In contrast, nonsignificant coefficients on labour market tightness and organizational ageism did not support H1 or H3a.

Our remaining hypotheses predicted that the decision to target older applicants would be positively associated with the use of other targeted recruitment strategies. As our preliminary analyses showed evidence for data source effects on recruiting strategies, we performed separate analyses for the Web and paper survey sample respondents. This allowed us to assess whether the pattern of results differed as a function of data collection method. Our predictions received partial support. After accounting for the control variables, as predicted by H5, the decision to target older workers was significantly associated with

the number of recruitment sources used, $\beta = .28$; $p < .01$, in the paper sample; however, the relationship was not significant in the Web sample. The remaining hypotheses predicted that the decision to target older worker would be associated with recruiter age (H4), and increased emphasis on benefits relating to financial stability (H6a) and work environment (H6b). These were not supported.

DISCUSSION

Looking at our findings through the "big picture" lens provided by Rynes and Barber's (1990) model, there are several important take-away points. First, contingencies do, indeed, affect the decision to target older workers, though it appears that those over which organizations can exert control (incumbent age and valuing diversity) may have stronger effects than those over which they cannot (i.e., labour market conditions). Second, although we found some significant relationship between the decision to target older workers and other attraction strategies, the mixed support and generally modest effect sizes imply that organizations that wish to target older workers may not be managing their impressions with these candidates as effectively as they could be. To the extent that recruiting older workers is an important organizational strategy for acquiring future workers (Doverspike et al., 2000; Fandray, 2000), it is important to identify the factors that facilitate or impede this strategy as well as the recruitment strategies that organizations tend to use with targeted older worker recruitment. We discuss our findings more specifically next.

Predictors of targeted older worker recruitment

We found no support for a relationship between labour market tightness (H1) or organizational ageism (H3b) and the decision to target older workers. However, consistent with study hypotheses, there was a significant relationship between targeted older worker recruitment and incumbent age (H2) and valuing diversity (H3a), respectively.

Study results suggest that where current job holders are older, mature applicants are less likely to be perceived as nontraditional; therefore, there should be less resistance to pursuing them in recruitment for these jobs. This finding is consistent with research that finds that individuals are more likely to perceive a fit between younger applicants and young-typed jobs (Perry, 1994; Perry & Bourhis, 1998) and more broadly, to the Attraction–Selection–Attrition model (Schneider, 1987), which suggests that organizations attract applicants who are similar to the existing employee population. Ironically, it

TABLE 2

Means, standard deviations, and correlations among variables

Variable	1	2	3	4	5	6	7	8	9	10	11	12	13
1. Compensation	–												
2. Org. reputation	.20**	(.74)											
3. Org. size	-.04	-.03	–										
4. Job level	.11*	-.07	-.01	–									
5. Labour market tightness	.01	-.05	-.01	.20**	(.83)								
6. Incumbent age	.12*	.13*	-.05	.18**	.06	–							
7. Value diversity	.04	.39**	.04	.04	-.06	.03	(.72)						
8. Org. ageism	-.05	-.26**	.14*	.04	-.02	-.06	-.14	(.80)					
9. Target older workers	.04	.07	.10	.00	.04	.14*	.20**	-.07	–				
10. Recruiter age[1]	.11/.11	.14/-.02	-.06/-.09	.12/.06	-.08/-.01	.26**/.01	-.03/-.09	.03/.00	-.13/-.03	–			
11. No. of sources	.02	.03	.14*	-.03	.14**	-.06	.11	.01	.19**	-.11/-.12	–		
12. Financial stability benefits	.19**	.11	.12*	.18**	.05	.19*	.11	.00	.06	.20/-.01	.08	–	
13. Work environment benefits	.14*	.20**	.06	.31**	.16**	.05	.17**	-.17**	.05	.32**/.02	.21**	.30**	–
Mean	3.15	5.86	2.91	6.91	4.79	37.42	4.22	2.55	2.47	41.26/5.12	7.60	4.12	4.06
SD	0.73	1.12	1.54	1.27	1.59	6.96	1.26	1.12	1.75	9.56/2.33	3.96	1.47	1.50

n = 374.
*p < .05.
**p < .01. Reliabilities for multiitem measures are presented in parentheses along the diagonal.
[1]Due to coding differences, correlations between study variables and recruiter age are presented separately for each sample. Correlations in the paper sample (n = 130) are presented before those in the Web sample (n = 244).

TABLE 3
Results of regression analyses

	Decision to target older workers		Recruiter age[1]		No. of sources[1]		Financial stability benefits[1]		Work environment benefits[1]	
	β	ΔR^2	β	ΔR^2	β	ΔR^2	β	ΔR^2	β	ΔR^2
Step 1		.02		.04/.02		.04*/.07*		.07/.12**		.18**/.15**
Data collection method	−.06		—							
Compensation package	.02		.08/.11		−.03/.05		.21/.12		.24*/.04	
Org. reputation	−.03		.14/−.04		−.17/.12		.01/.13		.24*/.18*	
Org. size	.10		−.04/−.09		.06/.19**		−.05/.20**		.02/.09	
Job level	−.04		.12/.05		−.05/−.04		.11/.20**		.21/*.33**	
Step 2		.06**		.02/.00		.08*/.02		.00/.00		.01/.02
Labour market tightness	.04									
Incumbent age	.14*									
Valuing diversity	.19**									
Org. ageism	−.07									
Decision to target older workers			−.14/−.02		.28**/.13		.04/.03		−.10/.13	
Total R^2	.08		.06/.02		.12/.09		.07/.12		.19/.17	

$n = 374$.
*$p < .05$,
**$p < .01$,
†$p < .10$.
[1]Results exploring the impact of the decision to target older workers on recruiter age, number of sources, financial stability benefits, and work environment benefits were conducted separately for each sample. Paper sample statistics ($n = 130$) are presented before Web sample statistics ($n = 244$).

appears that organizations that stand the most to benefit from targeted older worker recruitment (in terms of increasing their diversity) are the least likely to use this strategy. These organizations may be missing a valuable source of potential employees if they overlook older applicants for jobs that are traditionally held by younger incumbents.

We argue that those responsible for developing a recruiting strategy (HR, line managers) need to be mindful to consider applicant pools whose members do not necessarily look like current job incumbents. This can be done directly by informing recruiters about their potential biases and providing them with examples of successful older workers who currently hold "younger-typed" jobs. If older applicants are recruited along with younger applicants for these jobs, the eventual incumbent demographic composition should ultimately cease to necessitate the use of a targeted recruitment strategy, as both older and younger applicants will be perceived as equally suitable for the job.

We also found that organizations that value diversity generally are more inclined to engage in the targeted recruitment of older workers. This finding is consistent with the work of researchers who have reported that targeted recruitment is more likely to be successful when the organization is truly committed to diversity (Avery & McKay, 2006; Richard & Kirby,

1998). However, we found it surprising that the more global valuing diversity measure was related to targeted older worker recruitment, whereas the more specific organizational ageism construct was not. One possible explanation for the lack of a significant effect for organizational ageism may, in part, be attributable to the fact that the organizations in our sample were not viewed as particularly ageist ($M = 2.54$, $SD = 1.12$ on a 7-point scale), thereby restricting the range of this variable. In addition, this measure captured organizations' attitudes about older individual rather than organizational strategic behaviours per se. As such, it may have been more vulnerable than the valuing diversity measure, to social desirability. By contrast, the global valuing diversity climate measure tapped organizations' behaviours related to a more general diversity climate. Consistent with this view, Rynes and Rosen (1995) found that organizations that value diversity engage in a cluster of practices and espouse a number of beliefs that support diversity, including age diversity.

Finally, we found no evidence that labour market conditions were associated with the decision to target older workers. This nonsignificant finding runs counter to Becker's (1957) view of discrimination as a function of the availability of labour. In our sample, labour market tightness was moderate ($M = 3.15$) but the variance on this variable was relatively small

($SD = 0.73$). Thus, the lack of significant labour market effects may be attributable to the fact that there was insufficient variance on market tightness across the jobs for which respondents were recruiting to detect a relationship between this variable and the targeted recruitment of older workers measure.

Outcomes of targeted older worker recruitment

Rynes and Barber's (1990) and Avery and McKay's (2006) work suggest that targeted older worker recruitment *should* be related to the age of the recruiter(s) employed, the number of recruitment sources used, and the benefits and inducements emphasized in recruitment. We were interested to learn whether this was, in fact, the case. Contrary to expectations, we found no support for a relationship between targeted older worker recruitment and age of organizational representative (H4) or emphasizing financial stability benefits (H6a). However, there was some evidence that it was significantly associated with the number of recruitment sources used (H5). That targeted recruitment was positively related to the number of recruitment sources used is encouraging, given that nontraditional applicants are less likely to come from more traditional recruiting sources. Thus, employers who want to target older applicant pools are wise to cast a wide enough net to capture other pools as well. As we noted earlier, efforts aimed at targeting a specific group are likely to be more effective when they suggest inclusiveness towards all groups.

Although our findings indicate that more recruiting sources are likely to be used, to date, very little empirical research has explicitly examined the extent to which various recruitment sources actually attract older workers. We encourage future research in this area. Nakai et al.'s (2011) work suggests that future researchers also consider that different sources may be appropriate for different categories of older job seekers (e.g., those who have to work vs. those who work for personal satisfaction and growth).

That the decision to target older applicants was unrelated to emphasizing financial stability and work environment benefits is also worth noting. Other researchers (cf. Pitt-Castouphes & Smyer, 2005; Taylor et al., 2005) have demonstrated that older candidates favour financial stability and work environment benefits; however, as with many areas in HR, there is often a significant lag between the publication of research findings and the implementation of those findings, in practice. The lack of relationship may also be due to the fact that recruiters have little flexibility in the financial benefits that they offer recruits because of their relatively high costs. Thus, organizations may not be able to afford to offer financial benefits that are likely to obligate them to costly future financial commitments (e.g., health insurance, retirement contributions).

The ASA model (Schneider, 1987), coupled with the signalling role played by recruiters (Highhouse et al., 1999; McKay & Avery, 2006) suggest that organizations wishing to target older applicants should rely more heavily on older recruiters. Contrary to expectation, there was no significant relationship between the decision to target older applicants in recruitment and the use of older recruiters. Perhaps employers understand intuitively, what some researchers have found which is that recruiter age may have limited importance in applicant attraction. Specifically, Thomas and Wise (1999) found that recruiter characteristics have less of an influence than job characteristics on job seekers. Moreover, Rynes, Heneman and Schwab (1980) suggested that job seekers with more work experience would be less influenced by recruiters. Thus, it may be that organizations do not see the age of the representative as an important element of their recruiting strategy once they have decided to target older applicants. Alternatively, it may be that organizations did not have the ability to use older organizational representatives. The organizations in the current study were small to medium-sized firms (more than two-thirds had fewer than 1000 employees). Thus, their HR departments were likely fairly small. As a result, even if an organization sought to match their representatives to the applicant pool they were targeting, it is quite possible that few viable organizational representatives were older. Future research is necessary to more fully understand when and whether applicant age similarity is effective for recruiting older applicants.

The foregoing paragraphs suggest that there are two strategies that theory and some research indicate may be important for attracting older applicants that respondents in our survey do not appear to be using: older recruiters and benefits. It is possible that organizations in our study did not have the financial or human resources needed to use these strategies or the knowledge to consider the potential benefits of such strategies. We encourage future research to explore whether these strategies are effective at recruiting older workers and encourage researchers to ensure that such findings are disseminated to the practitioner community.

Limitations and conclusions

Despite the fact that our study fills an important gap in the literature, it is not without limitations. Although we previously noted that our results do not appear to be attributable to common method bias, the fact that a single organizational respondent reported on the policies of the organization could raise a concern regarding the ability of a single person to accurately respond on behalf of the organization. However, issues concerning recruitment and climate are largely the business of the HR department, and therefore the HR professionals that comprised our sample should ostensibly be quite qualified to answer our survey questions.

Another limitation is that we cannot establish causality or rule out all alternative explanations for our results. For example, it is possible that firms make decisions at high levels to target older workers, which may lead people to believe that the organization values diversity. However, given that the respondents were HR professionals probably involved in such decisions, it seems unlikely that they interpreted the decision to target older workers for a particular job as the primary driver of the firm's more general values around diversity. Likewise, the relationship we observed between incumbent age and the decision to target older workers may reflect the fact that higher level jobs are seen as more suitable for older workers, yet this possibility seems unlikely given that our specific vocational preparation measure controls for job level.

An additional limitation of our study is that the decision to target older workers variable was a single-item measure; therefore, we cannot empirically assess the reliability of this measure. However, in contrast to complex assessments of individuals' attitudes, our measure was a very straightforward behavioural assessment of the extent to which the organization relied on a particular strategy, reducing the likelihood that there was much measurement error (Gardner, Cummings, Dunham, & Pierce, 1998; Wanous, Reichers, & Hudy, 1997).

Finally, although the current study begins to answer some important questions about the extent to which the decision to target older workers is related to the use of recruitment strategies and inducements to attract older workers, it does not address whether these strategies and inducements relate to organizational objectives. That is, the fact that respondents reported that their organizations did not use older recruiters when they made a decision to target older applicants may be based on organizations' experience that this strategy did not yield the desired results. Additional research from the organization's perspective is necessary to determine whether the strategies and inducements that older workers deem attractive actually result in increased numbers of older applicants.

Despite these limitations, this study made several contributions. By empirically testing some of the propositions offered by Rynes and Barber (1990) and Avery and McKay (2006), we add to the limited research on recruitment from the organization's perspective. In addition, by focusing on older applicant recruiting, the current study filled an important gap in the research on workforce ageing. Despite an abundance of research linking age to selection, performance, succession planning, and training, there has been a dearth of empirical research on recruitment of older applicants (Perry & Parlamis, 2005). Finally, in light of the predicted knowledge labour shortages that will occur as Baby Boomers retire (Kindelan, 1998), this study provides practical guidance for organizations needing to fill these vacancies.

REFERENCES

AARP (2005). *The business case for workers age 50+: Planning for tomorrow's talent needs in today's competitive environment.* Washington, DC: Author.

Avery, D. R., & McKay, P. F. (2006). Target practice: An organizational impression management approach to attracting minority and female job applicants. *Personnel Psychology, 59,* 157–188.

Becker, G. S. (1957). *The economics of discrimination.* Chicago, IL: University of Chicago Press.

Breaugh, J. A., & Starke, M. (2000). Research on employee recruitment: So many studies, so many remaining questions. *Journal of Management, 26,* 405–434.

Cable, D. M., & Judge, T. A. (1996). Person-organization fit, job choice decisions, and organizational entry. *Organizational Behavior and Human Decision Processes, 67,* 294–311.

Cable, D. M., & Turban, D. B. (2003). The value of organizational reputation in the recruitment context: A brand-equity perspective. *Journal of Applied Social Psychology, 33,* 2244–2266.

Cleveland, J. N., Shore, L. M., & Murphy, K. R. (1997). Person- and context-oriented perceptual age measures: Additional evidence of distinctiveness and usefulness. *Journal of Organizational Behavior, 18,* 239–251.

Clugston, M., Howell, J. P., & Dorfman, P. W. (2000). Dispositional influences on pay preferences. *Journal of Business and Psychology, 15,* 311–321.

Conway, J. M., & Lance, C. E. (2010). What reviewers should expect from authors regarding common method bias in organizational research. *Journal of Business and Psychology, 25,* 323–334.

Doverspike, D., Taylor, M. A., Shultz, K. S., & McKay, P. F. (2000). Responding to the challenge of a changing workforce: Recruiting nontraditional demographic groups. *Public Personnel Management, 29,* 445–459.

Elsbach, K. D., Sutton, R. I., & Principe, K. E. (1998). Averting expected challenges through anticipatory impression management: A study of hospital billing. *Organization Science, 9,* 68–86.

Employee Benefits Research Institute (2010). *The 2010 Retirement Confidence Survey: Confidence stabilizing, but preparations continue to erode (Issue Brief #340).* Washington, DC: Author.

Fandray, D. (2000). Gray matters. *Workforce, 79*(7), 26–31.

Fields, D., Chan, A., Akhtar, S., & Blum, T. (2006). Human resource management strategies under uncertainty: How do US and Hong Kong Chinese companies differ? *Cross Cultural Management, 13,* 171–186.

Fields, D. L., Goodman, J. S., & Blum, T. C. (2005). Human resource dependence and organizational demography: A study of minority employment in private sector companies. *Journal of Management, 31,* 167–185.

Fiske, S. T., & Taylor, S. E. (1991). *Social cognition* (2nd ed.). New York, NY: McGraw-Hill.

Fyock, C. D. (2005). Effective strategies for recruiting and retaining older workers. In P. T. Beatty & R. M. S. Visser (Eds.), *Thriving on an aging workforce: Strategies for organizational and systemic change* (pp. 51–59). Malabar, FL: Krieger Publishing.

Gardner, D. G., Cummings, L. L., Dunham, R. B., & Pierce, J. L. (1998). Single-item versus multiple-item measurement scales: An empirical comparison. *Educational and Psychological Measurement, 58,* 898–915.

Gilbert, J. A., & Ivancevich, J. M. (2000). Valuing diversity: A tale of two organizations. *Academy of Management Perspectives, 14,* 93–105.

Goldberg, C., Finkelstein, L., Perry, E., & Konrad, A. (2004). Job and industry fit: The effects of age and gender matches on career progress outcomes. *Journal of Organizational Behavior*, 25, 807–829.

Goldberg, C. B. (2003). Applicant reactions to the employment interview: A look at demographic similarity and social identity theory. *Journal of Business Research*, 56, 561–571.

Hedge, J. W., Borman, W. C., & Lammlein, S. E. (2006). *The aging workforce: Realities, myths, and implications for organizations.* Washington, DC: APA Press.

Hegarty, W. H., & Dalton, D. R. (1995). Development and psychometric properties of the organizational diversity inventory (ODI). *Educational and Psychological Measurement*, 55, 1047–1052.

Highhouse, S., Stierwalt, S. L., Bachiochi, P., Elder, A. E., & Fisher, G. (1999). Effects of advertised human resource management practices on attraction of African American applicants. *Personnel Psychology*, 52, 425–442.

Hirshorn, B. A., & Hoyer, D. T. (1994). Private sector hiring and use of retirees: The firm's perspective. *The Gerontologist*, 34, 50–58.

Kindelan, A. (1998). Older workers can alleviate labor shortages. *HR Magazine*, 43(10), 200.

Kirnan, J. P., Farley, J. A., & Geisinger, K. F. (1989). The relationship between recruiting source, applicant quality, and hire performance: An analysis by sex, ethnicity, and age. *Personnel Psychology*, 42, 293–308.

Kulik, C. T., & Roberson, L. (2008). Diversity initiative effectiveness: What organizations can (and cannot) expect from diversity recruitment, diversity training, and formal mentoring programs. In A. P. Brief (Ed.), *Diversity at work* (pp. 265–317). Cambridge, UK: Cambridge University Press.

Lindell, M. K., & Whitney, D. J. (2001). Accounting for common method variance in cross-sectional designs. *Journal of Applied Psychology*, 86, 114–121.

Loudin, A. (2000). Diversity pays. *Warehousing Management*, 7, 30–33.

Martins, L. L., & Parsons, C. K. (2007). Effects of gender diversity management on perceptions of organizational attractiveness: The role of individual differences in attitudes and beliefs. *Journal of Applied Psychology*, 92, 865–875.

Maurer, S. D., Howe, V., & Lee, T. W. (1992). Organizational recruiting as marketing management: An interdisciplinary study of engineering graduates. *Personnel Psychology*, 45, 807–833.

McKay, P. F., & Avery, D. R. (2006). What has race got to do with it? Unraveling the role of racioethnicity in job seekers' reactions to site visits. *Personnel Psychology*, 59, 395–429.

Nakai, Y., Chang, B., Snell, A., & Fluckinger, C. (2011). Profiles of mature job seekers: Connecting needs and desires to work characteristics. *Journal of Organizational Behavior*, 32, 155–173.

Parkinson, D. (2002). *Voices of experience: Mature workers in the future workforce* (Research Rep.). The Conference Board, New York, NY.

Perry, E. L. (1994). A prototype matching approach to understanding the role of applicant gender and age in the evaluation of job applicants. *Journal of Applied Social Psychology*, 24, 1433–1473.

Perry, E. L. (1997). A cognitive approach to understanding discrimination: A closer look at applicant gender and age. In G. R. Ferris (Ed.), *Research in personnel and human resources management* (Vol. 15, pp. 175–240). Greenwich, CT: JAI Press.

Perry, E. L., & Bourhis, A. C. (1998). A closer look at the role of applicant age in selection decisions. *Journal of Applied Social Psychology*, 28, 1670–1697.

Perry, E. L., & Finkelstein, L. M. (1999). Toward a broader view of age discrimination in employment-related decisions: A joint consideration of organizational factors and cognitive processes. *Human Resource Management Review*, 9, 21–49.

Perry, E. L., & Parlamis, J. D. (2005). Age and ageism in organizations: A review and consideration of national culture. In A. M. Konrad, P. Prasad, & J. K. Pringle (Eds.), *Handbook of workplace diversity* (pp. 345–370). London, UK: Sage.

Pitt-Catsouphes, M., & Smyer, M. A. (2005). *Older workers: What keeps them working?* (Issue Brief No. 01). Center on Aging and Work, Boston College, Boston, MA.

Podsakoff, P. M., MacKenzie, S. B., Lee, J., & Podsakoff, N. (2003). Common method biases in behavioral research: A critical review of the literature and recommended remedies. *Journal of Applied Psychology*, 88, 879–903.

Posthuma, R. A., & Campion, M. A. (2009). Age stereotypes in the workplace: Common stereotypes, moderators, and future research directions. *Journal of Management*, 35, 158–188.

Rau, B. L., & Adams, G. A. (2005). Attracting retirees to apply: Desired organizational characteristics of bridge employment. *Journal of Organizational Behavior*, 26, 649–661.

Richard, O. C., & Kirby, S. L. (1998). Women recruits' perceptions of workforce diversity program selection decisions: A procedural justice examination. *Journal of Applied Social Psychology*, 28, 183–188.

Rindova, V. P., Williamson, I. O., Petkova, A. P., & Sever, J. M. (2005). Being good or being known: An empirical examination of the dimensions, antecedents, and consequences of organizational reputation. *Academy of Management Journal*, 48, 1033–1049.

Riordan, C. M., & Wayne, S. H. (2008). A review and examination of demographic similarity measures used to assess relational demography within groups. *Organizational Research Methods*, 11, 562–592.

Rosen, B., & Jerdee, T. H. (1976). The influence of age stereotypes on managerial decisions. *Journal of Applied Psychology*, 62, 428–432.

Rynes, S. L., & Barber, A. E. (1990). Applicant attraction strategies: An organizational perspective. *Academy of Management Review*, 15, 286–310.

Rynes, S. L., & Cable, D. M. (2003). Recruitment research in the twenty-first century. In W. C. Borman, D. R. Ilgen, & R. J. Klimosi (Eds.), *Handbook of psychology: Industrial and organizational psychology* (Vol. 12, pp. 55–76). New York, NY: Wiley.

Rynes, S. L., Heneman, H. G., & Schwab, D. (1980). Individual reactions to organizational recruiting: A review. *Personnel Psychology*, 33, 529–542.

Rynes, S. L., Orlitzky, M. O., & Bretz, R. D., Jr. (1997). Experienced hiring versus college recruiting: Practices and emerging trends. *Personnel Psychology*, 50, 309–339.

Rynes, S., & Rosen, B. (1995). A field survey of factors affecting the adoption and perceived success of diversity training. *Personnel Psychology*, 48, 247–270.

Schneider, B. (1987). The people make the place. *Personnel Psychology*, 40, 437–454.

Shalla, V. (2010). Ageing labour forces: Promises and prospects. *Labour*, 65, 248–251.

Shore, L. M., & Goldberg, C. B. (2005). Age discrimination in the workplace. In R. L. Dipboye & A. Colella (Eds.), *Psychological and organizational bases of discrimination at work* (SIOP Frontiers Series, pp. 203–225). Mahwah, NJ: Lawrence Erlbaum Associates, Inc.

Slaughter, J. E., Sinar, E. F., & Bachiochi, P. D. (2002). Black applicants' reactions to affirmative action plans: Effects of plan content and previous experience with discrimination. *Journal of Applied Psychology*, 87, 333–344.

Sullivan, S. E., & Duplaga, E. A. (1997). Recruiting and retaining older workers for the new millennium. *Business Horizons*, 40(6), 65–69.

Taylor, M., & Bergmann, T. (1987). Organizational recruitment activities and applicants' reactions at different stages of the recruitment process. *Personnel Psychology*, 40, 261–285.

Taylor, M. A., Shultz, K. S., & Doverspike, D. (2005). Academic perspectives on recruiting and retaining older workers. In P. T. Beatty & R. M. S. Visser (Eds.), *Thriving on an aging workforce: Strategies for organizational and systemic change* (pp. 1697–1725). Malabar, FL: Krieger Publishing.

Taylor, P., & Walker, A. (1998). Employers and older workers: Attitudes and employment practices. *Ageing and Society, 18*, 641–658.

Thomas, K. M., & Wise, P. G. (1999). Organizational attractiveness and individual differences: Are diverse applicants attracted by different factors? *Journal of Business and Psychology, 13*, 375–390.

Tourangeau, R., Rips, L. J., & Rasinski, K. (2000). *The psychology of survey response.* Cambridge, UK: Cambridge University Press.

Turban, D. B., & Cable, D. M. (2003). Firm reputation and applicant pool characteristics. *Journal of Organizational Behavior, 24*, 733–751.

United States Government Accountability Office. (2005). *Older workers: Labor can help employers and employees plan better for the future* (GAO Publication No. 06-80). Washington, DC: Author.

Vecchio, R. P. (1995). The impact of referral sources on employee attitudes: Evidence from a national sample. *Journal of Management, 21*, 953–965.

Wanous, J. P., Reichers, A. E., & Hudy, M. J. (1997). Overall job satisfaction: How good are single-item measures? *Journal of Applied Psychology, 82*, 247–252.

Williams, M. L., & Bauer, T. N. (1994). The effect of a managing diversity policy on organizational attractiveness. *Group and Organization Management, 19*, 295–308.

Young, I. P., Place, A. W., Rinehart, J. S., Jury, J. C., & Baits, D. F. (1997). Teacher recruitment: A test of the similarity-attraction hypothesis for race and sex. *Education Administration Quarterly, 33*, 86–106.

Zimmy, F. (2011). Fostering innovation through a diverse workforce. *Forbes*, July 19. Retrieved from www.slideshare.net/fred.../forbes-innovation-through-diversity

APPENDIX: SURVEY MEASURES

Labour market tightness (1–7 agreement)

1. It took a long time to fill this position.
2. There was a large pool of applicants from which to choose.
3. It was difficult to find applicants qualified to fill this position.
4. There was a large shortage in the labour market for this job.

Organizational ageism (1–7 agreement)

1. Many people in my organization subscribe to the view that you can't teach an old dog new tricks.
2. In my organization, older workers are seen as less capable of adapting to changes in the work environment.
3. In my organization, older employees are viewed as being "dead wood".
4. My organization views investments in older workers as unlikely to yield a return.
5. In my organization, older workers are generally viewed as more technologically obsolete than younger workers.
6. When training opportunities arise in this organization, they are usually given to younger employees.

Valuing diversity (1–7 agreement)

1. Recruiting a diverse work force is a high priority in my organization.
2. Managers' efforts at recruiting a diverse workforce are rewarded.
3. Managing diversity has helped my organization become more effective.

Recruitment sources used (0/1 summative scale)

1. Organization's Web site (external)
2. Referral from current employees
3. Referral from business contacts
4. Organization's own recruiter
5. Locations (e.g., churches) targeted at particular demographic groups
6. Other sources targeted at particular demographic groups
7. Online services (Monster.com, etc.)
8. Employment agencies
9. Newspaper advertisements
10. Minority job fairs
11. General job fairs
12. Unsolicited applications/walk-ins
13. Telephone
14. Internal postings/intranet
15. Temps/contract workers
16. Other

Targeted financial and work environment benefits (1–7 extent)

Companies offer many different types of benefits. However, some of these benefits tend to be highlighted in recruitment more than others. Keeping in mind the job you noted in Question 1, please indicate the extent to which each of the following was highlighted in the recruitment process.

1. Retirement contributions (financial)
2. Retirement planning advice (financial)
3. Health insurance (financial)
4. Professional growth (work environment)
5. Varied work tasks (work environment)
6. Satisfying/meaningful work (work environment)
7. Friendly work environment (work environment)
8. Opportunities to mentor others (work environment)

Organizational reputation (1–7 agreement)

1. Most applicants would view this organization as an attractive employer.
2. Most applicants would view this organization as having a good reputation.

A lifespan perspective on psychological contracts and their relations with organizational commitment

P. Matthijs Bal[1], Annet H. de Lange[2], Hannes Zacher[3], and Beatrice I. J. M. Van der Heijden[4]

[1]Department of Management and Organization, VU University Amsterdam, Amsterdam, The Netherlands

[2]Department of Work and Organizational Psychology, Radboud University Nijmegen, Nijmegen, The Netherlands

[3]School of Psychology, University of Queensland, Brisbane, Australia

[4]Institute for Management Research, Radboud University Nijmegen, Nijmegen, The Netherlands, Open Universiteit, The Netherlands, University of Twente, Enschede, The Netherlands

The current study investigated the influence of age-related constructs on the psychological contract and its relationships with continuance and normative commitment. It was proposed that as people age, their future time perspective (FTP) decreases. Consequently, it was expected that contract fulfilment would be positively related to continuance commitment for workers with short FTP, while it would be positively related to normative commitment for workers with long FTP. Conversely, it was argued that, with age, workers' perceived work-related expertise increases, resulting in stronger reactions to obligation fulfilment on normative commitment. A study among 334 employees showed that FTP and work-related expertise indeed moderated the relationships between contract fulfilment and organizational commitment. The results showed that the influence of age on the relations between contract fulfilment with outcomes is dependent upon FTP and occupational expertise. The study shows the value of a lifespan perspective on psychological contracts and their relations with organizational commitment.

Due to the ageing of the workforce, governments and organizations are increasingly aware of the need to retain older workers in the labour market in order to ensure sufficient levels of staff in the long run (European Commission, 2010; Wang & Shultz, 2010). On the one hand, the large baby boom generation is currently reaching retirement; on the other hand, birth rates have considerably decreased during the last decades. These demographic changes imply a shortage of younger workers who enter the labour market in relation to the supply needed to fill the places of those employees retiring (Alley & Crimmins, 2007). Therefore, the ageing workforce has become one of the most important challenges in organizations nowadays and considerable research has been devoted to the topic (Shultz & Wang, 2011; Wang & Shultz, 2010). For instance, research has focused on how older workers can be motivated in

their work, and what causes them to remain committed to their organizations (Bal, Jansen, Van der Velde, De Lange, & Rousseau, 2010; Ng & Feldman, 2009).

A highly useful perspective on the motivation of older workers has been presented by psychological contract theory (Rousseau, 1995) which postulates that a high-quality relationship between the employee and the organization is necessary for employees to become committed to their organization (Zhao, Wayne, Glibkowski, & Bravo, 2007). Although some previous studies have looked at the role of age in psychological contracts and its relations with job attitudes (Bal, De Lange, Jansen, & Van der Velde, 2008; Bellou, 2009; Ng & Feldman, 2009), no previous empirical attempts have been made to explain *why* and *how* age affects the relations of psychological contracts with job attitudes. Stated differently, empirical research on the age-related processes that influence reactions to psychological contracts is lacking (Kooij, De Lange, Jansen, & Dikkers, 2008; Zacher, Heusner, Schmitz, Zwierzanska, & Frese, 2010).

The limited approach focusing on chronological age only has been criticized because age is an "umbrella" variable under which various changes in people's lives are subsumed. Moreover, the neglect of mediator and moderator variables in previous research is unfortunate, because research on ageing is often criticized for treating age as if it was a psychologically meaningful construct by itself (Schaie, 1986). Chronological age is only an index, and it is therefore of utmost importance to gain a better understanding of how age-related changes in psychological variables affect organizational outcomes (Ng & Feldman, 2008; Schwall, 2012). Moreover, up until now research has shown inconsistent findings with regard to the role of age in psychological contract reactions (Bal et al., 2008; Bellou, 2009). This inconsistency could be explained such that age can have both negative and positive effects, through decreases in future time perspective and through increases in experience and perceived work-related expertise. Therefore, the *total* effect of age on psychological contracts may be neutralized and, therefore, invisible.

Hence, it is imperative to investigate the underlying concepts to disentangle the complex role of age in the relations between psychological contract evaluations and presumed outcomes (Bal et al., 2008; Kooij et al., 2008). This article, therefore, introduces a lifespan perspective on psychological contracts, and shows the pivotal roles of future time perspective and perceived expertise in the relations of age with psychological contracts and job attitudes. Sterns and Miklos (1995; see also Kooij et al., 2008) introduced several theoretical perspectives on age to explain the various relationships of age-related concepts with attitudes and behaviours. Both a psychosocial perspective on age, describing how people perceive themselves in relation to their future, and an organizational perspective on age, describing how age influences perceived expertise in one's job, may explain why the relation of age with organizational outcomes such as psychological contracts is complex.

On the one hand, the psychosocial perspective on ageing focuses on how people, as they age, gain a different perception of their future (Carstensen, 2006). Socioemotional selectivity theory (Carstensen, Isaacowitz, & Charles, 1999) argues that older workers have less expansive time horizons, implying that they will react less intensely towards psychological contract fulfilments that aim at preserving their relationship with their employer (Bal et al., 2008). On the other hand, the

organizational perspective on age indicates that, with increasing age, people gain higher experience and expertise (Quinones, Ford, & Teachout, 1995). Because of this, people have higher expectations of their employer, and tend to respond more strongly to inducements offered by their employer (Bal et al., 2008).

In the current study, we integrate both of these perspectives in the relations between age, psychological contracts, and organizational commitment. We focus on organizational commitment as outcome of psychological contracts, because commitment has been identified as one of the strongest predictors of both employee performance and the motivation to continue working (Harrison, Newman, & Roth, 2006; Wang & Shultz, 2010). We differentiate between continuance and normative commitment since it is expected that FTP and expertise are differentially related to these types of commitment, and we do not focus on affective commitment, because it is equally important for low and high FTP and expert employees (Bal et al., 2008). Moreover, they tap different types of psychological linkages with the organizations, and are accordingly expected to be predicted through different processes (Allen & Meyer, 1990). In all, this study will reveal a piece of the complex puzzle that constitutes the, up to now, somewhat contradictory and not fully understood, relations between age, the psychological contract, and its relations with commitment (Ng & Feldman, 2009). Figure 1 shows the research model that guides the current research. The main purpose of the article is to show *how* age influences the relationships of psychological contract fulfilment with outcomes through its effects on both FTP and expertise. Hence, the aim of the article is to show that age has distinct effects on the relations of contract fulfilment with outcomes because it negatively relates to FTP and positively relates to expertise.

THE PSYCHOLOGICAL CONTRACT

According to Rousseau (1995, p. 9), "the psychological contract consists of individual beliefs regarding terms of an exchange agreement between individuals and their organization". An employee's psychological contract includes that person's understandings of his or her own and the employer's obligations (Dabos & Rousseau, 2004; Rousseau, 1995), and are subjective in nature and exist in the eye of the beholder, that is, the employee (Suazo, Martínez, & Sandoval, 2009). Psychological contracts include perceptions of the employee about employer obligations and the extent to which these obligations are fulfilled. Employees perceive the extent to which their employer has fulfilled its obligations towards them. Research has shown that it is through these perceptions of

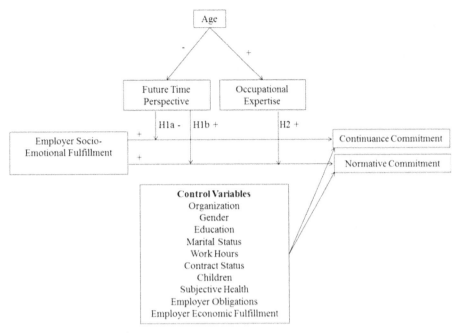

Figure 1. Research model of the current study.

fulfilment (i.e., employer fulfilment) that employees become more committed towards their organization (Zhao et al., 2007).

Theoretically, in line with social exchange theory and the norm of reciprocity (Gouldner, 1960), people engage in a social exchange relationship and form a psychological contract with their employer, and investments of one party are likely to be reciprocated by the other party. Hence, contract fulfilments by the employer are reciprocated by the employee with higher commitment.[1] In this study, we distinguish two types of employer fulfilment. In line with the framework of Bal et al. (2010; see also Foa, 1971), we distinguish employer economic and socioemotional fulfilment. *Economic fulfilment* refers to extent to which employees perceived that their organization fulfils its obligations concerning monetary resources, and these include fair pay compared to other employees and fringe benefits (Coyle-Shapiro & Conway, 2005; Shore et al., 2004). These obligations are limited in time frame such that they focus on the transactional relationship between the employee and the organization. *Socioemotional fulfilment* refers to the extent to which employees perceive that their organization has fulfilled its obligations concerning resources that are aimed to developing the employee and to build up a strong relationship (Bal et al., 2010). These resources include participation in decision making and support for development, and

are a form of support and socioemotional concern of the organization for the employee. Economic and socioemotional fulfilments are not opposites but complement each other in the psychological contract of employees with their organizations (Bal et al., 2010).

A LIFESPAN PERSPECTIVE ON PSYCHOLOGICAL CONTRACTS

Previous studies have shown that age plays a significant role in the development and consequences of psychological contracts (Bal et al., 2008; Ng & Feldman, 2009). For instance, Bal et al. (2008) showed that the impact of contract breach on commitment is weaker for older workers. However, the limitation of these earlier studies is that there have been few attempts to explain the specific role of age. Researchers have argued that ageing can be regarded as a proxy for different underlying age-related processes (e.g., De Lange et al., 2010; Kooij et al., 2008; Sterns & Miklos, 1995). More concretely, in this study, we examine differences in people's perceptions of possibilities for future goal attainment (future time perspective) and perceptions of their expertise at work (perceived work-related expertise), as potential explanations for differences in responses to contract fulfilments.

SOCIOEMOTIONAL SELECTIVITY THEORY AND THE PSYCHOLOGICAL CONTRACT

According to Socioemotional Selectivity Theory, when people grow older, they increasingly experience

---

[1]Theoretically, the psychological contract also consists of employee obligations; however, in the current study, we omit this part of the psychological contract, since it has been shown that, in particular, employer obligations and fulfilment influence organizational commitment (Zhao et al., 2007).

time as running out (Carstensen, 2006; Carstensen & Mikels, 2005). Related to work settings, ageing workers perceive a changing horizon in terms of the time and opportunities they have left until their retirement (Zacher & Frese, 2009). In contrast to objective calendar time, future time perspective (FTP) focuses on peoples' subjective experiences (Husman & Shell, 2008). FTP refers to how much time and opportunities individuals believe they have left in their personal future and comprises a process that is subject to large interindividual differences. FTP generally decreases with age, but the extent to which people see their future as open-ended or constrained may also vary among people of the same age (Bal et al., 2010; Zacher & Frese, 2009). This shifting time perspective has profound effects on human processes including motivation and emotion (Carstensen, 2006). People who see their future as open-ended are more likely to focus on long-term goals and a long-term relationship with their organization. In contrast, people who see their future as running out are more likely to focus on immediate rewards and on building up relationships with close others (Lang & Carstensen, 2002).

With respect to the psychological contract, we argue that differences in FTP will determine the strength of the relationships between contract fulfilment and commitment, as the salience of obligations as well as the type of commitment varies depending on whether people have low or high levels of FTP. In line with Bal and colleagues (2010), who argued that reactions to fulfilment of salient obligations are stronger compared to fulfilment of less important obligations, we expect that the relations of socioemotional fulfilment with organizational commitment are moderated by FTP, while we control for the extent to which employees perceived their economic obligations to be fulfilled. Theory on commitment (Allen & Meyer, 1990; Meyer et al., 2002) postulates that employees form psychological linkages with their organization because they have to do so due to the costs of leaving the organization (i.e., they have to remain; continuance commitment), or because they feel obligated to remain with their organization (i.e., they believe they ought to stay; normative commitment). Previous research has shown that these forms are distinct and are predicted by different antecedents (Meyer et al., 2002). Hence, we expect specific interactions to occur between FTP, contract fulfilment, and commitment.

Socioemotional fulfilment should generally strengthen the relationship between employee and organization, and thus they are expected to enhance commitment (Zhao et al., 2007). However, short FTP workers (who, in general, are older workers) perceive fewer opportunities in the future, and are more focused on maintaining what they have and on strengthening their relationship with their

organization (Bal et al., 2010; Zacher & Frese, 2011). Hence, when they receive socioemotional resources, they will be more likely to feel increased costs of leaving the organization because they perceive that other organizations are less likely to offer these inducements to them. Thus, for short FTP workers, socioemotional fulfilments relate to higher continuance commitment. This is consistent with findings of Markovits et al. (2008), who found that employees with a high prevention focus (cf. short FTP workers; Zacher & De Lange, 2011) are higher in continuance commitment than employees with a promotion focus, indicating that employees with a stronger focus on preventing losses are more inclined to hold a strong relationship with their current organization. Furthermore, a meta-analysis has shown that older workers value job security higher than younger workers (Kooij, De Lange, Jansen, Kanfer, R., & Dikkers, 2011), indicating that older workers will be more highly focused on resources that contribute to their continuance commitment.

In contrast, long FTP workers are focused on the future and on rewards that will be obtained in the future (Zacher et al., 2010). People who experience their future as open-ended are more likely to see many remaining opportunities in life and work. Therefore, they are more inclined to look for organizations and employment opportunities that fulfil their needs for relational exchanges, and they strive to work for organizations that offer them resources that fulfil their needs for challenging jobs and development. Hence, when long FTP workers receive socioemotional fulfilments, they will not perceive increased costs of leaving their organization (i.e., continuance commitment) because they perceive that they are employable and will easily find a new job. However, because of the resources they received from their employer, they will feel obligated to remain in their organization. These organizational investments in them enhance felt obligations and norms to stay in their organization, even though they feel low costs of leaving their organization (Markovits et al., 2008). This is only expected for socioemotional fulfilments, since they tap into the relational aspects of the employment exchange relationship, whereas economic fulfilments refer to transactional elements, indicating universal resources that employees can obtain through different means, and in different organizations (Bal et al. 2010; Foa, 1971). Hence, socioemotional fulfilment increases high continuance commitment for short FTP workers, and increases normative commitment among long FTP workers.

Hypothesis 1a: FTP moderates the relationship between socioemotional fulfilment and continuance commitment, with a stronger relationship for employees low in FTP compared to employees high in FTP.

Hypothesis 1b: FTP moderates the relationship between socioemotional fulfilment and normative commitment, with a stronger relationship for employees high in FTP compared to employees low in FTP.

PERCEIVED WORK-RELATED EXPERTISE AND THE PSYCHOLOGICAL CONTRACT

Across their lifespan, people not only perceive their future being more constraint as they age, they also develop themselves and may become more experienced in their work and experts in their occupation (Ackerman, 1996). Consequently, older workers become better in adapting to their environment. Research has indeed shown that older workers become better in adapting to environmental challenges until late adulthood (Heckhausen, Wrosch, & Schulz, 2010; Zacher & Frese, 2011). Hence, this increased experience may determine to a large extent how workers respond to contract fulfilments. In this study, we focus on *perceived work-related expertise*, which we define as employees' perceptions of their accumulated professional skills and knowledge (Van der Heijde & Van der Heijden, 2006). It is deemed appropriate to assess employees' own perceptions of their skills and knowledge, since previous research has shown that generally people can accurately assess their level of knowledge and abilities (Ackerman, Beier, & Bowen, 2002). It is expected that over the life course, people develop more expertise in relation to their work and occupation. Consequently, because their expertise is a form of valuable human capital, they gain a sense of entitlement towards their organization (Rousseau & Parks, 1993; Van der Heijde & Van der Heijden, 2006).

We argue that perceived expertise moderates the relationship between socioemotional fulfilment and normative commitment. We do not expect expertise to moderate the relationship between contract fulfilment and continuance commitment, because for high expertise employees it will be easier to find a new job, and hence continuance commitment is less likely to be an issue for experienced employees (Van der Heijde & Van der Heijden, 2006). Employees with high levels of perceived expertise are expected to see more obligations from their employer, because of a sense of entitlement they have towards their organization in return for the value they bring in the organization with their knowledge and skills (Farr & Ringseis, 2002; Rousseau & Parks, 1993). Therefore, they are more highly focused on, will more strongly monitor the inducements they receive from their organization, and will prioritize their long-term relationship with their organization (Wright & Bonett, 2002). As such, fulfilment of obligations that stress the socioemotional relationship is expected to have stronger effects on normative commitment for people with a high amount of perceived expertise. Because experts feel a sense of entitlement, and have a high amount of employability (Van der Heijde & Van der Heijden, 2006), organizational investments in the long-term relationship between the two parties indicates that the organization cares for the employee, and wants to retain the employee (Cassar & Briner, 2011; Restubog, Hornsey, Bordia, & Esposo, 2008). Consequently, these employees will feel more normatively committed to the organization when fulfilment is high. In contrast, resources that stress the transactional relationship, such as economic fulfilments, have no or little indicative value for the strength of the relationship, and hence do not promote commitment, neither for experts nor for low-expertise employees (Mathieu & Zajac, 1990). Thus, we only expect the relations of socioemotional fulfilment with normative commitment to be moderated by perceived expertise.

Hypothesis 2: Perceived work-related expertise moderates the relationship between socioemotional fulfilment and normative commitment, with a stronger relationship for employees with a high perceived expertise compared to those with a low perceived expertise.

METHOD

Participants and procedure

We included two samples in the current study. For Sample A, a questionnaire was distributed among employees in two departments of a large telecommunications company in Belgium. One hundred and seventeen respondents responded to a digital invitation to participate in an online questionnaire (response rate 68%). The respondents were on average 37 years old and 44% were male; 91% worked full time. For Sample B, a questionnaire was distributed in five Dutch cities among 1012 bus and taxi drivers employed by a transport company. Two hundred and seventeen employees filled out the questionnaire (response rate 21%). The employees' ages ranged from 21 to 70 years, with a mean age of 54.8 years; 67% were male, 79% were cohabiting or married, and 65% worked full time. The respondents can be considered representative for the entire population of drivers, who show similar demographic statistics (e.g., 65.3% men; 47.5% aged 55 or older). Later, we present evidence to justify the aggregation of the samples into one dataset ($N = 334$).

Measures

Psychological contract

Employer fulfilment was measured by indicating the extent to which employees believed their employer had fulfilled a range of obligations (on a 5-point Likert scale: 1 = "not at all", 5 = "to a very great extent"). Previous studies have shown good psychometric qualities, i.e., the reliability and validity of these scales (Bal et al., 2010; Coyle-Shapiro & Conway, 2005). Economic fulfilment was measured with six items referring to financial aspects of employees' jobs, an example item being "pay for performance", and socioemotional fulfilment was also measured by means of six items, an example item being "participation in decision making". Both scales were found to be reliable measures: economic fulfilment, $\alpha = .90$; socioemotional fulfilment, $\alpha = .84$.

Age. This was measured by the chronological age of the respondent. Future time perspective was measured with the 10-item scale developed by Lang and Carstensen (2002). Participants rated on a 7-point scale (1 = "not at all", 7 = "to a very great extent") the degree to which they agreed with each of the items. Examples were: "I have the sense that time is running out" (reverse coded), and "Many opportunities await me in the future" ($\alpha = .89$). Perceived work-related expertise was measured with the 15-item scale from Van der Heijde and Van der Heijden (2006) indicating the level of knowledge and skills employees perceive to have in their work. Answers were provided on a 6-point scale, with examples of scale extremes ranging from 1 = "not at all" to 6 = "to a very great extent". An example item was: "My competencies are qualitatively of a high level" ($\alpha = .92$).

Organizational commitment. This was measured using two subscales from Allen and Meyer (1990). Continuance and normative commitment were each measured with eight items. An example item of continuance commitment was: "It would be very hard for me to leave my organization right now, even if I wanted to" ($\alpha = .81$). Normative commitment appeared to be also reliably measured ($\alpha = .74$), with an example item being: "I was taught to believe in the value of remaining loyal to one organization."

Control variables

In the analyses, we controlled for the effects of organization (dummy coded), gender, education, marital status, work hours, contract status, children, subjective health, and employer obligations, as these variables have been identified in previous empirical research to be confounders of the relations between age-related variables and psychological contract and organizational commitment (Bellou, 2009; Mathieu & Zajac, 1990). Gender was measured as follows: 0 = female, 1 = male. Education was measured using the highest finished educational degree (1 = primary school; 4 = university degree). Marital status measured whether people were married or cohabiting (0), or whether they were single, divorced, or something else (1). Work hours indicated how many hours the respondent worked per week. Contract status indicated whether one had a temporary or a permanent contract. Respondents were asked how many children they had. They were also asked to indicate their subjective health on a 5-point scale ranging from 1 = "poor" to 5 = "excellent". Finally, we controlled for perceived employer obligations, because the impact of psychological contract fulfilment may be dependent upon the extent to which employees perceive something as an obligation by the employer (Rousseau, 1995). Economic obligations and socioemotional obligations were measured using scales from Bal et al. (2010) asking the respondent to which extent their employer is obligated to provide a range of items, using the same list of items as the employer fulfilment scale. Both scales were found to be reliable: economic obligations, $\alpha = .88$; socioemotional obligations, $\alpha = .84$.

Analyses

First, confirmatory factor analyses were conducted to test the factor structure underlying the data (CFA with LISREL 8.80; Jöreskog & Sörbom 2008). The hypothesized model was tested with the proposed nine multiitem factors under study, and was compared to alternative models. Moderated mediation analyses were conducted to test the hypotheses (Hayes, 2012; Preacher, Rucker, & Hayes, 2007). The independent variables were mean-centred to avoid multicollinearity (Cohen, Cohen, West, & Aiken, 2003). First, we tested a model in which age was related to FTP and perceived expertise, to ascertain whether FTP and perceived expertise mediated the moderation of age in the relations between contract fulfilment and commitment. Subsequently, we tested a moderated mediation model with relations of age with FTP and expertise, as well as the proposed interactions between FTP/expertise and contract fulfilment in relation to commitment (see Figure 1). To rule out the possibility of any alternative interaction effects of the age-related variables with contract fulfilment, we included interactions of FTP/expertise with economic fulfilment (not hypothesized). For the significant interaction effects, we performed simple slopes analyses, and calculated the coefficients for the slopes one SD below and above the mean (Cohen et al., 2003).

Moreover, indirect effects of age on the outcomes variables through FTP and expertise were estimated with the recommended bias-corrected and accelerated bootstrapped confidence intervals (Preacher et al., 2007).

RESULTS

Table 1 shows the results of the CFA. The proposed nine-factor model had an acceptable fit, and all of the alternative models had a significantly worse fit compared to the measurement model (Hu & Bentler, 1999). Therefore, it was concluded that the measures were adequate for the current study. Moreover, we tested whether it was appropriate to aggregate the two samples in one dataset through multigroup CFA. First, we tested a model in which the factor loadings were set invariant for the two organizations, and compared this model to a model in which the factor loadings were freely estimated for each organization. Table 1 shows that the invariant model obtained the best fit, and the free-parameter model did not obtain a significant better fit. Thus, we proceeded by aggregating the two samples.

Table 2 shows the correlations of all variables under study. In the telecommunications company, there were more women, and more highly educated, they were younger and healthier, and more were employed part time. They tended to work fewer hours per week, have fewer children, and reported more FTP and lower expertise than the employees in the taxi company. Moreover, employees in the telecommunications company reported higher economic fulfilment, lower socioemotional fulfilment, and lower normative commitment. Age was negatively related to FTP and positively to occupational expertise and normative commitment. FTP was negatively related to expertise and continuance commitment. Furthermore, expertise was not correlated with commitment. Socioemotional fulfilment was positively related to both forms of commitment, and the two commitment types were moderately intercorrelated. In sum, correlations were in line with expectations.

Hypothesis testing

We first tested whether age was related to FTP and perceived expertise. Table 3 presents the results of these analyses. All of the control variables were included in the analyses (organization, gender, education, marital status, contract status, work hours, children, and health), but for clarity of presentation purposes only significant predictors are shown. Age was significantly related to FTP, $B = -.028$, $p < .001$, and age was also related positively to perceived expertise, $B = .015$, $p < .001$. Hence, the first step for the mediated moderation hypotheses was fulfilled with age being negatively related to FTP and positively to perceived expertise.

Hypotheses 1 stated that FTP moderated the relations between socioemotional fulfilment and continuance and normative commitment. Tables 4 and 5 show the results of the moderated regression analyses. All of the control variables were included in the analyses, but for clarity of presentation purposes, only significant predictors are shown. The interaction between socioemotional fulfilment and FTP was significantly related to continuance commitment, $B = -.204$, $p < .01$. Figure 2 shows the interaction pattern. In line with the hypothesis, the relation was positive for short FTP workers, $B = .30$, $p < .01$, but nonsignificant for long FTP workers, $B = -.12$, ns. Thus, with these outcomes Hypothesis 1a was supported.

FTP also moderated the relationship between socioemotional fulfilment and normative commitment, $B = .112$, $p < .05$. Figure 3 shows that the relationship

TABLE 1
Results of scale analyses

Model	CFA	X^2	df	RMSEA	CFI	IFI	Δdf	$\Delta\chi^2$
Baseline	8 factors	5421.94***	2089	.069	.92	.92		Baseline
Alt. 1	7 factors	6484.68***	2096	.079	.91	.91	7	1062.74***
Alt. 2	7 factors	6039.57***	2096	.075	.91	.91	7	627.63***
Alt. 3	7 factors	6024.87***	2096	.075	.91	.91	7	602.93***
Alt. 4	1 factor	18641.37***	2117	.15	.79	.79	28	13291.43***
Organization comparison								
Invariant	8 factors	7078.32***	4078	.067	.90	.90		Baseline
Free estimated	8 factors	7072.38***	4040	.067	.93	.93	38	5.94 *ns*
Organization A	8 factors	812.23	2089	.010	.99	.99		
Organization B	8 factors	4290.57***	2089	.070	.90	.90		

Eight factors refer to the proposed eight factors under study. Alt 1: psychological contract obligations as one factor; Alt. 2: psychological contract fulfilment as one factor; Alt. 3: Commitment as one factor; Alt 4: all items together. CFA = Confirmatory Factor Analysis; RMSEA = Root Mean Square Error of Approximation; CFI = Comparative Fit Index; IFI = Incremental Fit Index. ***$p < .001$.

TABLE 2

Means, standard deviations, reliabilities, and correlations of the study variables

Variable	M	SD	1	2	3	4	5	6	7	8	9	10	11	12	13	14	15	16	17
1. Organization	0.65	—	—																
2. Gender	0.59	—	.22**	—															
3. Education	2.64	1.04	-.37**	-.09	—														
4. Marital status	0.77	—	.05	.12	-.06	—													
5. Contract status	0.75	—	-.31**	-.17**	.22**	-.02	—												
6. Work hours	31.56	10.46	.47**	-.09	.37**	-.07	.34**	—											
7. Children	1.58	1.25	.24**	.08	-.19**	.20**	-.06	-.20**	—										
8. Health	3.43	0.84	-.41**	-.03	.41**	-.08	.07	-.27**	-.14**	—									
9. Age	47.92	12.27	.46**	.33**	-.46**	.16**	-.27**	-.48**	.47**	-.37**	—								
10. Future time perspective	3.00	0.77	-.35**	-.15*	.27**	-.11	.16**	.30**	-.21**	-.28**	-.53**	.89							
11. Perceived expertise	4.64	0.61	.64**	.20**	-.42**	.07	-.14*	-.32**	.08	.23**	.46**	-.12*	.95						
12. Economic obligations	3.95	0.65	.11	.06	-.12*	.04	-.00	-.02	.04	.03	-.02	.06	.29**	.87					
13. Socioemotional obligations	3.74	0.61	-.09	-.05	.03	.09	.09	.05	.03	.08	-.13*	.20***	.17**	.59**	.81				
14. Economic fulfilment	2.82	0.91	-.38**	.07	.24**	.00	.08	.14*	-.11	.21***	-.23**	.31***	-.33***	-.12*	.05	.92			
15. Socioemotional fulfilment	2.95	0.65	.39**	-.07	-.31**	-.02	-.02	-.14*	.06	-.07	.17**	.20***	.38**	.18***	.22**	.27**	.86		
16. Continuance commitment	3.10	0.71	.08	-.08	-.19**	.02	.02	.12*	.04	-.13*	.12*	-.18**	.04	.13*	.16**	.08	.16**	.80	
17. Normative commitment	2.82	0.56	.15*	.03	-.26**	-.04	-.03	-.03	.04	-.05	.08	.01	.09	.07	.21**	.13*	.38***	.29**	.74

Reliabilities are reported along the diagonal. $N = 334$. Organization dummy (0 = telecommunications company, 1 = transport company); gender: 0 = female, 1 = male; marital status: 0 = single, divorced, or something else, 1 = married or cohabiting; contract status: 0 = part-time, 1 = full-time. *$p < .05$, **$p < .01$.

was positive for long FTP workers, $B = .30$, $p < .01$, but nonsignificant for short FTP workers, $B = .08$, *ns*. Hence, Hypothesis 1b was also supported. We also found two nonhypothesized interaction effects of economic fulfilment with FTP in relation to continuance

commitment, $B = .111$, $p < .10$, and normative commitment, $B = -.113$, $p < .05$. Figures 4 and 5 show the interaction patterns. Economic fulfilment was positively related to continuance commitment for long FTP workers, $B = .21$, $p < .05$, but not for short FTP workers, $B = -.02$, *ns*. For normative commitment, we found an opposite interaction pattern: The relation was positive for short FTP workers, $B = .14$, $p < .01$, but nonsignificant for long FTP workers, $B = -.09$, *ns*.

Hypothesis 2 stated that perceived expertise moderated the relation between socioemotional fulfilment and normative commitment. Table 4 shows that perceived expertise moderated the relationship between socioemotional fulfilment and normative commitment, $B = .314$, $p < .001$. Figure 6 shows the interaction pattern. While the relationship was nonsignificant for employees with low expertise, $B = -.12$, *ns*, it was positive for employees with high expertise, $B = .50$, $p < .001$. In sum, Hypothesis 2 was supported; the relationship between socioemotional fulfilment and normative commitment was stronger for high expertise employees.

TABLE 3
Bootstrap regression analyses predicting FTP and perceived expertise ($N = 334$)

	Dependent variables	
	Future time perspective B (SE)	*Perceived expertise* B (SE)
Control variables		
Education		−.174 (.033)*
Independent variables		
Age	−.028 (.004)*	.015 (.003)*
F	18.98*	16.68*
R^2	.32	.29

Bootstrap sample size = 5000. *$p < .001$. All predictors were mean-centred. For clarity of presentation, only significant results of the control variables are shown.

TABLE 4
Moderated regression analyses predicting organizational commitment ($N = 334$)

	Dependent variables	
	Continuance commitment B (SE)	*Normative commitment* B (SE)
Control variables		
Organization dummy	−.127 (.028)***	
Gender	−.218 (.077)**	
Education	−.144 (.043)***	−.176 (.034)***
Work hours	.022 (.004)***	.007 (.003)*
Socioemotional obligations		.227 (.058)***
Independent variables		
Age	.011 (.005)*	.002 (.004)
Future time perspective (FTP)	−.222 (.060)***	−.103 (.047)*
Perceived expertise (Occ. Exp.)	.004 (.076)	−.014 (.059)
Economic fulfilment (Ec. Ful.)	.095 (.054)	.025 (.042)
Socioemotional fulfilment (S-E. Ful.)	.108 (.080)	.185 (.063)**
Interaction terms		
Ec. Ful. × FTP	.111 (.064)†	−.113 (.050)*
S-E. Ful. × FTP	−.204 (.070)**	.112 (.055)*
Ec. Ful. × Occ. Exp.	−.078 (.084)	−.066 (.066)
S-E. Ful. × Occ. Exp.	.099 (.113)	.314 (.088)***
F^1	5.99***	6.44***
R^2	.26	.27

LL = lower limit; CI = confidence interval; UL = upper limit. Bootstrap sample size = 5000. *$p < .05$, **$p < .01$, ***$p < .001$. All predictors were mean-centred. For clarity of presentation, only significant results of the control variables are shown. †$p < .10$.

TABLE 5
Indirect effects of age on organizational commitment

Indirect effect of age	*Effect (SE)*	*LL 95% CI*	*UL 95% CI*
Continuance commitment			
Mediator: Future time perspective			
−1 SD of economic fulfilment	.009 (.003)	.004	.015
Mean economic fulfilment	.006 (.002)	.002	.010
+1 SD of economic fulfilment	.003 (.003)	−.002	.009
−1 SD of socioemotional fulfilment	.002 (.003)	−.003	.008
Mean socioemotional fulfilment	.006 (.002)	.002	.010
+1 SD of socioemotional fulfilment	.010 (.003)	−.005	.017
Normative commitment			
Mediator: Future time perspective			
−1 SD of economic fulfilment	.000 (.002)	−.004	.004
Mean economic fulfilment	.003 (.002)	.000	.006
+1 SD of economic fulfilment	.006 (.002)	.001	.011
−1 SD of socioemotional fulfilment	.005 (.002)	.001	.010
Mean socioemotional fulfilment	.003 (.002)	.000	.006
+1 SD of socioemotional fulfilment	.001 (.002)	−.003	.005
Mediator: Perceived expertise			
−1 SD of socioemotional fulfilment	−.004 (.002)	−.008	−.001
Mean socioemotional fulfilment	.000 (.001)	−.003	.002
+1 SD of socioemotional fulfilment	.004 (.002)	.000	.008

LL=lower limit; CI=confidence interval; UL=upper limit. Bootstrap sample size=5000.

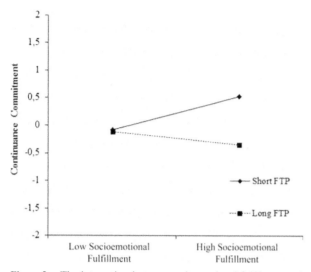

Figure 2. The interaction between socioemotional fulfilment and future time perspective on continuance commitment.

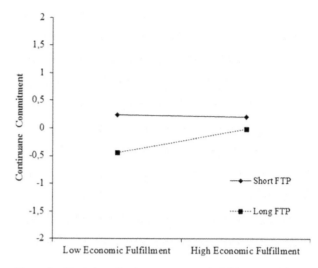

Figure 4. The interaction between economic fulfilment and future time perspective on continuance commitment.

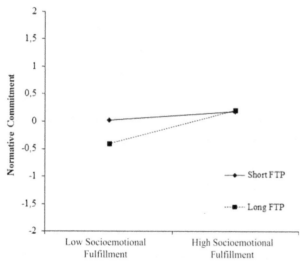

Figure 3. The interaction between socioemotional fulfilment and future time perspective on normative commitment.

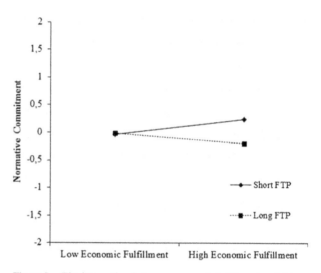

Figure 5. The interaction between economic fulfilment and future time perspective on normative commitment.

DISCUSSION

The current study investigated *how* age influences the relations between psychological contract fulfilment and different forms of organizational commitment. As suggested by a number of scholars (e.g., Kooij et al., 2008; Sterns & Miklos, 1995), it is imperative to study the underlying processes of age-related differences in the workplace. Through investigation of the relations between age and future time perspective and perceived work-related expertise, on the one hand, and the moderating effects of FTP and perceived expertise on the relations between psychological contract fulfilment and organizational commitment on the other hand, we have gained a better understanding on the processes underlying the effects of age in the workplace.

We have shown that age is related to decreased FTP and to increased perceived expertise. When people age, they experience both gains (in experience and expertise), and losses (in their perceived remaining time and opportunities). Hence, while individual differences exist among people of the same age, we observe changes in FTP and perceived expertise with increasing age.

The study also showed that FTP and perceived expertise moderate the relationships between contract fulfilment and organizational commitment. We found that the relations between contract fulfilment and continuance and normative commitment are complex. The extent to which employees feel that the costs of leaving their organization are too high, or to which they feel high normative obligations to stay with their organization, are dependent upon

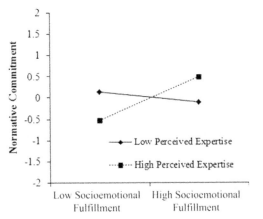

Figure 6. The interaction between socioemotional fulfilment and perceived expertise on normative commitment.

employees' levels of FTP and perceived work-related expertise.

Socioemotional fulfilment contributes to higher continuance commitment only for short FTP workers. Because short FTP workers (and hence in general older workers) perceive fewer opportunities to pursue in their future, they tend to focus on present relationships with others (Carstensen, 2006), and hence when they receive resources that promote their relationship with their employer, such as socioemotional fulfilments, they will perceive that the sacrifices they have to give up when leaving their organization become even higher. For long FTP workers, however, continuance commitment is less important, because they perceive more remaining opportunities, are more focused on proactivity (Zacher & Frese, 2011), and hence, when they receive socioemotional fulfilments, their continuance commitment does not increase but their normative commitment does. In other words, they know that they are independent of their organization, but the resources they receive from their organization enhance their perceptions of reciprocity, or the norm to stay in their organization.

Hence, socioemotional fulfilment appeared to be particularly related to the cognitive, moral form of commitment among long FTP workers, but not to their level of continuance commitment. In other words, although long FTP workers realize that these incentives from the organization *should* enhance their commitment to the organization, they may have more problems with actually *wanting* to stay with their organization. Long FTP workers may perceive new chances and opportunities (Bal et al., 2010), yet they might be more likely to see these not only in their current organization, but also outside of their current organization, even though they know that they should stay in their current organization, because of the investments made by their employer in terms of enhancing their work motivation. We found similar results for perceived work-related expertise, which moderated the relationship between socioemotional fulfilment and normative commitment, such that these relations were stronger for those employees with a high amount of expertise. Our outcomes also partly answer the so-called employability paradox: Long-term investments through socioemotional fulfilments cause highly skilled employees to become even more employable (Van der Heijde & Van der Heijden, 2006), and although these investments are reciprocated through a higher level of felt normative commitment (Gaspersz & Ott, 1996), it is not merely accompanied with a higher emotional bond with the organization, and the desire to stay with it, herewith supporting the fear of employers to lose their high potentials.

On the other hand, short FTP workers might not have expected to receive socioemotional inducements, and, therefore, fulfilment comes as a surprise to them, presumably making them more likely to stay. Offering socioemotional inducements aimed at a long-term relationship to short FTP workers may create new opportunities for these employees to pick up new challenges in their work, and to invest in their career. For these people, organizational incentives are direct signals that the organization cares for them, and values their contribution to the organization (Conway & Coyle-Shapiro, 2012), and, hence, they reciprocate through higher continuance commitment. Thus, socioemotional inducements may increase short FTP workers' perceptions of being in control (Heckhausen et al., 2010), through investments in their skills, knowledge, and participation in the organization.

With regard to economic fulfilments, we found that the interaction patterns were opposite to those of socioemotional fulfilments, indicating a reversed signal sent through these resources compared to socioemotional resources. Economic fulfilments may increase continuance commitment for long FTP workers, because it may become harder for them to find a new job which delivers them the same amount of economic rewards. However, since economic fulfilments do not contribute to emotional attachment to the organization, it can be questioned whether these expensive resources provide the desired results in terms of productivity and performance (Harrison et al., 2006). Moreover, we found that economic fulfilment related to higher normative commitment for short FTP workers. This can be explained by the fact that the cognitive discrepancy of high economic resources, as experienced by short FTP workers, is responded to by feeling more obligated to stay. Short FTP workers tend to prioritize immediate rewards from their work; hence, economic fulfilment, stressing the transactional nature of the relationship, appears to increase the feeling among employees that they ought to be committed to their organization. This also supports the propositions of socioemotional selectivity theory (Carstensen, 2006), which postulates that when people have a short FTP, they tend to prioritize short-term goals rather than long-term goals. Hence, the short-term, transactional utility of economic fulfilment may fulfil the needs of employees with a decreasing FTP.

This article contributes to previous research on the relationship between age and psychological contracts in a number of ways. First, it sheds light on the various roles of age-related variables in relations between psychological contracts and, more specifically, organizational commitment, including future time perspective and perceived work-related expertise. As a result, it furthers our understanding of the role of age in the workplace by simultaneously investigating a psychosocial perspective and an organizational perspective on age (Kooij et al., 2008). Thereby, this empirical study offers explanations for the inconsistent results on the role of age in psychological contracts (Bal et al., 2008, 2010; Ng & Feldman, 2009).

Second, by looking at two less often investigated forms of commitment (Allen & Meyer, 1990), this study extends our insight into the effects of age and psychological contracts on commitment (Bal et al., 2008). For researchers of the effects of psychological contracts on commitment, it is important to acknowledge that fulfilment may differentially relate to various types of organizational commitment, depending whether it concerns a cost-based or a normative form of commitment. Finally, this article adds to previous research by focusing on the roles of age-related variables in both content and fulfilment of the psychological contract, thereby extending previous research, which has primarily focused on interactions of age with perceptions of contract breach (Bal et al., 2008).

Limitations of the present study

This study also has some limitations. First, all data were collected through self-reports, which might have led to potential problems of common-method bias (Podsakoff, MacKenzie, & Podsakoff, 2012). This may have affected our results, and future research should also include other-reports such as from colleagues or supervisors. However, moderated relationships are less likely to be affected by common-method bias (Siemsen, Roth, & Oliviera, 2010). Second, the study was cross-sectional, and therefore causal interpretations must be made cautiously. It could for instance be that more highly committed employees receive more contract fulfilments by their organization, as a way of reciprocation of employee

loyalty to the organization (Conway & Coyle-Shapiro, 2012). Finally, further research is needed to be able to conclude on the generalizability of our outcomes to a broader population. The sample included call-centre employees and drivers, and the work that these employees conduct may be different from other types of job where more possibilities might exist for people to influence both their levels of future time perspective and their work-related expertise (Bal et al., 2010). Even though we found that the factor structure was similar for both samples, we also found differences between the two samples in many variables. Because jobs in the telecommunications company primarily concerned office work, these employees were more likely to be female, younger, and more highly educated, whereas employees in the taxi company were more likely to be male, older, and less educated. Because younger workers tend to value economic rewards more than older workers, the employees in the telecommunications company might be more focused on economic fulfilment, whereas employees in the taxi company were more focused on socioemotional fulfilments. Moreover, the somewhat older employees in the taxi company may be more normatively committed. Thus, further research is needed to investigate the robustness of our findings, and to determine the extent to which our findings generalize to other occupational settings and/or to other countries (Fouad & Arbona, 1994).

Suggestions for future research

This study focused on the moderating effects of FTP and perceived expertise on the relationships between psychological contracts and organizational commitment. Future research should also investigate objective measures of work behaviours, such as job performance, absenteeism, and turnover (Shaw, Dineen, Fang, & Vellella, 2009). A potential avenue for research is whether these concepts also influence how people actually behave at work, to obtain more insight into actual work outcomes of psychological contract dynamics. Further, due to shortages at the labour market, and recent changes in retirement ages, more people will be working after the age of 65 (Bal, De Jong, Jansen, & Bakker, 2012). However, older workers (> 50 years) are underrepresented in psychological contract research to date. We therefore need additional research that includes employees with a wider age range, to investigate more specifically how older workers perceive their psychological contracts. It is also important to investigate how psychological contracts develop when people continue working after retirement, since it is likely that more and more workers will be active at a higher age (Bal et al., 2010).

Practical implications and conclusion

The results of the current study also have important practical implications. First, organizations focusing on implementing age-conscious Human Resource policies should be aware of the interindividual differences among employees of the same age. We have shown that it is not age per se, but the extent to which people perceive their future as open-ended or limited that determines how they react towards psychological contract fulfilments. Moreover, the same applies to work-related expertise; the extent to which employees perceive that they have built up expertise in their specific occupation determines how they react normatively towards contract fulfilments. Hence, to motivate employees in their work, and to keep employees committed to their organization, managers have to ascertain how employees perceive their future, and they have to seriously acknowledge and value the amount of expertise they have gained throughout their career. Moreover, organizations will benefit from including socioemotional elements in the psychological contract, such that it motivates employees in their work, and to become more committed to the organization. Although, as shown, economic fulfilments (e.g., high pay) will be beneficial in the recruitment of employees for the firm, it is the socioemotional part of the job that causes employees to become more committed to the goals of the organization and to stay. Hence, socioemotional obligations are very important elements of the psychological contract, as they send out positive signals to employees about the long-term relationship between the employee and the organization.

This study showed that age-related variables, such as FTP and perceived expertise, play an important role in how age relates to the development of psychological contracts and their impact upon organizational commitment. We integrated theoretical perspectives from socioemotional selectivity theory (Carstensen, 2006) with psychological contract research (Rousseau, 1995), and found that socioemotional fulfilments appeared to be more strongly related to continuance commitment for short FTP workers, and to normative commitment for long FTP and high expertise workers.

REFERENCES

Ackerman, P. L. (1996). A theory of adult intellectual development: Process, personality, interest, and knowledge. *Intelligence, 22*, 227–257.

Ackerman, P. L., Beier, M. E., & Bowen, K. R. (2002). What we really know about our abilities and our knowledge. *Personality and Individual Differences, 33*, 587–605.

Allen, N. J., & Meyer, J. P. (1990). The measurement and antecedents of affective, continuance and normative commitment to the organization. *Journal of Occupational Psychology, 63*, 1–18.

Alley, D., & Crimmins, E. (2007). The demography of aging and work. In K. S. Shultz & G. A. Adams (Eds.), *Aging and work in the 21st century* (pp. 7–23). New York, NY: Psychology Press.

Bal, P. M., De Jong, S. B., Jansen, P. G. W., & Bakker, A. B. (2012). Motivating employees to work beyond retirement: A multi-level study of the role of I-deals and unit climate. *Journal of Management Studies, 49*, 306–331.

Bal, P. M., De Lange, A. H., Jansen, P. G. W., & Van der Velde, M. E. G. (2008). Psychological contract breach and job attitudes: A meta-analysis of age as a moderator. *Journal of Vocational Behavior, 72*, 143–158.

Bal, P. M., Jansen, P. G. W., Van der Velde, M. E. G., De Lange, A. H., & Rousseau, D. M. (2010). The role of future time perspective in psychological contracts: A study among older workers. *Journal of Vocational Behavior, 76*, 474–486.

Bellou, V. (2009). Profiling the desirable psychological contract for different groups of employees: Evidence from Greece. *International Journal of Human Resource Management, 20*, 810–830.

Carstensen, L. L. (2006). The influence of a sense of time on human development. *Science, 312*, 1913–1915.

Carstensen, L. L., Isaacowitz, D. M., & Charles, S. T. (1999). Taking time seriously: A theory of socioemotional selectivity. *The American Psychologist, 54*, 165–181.

Carstensen, L. L., & Mikels, J. A. (2005). At the intersection of emotion and cognition: Aging and the positivity effect. *Current Directions in Psychological Science, 14*, 117–121.

Cassar, V., & Briner, R. B. (2011). The relationship between psychological contract breach and organizational commitment: Exchange imbalance as a moderator of the mediating role of violation. *Journal of Vocational Behavior, 78*, 283–289.

Cohen, J., Cohen, P., West, S. G., & Aiken, L. S. (2003). *Applied multiple regression/correlation analysis for the behavioral sciences* (3rd ed.). Mahwah, NJ: Lawrence Erlbaum Associates, Inc.

Conway, N., & Coyle-Shapiro, J. A. M. (2012). The reciprocal relationship between psychological contract fulfilment and employee performance and the moderating role of perceived organizational support and tenure. *Journal of Occupational and Organizational Psychology, 85*, 277–299.

Coyle-Shapiro, J. A. M., & Conway, N. (2005). Exchange relationships: Examining psychological contracts and perceived organizational support. *Journal of Applied Psychology, 90*, 774–781.

Coyle-Shapiro, J. A. M., & Kessler, I. (2002). Exploring reciprocity through the lens of the psychological contract: employee and employer perceptions. *European Journal of Work and Organizational Psychology, 11*, 69–86.

Dabos, G. E., & Rousseau, D. M. (2004). Mutuality and reciprocity in psychological contracts of employees and employers. *Journal of Applied Psychology, 89*, 52–72.

De Lange, A. H., Taris, T. W., Jansen, P., Kompier, M. A. J., Houtman, I. L. D., & Bongers, P. M. (2010). On the relationships among work characteristics and learning-related behavior: Does age matter? *Journal of Organizational Behavior, 31*, 925–950.

European Commission. (2010). *Green paper: Toward adequate, sustainable and safe European pension systems.* Brussels, Belgium: Author.

Farr, J. L., & Ringseis, E. L. (2002). The older worker in organizational context: Beyond the individual. In C. L. Cooper & I. T. Robertson (Eds.), *International review of industrial and organizational psychology* (Vol. 17, pp. 31–75). New York, NY: Wiley.

Foa, U. G. (1971). Interpersonal and economic resources. *Science, 171*, 345–351.

Fouad, N. A., & Arbona, C. (1994). Careers in a cultural context. *Career Development Quarterly, 43*, 96–104.

Gaspersz, J., & Ott, M. (1996). Management van employability [Management of employability]. Assen, The Netherlands: Van Gorcum/Stichting Management Studies (SMS).

Gouldner, A. W. (1960). The norm of reciprocity: A preliminary statement. *American Sociological Review, 25,* 161–178.

Harrison, D. A., Newman, D. A., & Roth, P. L. (2006). How important are job attitudes? Meta-analytic comparisons of integrative behavioral outcomes and time sequences. *Academy of Management Journal, 49,* 305–325.

Hayes, A. F. (2012). *PROCESS: A versatile computational tool for observed-variable mediation, moderation, and conditional process modeling.* Manuscript submitted for publication.

Heckhausen, J., Wrosch, C., & Schulz, R. (2010). A motivational theory of life-span development. *Psychological Review, 117,* 32–60.

Hu, L., & Bentler, P. M. (1999). Cutoff criteria for fit indexes in covariance structure analysis: Conventional criteria versus new alternatives. *Structural Equation Modeling, 6,* 1–55.

Husman, J., & Shell, D. F. (2008). Beliefs and perceptions about the future: A measurement of future time perspective. *Learning and Individual Differences, 18,* 166–175.

Jöreskog, K., & Sörbom, D. (2008). *LISREL 8.80.* Chicago, IL: Scientific Software International.

Kooij, D., De Lange, A., Jansen, P., & Dikkers, J. (2008). Older workers' motivation to continue to work: Five meanings of age. *Journal of Managerial Psychology, 23,* 364–394.

Kooij, D., De Lange, A. H., Jansen, P. G. W., Kanfer, R., & Dikkers, J. (2011). Age and work-related motives: Results of a meta-analysis. *Journal of Organizational Behavior, 32,* 197–225.

Lang, F. R., & Carstensen, L. L. (2002). Time counts: Future time perspective, goals, and social relationships. *Psychology and Aging, 17,* 125–139.

Markovits, Y., Ullrich, J., Van Dick, R., & Davis, A. J. (2008). Regulatory foci and organizational commitment. *Journal of Vocational Behavior, 73,* 485–489.

Mathieu, J. E., & Zajac, D. M. (1990). A review and meta-analysis of the antecedents, correlates, and consequences of organizational commitment. *Psychological Bulletin, 108,* 171–194.

Meyer, J. P., Stanley, D. J., Herscovitch, L., & Topolnytsky, L. (2002). Affective, continuance, and normative commitment to the organization: A meta-analysis of antecedents, correlates, and consequences. *Journal of Vocational Behavior, 61,* 20–52.

Ng, T. W. H., & Feldman, D. C. (2008). The relationship of age to ten dimensions of job performance. *Journal of Applied Psychology, 93,* 392–423.

Ng, T. W. H., & Feldman, D. C. (2009). Age, work experience, and the psychological contract. *Journal of Organizational Behavior, 30,* 1053–1075.

Podsakoff, P. M., MacKenzie, S. B., & Podsakoff, N. P. (2012). Sources of method bias in social science research and recommendation on how to control it. *Annual Review of Psychology, 63,* 539–569.

Preacher, K. J., Rucker, D. D., & Hayes, A. F. (2007). Addressing moderated mediation hypotheses: Theory, methods, and prescriptions. *Multivariate Behavioral Research, 42,* 185–227.

Quinones, M. A., Ford, J. K., & Teachout, M. S. (1995). The relationship between work experience and job performance: A conceptual and meta-analytic review. *Personnel Psychology, 48,* 887–910.

Restubog, S. L. D., Hornsey, M., Bordia, P., & Esposo, S. (2008). Effects of psychological contract breach on organizational citizenship behaviour: Insights from the group value model. *Journal of Management Studies, 45,* 1377–1400.

Rousseau, D. M. (1995). *Psychological contracts in organizations: Understanding written and unwritten agreements.* Thousand Oaks, CA: Sage.

Rousseau, D. M., & Parks, J. M. (1993). The contracts of individuals and organizations. In L. L. Cummings & B. M. Staw (Eds.), *Research in organizational behavior* (Vol. 15, pp. 1–43). Greenwich, CT: JAI Press.

Schaie, K. W. (1986). Beyond calendar definitions of age, time, and cohort: The general developmental model revisited. *Developmental Review, 6,* 252–277.

Schwall, A. R. (2012). Defining age and using age-relevant constructs. In J. W. Hedge & W. C. Borman (Eds.), *The Oxford handbook of work and aging* (pp. 169–186). New York, NY: Oxford University Press.

Shaw, J. D., Dineen, B. R., Fang, R., & Vellella, R. F. (2009). Employee-organization exchange relationships, HRM practices, and quit rates of good and poor performers. *Academy of Management Journal, 52,* 1016–1033.

Shore, L. M., Tetrick, L. E., Taylor, M. S., Coyle-Shapiro, J. A. M., Liden, R. C., Parks, J. M., ...Van Dyne, L. (2004). *The employee–organization relationship: A timely concept in a period of transition.* In J. J. Martocchio (Ed.), *Research in personnel and human resources management* (Vol. 23, pp. 291–370). Oxford, UK: Elsevier.

Shultz, K. S., & Wang, M. (2011). Psychological perspectives on the changing nature of retirement. *The American Psychologist, 66,* 170–179.

Siemsen, E., Roth, A., & Oliveira, P. (2010). Common method bias in regression models with linear, quadratic, and interaction effects. *Organizational Research Methods, 13,* 456–476.

Sterns, H. L., & Miklos, S. M. (1995). The aging worker in a changing environment: Organizational and individual issues. *Journal of Vocational Behavior, 47,* 248–268.

Suazo, M. M., Martinez, P. G., & Sandoval, R. (2009). Creating psychological and legal contracts through human resource practices: A signaling theory perspective. *Human Resource Management Review, 19,* 154–166.

Van der Heijde, C. M., & Van der Heijden, B. I. J. M. (2006). A competence-based and multidimensional operationalization and measurement of employability. *Human Resource Management, 45,* 449–476.

Wang, M., & Shultz, K. S. (2010). Employee retirement: A review and recommendations for future investigation. *Journal of Management, 36,* 172–206.

Wright, T. A., & Bonett, D. G. (2002). The moderating effects of employee tenure on the relation between organizational commitment and job performance: A meta-analysis. *Journal of Applied Psychology, 87,* 1183–1190.

Zacher, H., & De Lange, A. H. (2011). Relations between chronic regulatory focus and future time perspective: Results of a cross-lagged structural equation model. *Personality and Individual Differences, 50,* 1255–1260.

Zacher, H., & Frese, M. (2009). Remaining time and opportunities at work: Relationships between age, work characteristics, and occupational future time perspective. *Psychology and Aging, 24,* 487–493.

Zacher, H., & Frese, M. (2011). Maintaining a focus on opportunities at work: The interplay between age, job complexity, and the use of selection, optimization, and compensation strategies. *Journal of Organizational Behavior, 32,* 291–318.

Zacher, H., Heusner, S., Schmitz, M., Zwierzanska, M. M., & Frese, M. (2010). Focus on opportunities as a mediator of the relationships between age, job complexity, and work performance. *Journal of Vocational Behavior, 76,* 374–386.

Zhao, H., Wayne, S. J., Glibkowski, B. C., & Bravo, J. (2007). The impact of psychological contract breach on work-related outcomes: A meta-analysis. *Personnel Psychology, 60,* 647–680.

From "getting" to "giving": Exploring age-related differences in perceptions of and reactions to psychological contract balance

Tim Vantilborgh[1], Jemima Bidee[1], Roland Pepermans[1], Jurgen Willems[2], Gert Huybrechts[2], and Marc Jegers[2]

[1]Department of Work & Organizational Psychology, Vrije Universiteit Brussel, Brussels, Belgium
[2]Department of Applied Economics, Vrije Universiteit Brussel, Brussels, Belgium

We assess how age relates to the degree of balance in volunteers' psychological contracts (PCs). Research on PCs treating age as a substantive variable remains scarce in the literature. Nonetheless, this seems important in light of the increasing age-diversity in the voluntary workforce, as several theories suggest that younger and older individuals may prefer different degrees of balance in their PC. Moreover, previous studies have empirically shown that age influences how people respond to other aspects of the PC, such as breach and fulfilment. We hypothesize that volunteers perceive different levels of PC imbalance depending upon their age. More specifically, we argue that older volunteers tend to perceive organization underobligation, whereas younger volunteers tend to perceive organization overobligation. In addition, we hypothesize that age moderates the effects of PC imbalance on the intention to stop volunteering in an organization. We use polynomial regressions and response surface analysis to examine survey data of 401 volunteers. Our results support our hypotheses, thus emphasizing the importance of including individual differences, such as age, in future research on PC balance.

Volunteers—people performing an activity out of free will, for a formal organization, benefiting others and for no wage (Ziemek, 2006)—form an invaluable asset for many nonprofit organizations (NPOs) and for society as a whole (Salamon, Sokolowski, & Haddock, 2011). A recent inquiry estimates that 92 to 94 million adults in the European Union (EU) volunteer, thereby contributing between 0.5 and 3.0% of the EU's gross domestic product (EU, 2011). However, demographic changes in the population's age pyramid create challenges for NPOs. As the baby-boomer generation prepares for retirement, the average age of volunteers steadily increases as a cohort of healthy people with ample spare time becomes available to NPOs (Einolf, 2008). Consequently, NPOs have to manage both younger and older individuals[1] (Caldwell, Farmer, & Fedor,

2008), who volunteer to satisfy distinct motives (Kooij, De Lange, Jansen, Kanfer, & Dikkers, 2011; Okun & Schultz, 2003) and hence perceive different obligations in their exchange agreement with the NPO (Bal, De Lange, Jansen, & Van Der Velde, 2008). We therefore focus on volunteers' psychological contracts (PCs), which can be defined as the mutual obligations between two parties as perceived by an individual (Rousseau, 1989). In particular, we scrutinize an element of the PC that has received little attention in empirical research to date, namely the degree of balance in the PC. The goal of this study is to ascertain whether differences in perceptions of and reactions to the degree of balance in volunteers' PCs can be related to differences in age.

The bulk of the literature focused on PC breach and fulfilment—the degree to which the organization or the volunteer upholds promises made in terms of inducements or contributions. In comparison, relatively few studies examined the degree of

---

[1] We approach the terms "younger" and "older" from a relative point of view. Hence, we only use these terms to compare two individuals with different ages and to denote who is eldest.

balance in the PC, which captures the interplay between the promises made by the two parties in the exchange agreement. As can be seen in Figure 1, studies can focus on promise-based balance—i.e., the comparison between inducements and contributions that have been promised by both parties (e.g., De Cuyper, Rigotti, De Witte, & Mohr, 2008)—and/or fulfilment-based balance—i.e., the comparison between inducements and contributions that were actually delivered by both parties (e.g., de Jong, Schalk, & De Cuyper, 2009). In line with previous studies (e.g., De Cuyper et al., 2008; Payne, Culbertson, Boswell, & Barger, 2008; Shore & Barksdale, 1998) and with the promissory nature of the PC (Rousseau, 2000), we focus on perceptions of promise-based balance—in a context of volunteering. The concept of PC balance is of general importance in exchange agreements as previous studies demonstrated that it explains several employee attitudes and behaviours, such as turnover intentions and job satisfaction (de Jong et al., 2009; De Cuyper et al., 2008; Payne et al., 2008). While empirical research on volunteers' reactions to PC balance remains scarce, it may be argued that PC balance is important to explain volunteers' attitudes and behaviours as balance captures a crucial element in the exchange agreement between the volunteer and the NPO, i.e., reciprocity. It could be argued that even altruistic volunteers are likely to leave an NPO if their efforts are never reciprocated by the NPO with certain inducements, such as recognition or support. Moreover, the few studies to date that examined the degree of balance in the PC did not consider age as a substantive variable (e.g., De Cuyper et al., 2008; de Jong et al., 2009; Payne et al., 2008). This implies that they made the implicit assumption that perceptions of, and reactions to, PC balance are unrelated to age.

Building on socioemotional selectivity theory (Carstensen, 1992), generativity theory (McAdams, de St Aubin, & Logan, 1993), and a life-span view on changes in work motivation (Kanfer & Ackerman, 2004), we argue that age plays a key role in PC balance: Volunteers with different ages perceive different degrees of balance in their PC and react differently, in terms of intention to leave their NPO. Our study's contributions are threefold. First, from a theoretical perspective, by integrating age-related differences into perceptions of and reactions to PC balance, we add to previous studies that examined age-related differences and processes in the PC, such as future time perspective and regulatory focus (Bal et al., 2008; Bal, Jansen, van der Velde, de Lange, & Rousseau, 2010; de Lange, Bal, & Van der Heijden, 2011). Second, from a practical perspective, our study helps NPO managers to gain a better understanding of what volunteers of different ages expect from their organization, which may help them to reduce turnover rates. Third, from a methodological perspective, previous studies considered PC balance as a categorical variable (e.g., De Cuyper et al., 2008; de Jong et al., 2009) obtained by dichotomizing two continuous variables (promised inducements and promised contributions). Scholars have warned against the practice of dichotomizing variables (e.g., MacCallum, Zhang, Preacher, & Rucker, 2002). Yet, with the exception of Payne et al. (2008), this practice continues to be used in PC balance research. We apply polynomial regressions combined with response surface analyses—techniques described by Edwards and Parry (1993)—which allows us to treat PC balance as the interplay between two continuous variables.

VOLUNTEERS' PSYCHOLOGICAL CONTRACTS

Farmer and Fedor (1999) were among the first to propose that the PC can also be applied to volunteers. They argued that people volunteer to fulfil certain motives and, hence, perceive mutual obligations related to these motives. Although volunteers' and paid employees' PCs share many similarities (Liao-Troth, 2001; Vantilborgh, Bidee, Pepermans, Willems, Huybrechts, & Jegers, 2011a), there are some differences due to the nature of voluntary work (Farmer & Fedor, 1999). For example, volunteers do not perceive obligations related to receiving a wage (Liao-Troth, 2001). The majority of the studies on volunteers' PCs remain limited to describing the specific obligations that volunteers perceive, such as fair treatment and skill development (e.g., Nichols & Ojala, 2009; Taylor, Darcy, Hoye, & Cuskelly, 2006). A recent study further demonstrated that commonly used PC typologies that were originally developed for paid employees—i.e., the distinction between

Figure 1. The four elements of the psychological contract framework.

transactional, relational and ideological PCs—can also be applied to volunteers and provided an overview of the obligations that volunteers reported as being breached or fulfilled (Vantilborgh et al., 2011a). The fact that PC breach is relevant for volunteers was demonstrated by Starnes (2007), who showed that volunteers worked fewer hours when they had experienced a breach. In general, research on volunteers' PCs is still at an early phase and the degree of balance in volunteers' PCs has not yet received attention. Hence, our study attempts to fill this gap in the literature.

PERCEPTIONS OF THE DEGREE OF BALANCE IN THE PSYCHOLOGICAL CONTRACT

The degree of balance captures the exchange in the PC: A volunteer perceives that an NPO promised certain inducements and that she or he promised to provide certain contributions in return. The concept of reciprocity lies at the heart of PC balance (Gouldner, 1960): One party's efforts are expected to be reciprocated by the other party in order to create balance. Both balanced and imbalanced PCs can be discerned when considering the degree of balance in the PC, and a 2 × 2 typology has been used accordingly in prior studies (see Figure 2), distinguishing between mutual-low obligations (few inducements in return for few contributions), mutual-high obligations (many inducements in return for many contributions), organization overobligation (few contributions in return for many inducements), and organization underobligation (many contributions in return for few inducements) (Shore & Barksdale, 1998; Tsui, Pearce, Porter, & Tripoli, 1997). Whereas previous studies treated this typology as four distinct categories, we consider promise-based PC balance and imbalance as distinct continua,

ranging from mutual-low to mutual-high obligations and from organization over- to organization under-obligation, respectively.

Studies treating age as a substantive variable in PC research are scarce, as most consider it merely as a control variable (e.g., Raja, Johns, & Ntalianis, 2004). Nonetheless, a meta-analysis by Bal et al. (2008) demonstrated that age moderates reactions to PC breach. Similarly, Ng and Feldman (2009) explained in their theoretical article how age shapes experiences of PC breach. However, the relationship between age and the degree of balance in the PC has not yet received attention in the literature. We believe that an argument for such a relationship can be made, as (1) there is theoretical and empirical support for age-related differences in goals, motives, and values (e.g., Kooij et al., 2011; Okun & Schultz, 2003) and (2) people choose to volunteer in exchange agreements with a specific degree of PC balance, matching these goals, motives, and values (Clary et al., 1998).

Theoretical arguments for age-related differences in goals, motives, and values can be found in socioemotional selectivity theory (Carstensen, 1992; Carstensen & Löckenhoff, 2004), generativity theory (McAdams et al., 1993), and in Kanfer and Ackerman's (2004) life-span view on changes in work motivation. First, socioemotional selectivity theory states that people become aware that their time left to live is limited as they grow older. As a result, they start to attach less importance to achievement-oriented goals and instead focus on social goals and emotional gratification. Supporting this theory, Okun and Schultz (2003) demonstrate that younger volunteers emphasized career- and knowledge-related motives, whereas older volunteers emphasize social motives. Second, generativity theory describes that people develop a need to make lasting contributions and to feel connected with others as they undergo a midlife crisis (McAdams et al., 1993). Grant and Wade-Benzoni (2009) explain that generativity is also related to a growing awareness of less time left in life, and that it strengthens prosocial motivation. Omoto, Snyder, and Martino's (2000) finding that age relates positively with value-related motives for volunteering offers empirical support for this theory. Third, Kanfer and Ackerman's theory describes how work motivation changes over an individual's life span. They argue that age-related changes in personal characteristics lead to a declining strength of achievement and openness-to-experience motives, and an increasing strength of motives that promote positive affect and that protect the self-image. In sum, there are compelling theoretical arguments that people's goals, motives, and values change as they age. These theoretical arguments are further corroborated by a recent meta-analysis by Kooij et al. (2011), which showed that paid employees' age related positively to

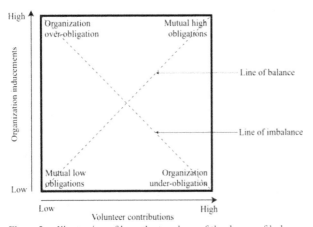

Figure 2. Illustration of how the typology of the degree of balance in the PC (based on Shore & Barksdale, 1998; Tsui et al., 1997) relates to balance and imbalance as continua.

intrinsic motives and negatively to growth and extrinsic motives.

Clary et al. (1998) argue that people engage in voluntary activities in line with their motives. For example, an individual with a strong career motive is more likely to volunteer in an NPO where she or he can build a strong network, gain work-related skills, and enhance her or his CV. Hence, in line with the attraction–selection–attrition (ASA) model (Schneider, 1987) and the person–organization fit literature (De Cooman et al., 2009), we argue that volunteers seek out exchange agreements with a specific degree of PC balance matching their goals, motives, and values. Given that the theoretical and empirical evidence mentioned earlier asserts that age-related differences exist in these goals, motives, and values (Kooij et al., 2011; Okun & Schultz, 2003; Omoto et al., 2000), it stands to reason that age-related differences can also be discerned in the degree of balance of volunteers' PCs.

Older volunteers will be attracted to exchange agreements in NPOs in which they can express their prosocial motivation (Grant & Wade-Benzoni, 2009)—to express a generativity concern—and value-driven motives (Omoto et al., 2000)—to derive socioemotional gratification. Hence, they will prefer "prosocial" exchange agreements in which they expect to receive few inducements from the NPO in return for making many contributions. In view of the degree of balance in the PC, this situation can be described as organization underobligation. In contrast, younger volunteers will seek out exchange agreements with NPOs allowing them to satisfy achievement- and growth-related motives (Kanfer & Ackerman, 2004; Okun & Schultz, 2003), because they do not yet face a generativity concern (McAdams et al., 1993) and still have a long-term time perspective (Carstensen & Löckenhoff, 2004). For example, they will seek out NPOs that offer them training opportunities, skill development, a professional network, and relevant work-related experience. Put differently, younger volunteers will be more concerned about the inducements they can derive from volunteering than about the contributions they can make to the NPO. Consequently, they will seek out exchange agreements in which they expect to receive many inducements from the NPO in return for few contributions. In view of the degree of balance in the PC, this situation can be described as organization overobligation. As we consider PC imbalance to be a continuum ranging from organization over- to organization underobligation, we propose:

Hypothesis 1: Along the line of imbalance, age increases when moving from organization overobligation to organization underobligation.

REACTIONS TO THE DEGREE OF BALANCE IN THE PSYCHOLOGICAL CONTRACT

Social exchange theory (Blau, 1964) and equity theory (Adams, 1963) can help to explain the relationship between the degree of balance in the PC on the one hand and volunteers' attitudes and behaviours on the other hand. According to these theories, people strive for balance between the contributions and the inducements they perceive as promised. Upon perceiving imbalance, they may attempt to restore balance by adjusting their own contributions or by renegotiating the exchange with the NPO. For instance, paid employees experiencing organization overobligation tend to engage more in socialization activities as a means of restoring balance (Payne et al., 2008). As a result, most relationships tend to be balanced, and imbalanced relationships tend to be temporary (Shore & Barksdale, 1998). Although the number of studies investigating PC balance is limited, they do seem to agree that mutual-high obligations render the best outcomes as it relates positively to job satisfaction (De Cuyper et al., 2008; de Jong et al., 2009), perceived fairness (de Jong et al., 2009), perceived organization support (Shore & Barksdale, 1998), and organizational commitment (De Cuyper et al., 2008; Shore & Barksdale, 1998). Moreover, it relates negatively to PC violation (De Cuyper et al., 2008) and intention to quit (de Jong et al., 2009). The relationships between the three other balance categories and outcomes are less clear. According to Shore and Barksdale (1998), the most adverse effects on outcomes can be observed in case of employees perceiving organization overobligation as these employees perceive that they promised to provide few contributions to their organization and hence consider their relationship to be temporary. In contrast, De Cuyper et al. (2008) show that, for some outcome variables, mutual-low obligations might lead to worse outcomes.

However, we argued earlier that age-related differences may exist in perceptions of the degree of balance in the PC and that younger and older volunteers may actually seek out an imbalanced PC. As Payne et al. (2008) notice, some people may prefer imbalanced exchange agreements because it enables them to satisfy their needs and is therefore beneficial. If people are attracted to a certain exchange agreement, because its degree of balance matches their goals, motives, and values, then they will be more likely to remain in this exchange agreement. In contrast, if the degree of balance in a volunteer's PC does not match their goals, motives, and values, it is likely that they will have a higher intention to leave the NPO because of a lack of fit (De Cooman et al., 2009). Hence, we propose that age moderates the relationship between the degree of balance in volunteers' PCs and their intention to leave the NPO. In particular, we expect that younger volunteers will show a higher intention to leave the NPO when they experience organization underobligation, whereas older volunteers will show a higher intention to leave the NPO when they encounter organization overobligation, because these particular forms of PC imbalance are not aligned with the goals, motives, and values associated with their age (Kanfer & Ackerman, 2004; Kooij et al., 2011; Okun & Schultz, 2003; Omoto et al., 2000).

Hypothesis 2: Age moderates the relationship between the degree of balance in the PC and intention to leave the NPO: Along the line of imbalance, younger volunteers' intention to leave the NPO is lowest as the degree of balance approaches organization overobligation and increases as the degree of balance approaches organization underobligation; along the line of imbalance, older volunteers' intention to leave the NPO is lowest as the degree of imbalance approaches organization underobligation and increases as the degree of imbalance approaches organization overobligation.

METHOD

Sample and procedure

We contacted NPOs electronically and asked them to distribute an invitation email among their volunteers containing a link to our online survey. NPOs ($N = 150$) from various sectors were chosen randomly from a large database of a Flemish umbrella organization to get a diverse sample of volunteers with various ages. Participation in the survey was discretionary and respondents were guaranteed anonymity and confidentiality. We explained the purpose of the study at the outset of the survey. Volunteers ($N = 401$) from 129 Belgian NPOs took part in our survey. The majority of these respondents volunteered in an NPO active in the health sector (53.36%), followed by the education (17.79%), sport (9.88%), sociocultural (7.11%), developmental aid (5.14%), advocacy (4.74%), and political sectors (1.98%). Respondents' ages ranged from 16 to 82 years, with a median age of 49 years ($SD = 17.18$). Most respondents were women (58%) and most had maximally obtained a secondary school degree (40%), followed by a bachelor (39%) and master degree or higher (21%). On average, respondents had been active as a volunteer for 7 years, of which 5 years was in their current organization,

volunteering around 19 hours a week ($SD = 8.94$). Nearly half of the respondents (47%) combined volunteering with paid employment in another organization. This high amount of respondents without paid employment (53%) is due to the number of retired individuals and students within our sample.

Measures

We used Rousseau's (2000) Psychological Contract Inventory (PCI) to assess volunteers' perceptions of promised inducements (28 items) and promised contributions (28 items). We altered the wording of some items to make them more suitable for volunteers (i.e., "volunteer work" instead of "job"). Respondents had to indicate to what extent they perceived that each item had been promised to them on a 5-point Likert scale ranging from (1) "not at all" to (5) "to a great extent". An example of a volunteer contribution item is "Make personal sacrifices for this organization". An example of an organization inducement item is "Make decisions with my interests in mind". The scales for volunteer contributions ($\alpha = .86$) and organization inducements ($\alpha = .90$) both demonstrated good internal reliability.

We assessed age by asking the respondents' year of birth. Finally, we measured intention to leave their current organization with the corresponding subscale (three items) of the Michigan Organization Assessment Questionnaire (Cammann, Fichman, Jenkins, & Klesh, 1979). We again altered the wording of some items to make them more suitable for volunteers (i.e., "organization" instead of "employer"). Each item of this measure is scored on a 7-point Likert scale, ranging from (1) "strongly disagree" to (7) "strongly agree". An example item is "It is likely that I will actively look for a new organization to volunteer in the next year". Finally, this measure showed a good internal reliability ($\alpha = .71$).

Analyses

We use polynomial regressions and response surface analyses to test our hypotheses (Edwards & Parry, 1993). PC balance involves the (in)congruence between promised inducements and promised contributions and thus forms an ideal application for these techniques, offering a number of important advantages. First, dichotomizing continuous variables, based on a median-split or cluster analysis, results in a loss of information on individual differences, a loss of effect size, distorted effects, and sample-specific results (MacCallum et al., 2002). Polynomial regression analysis circumvents these issues, by using continuous independent variables. Second, assuming linear relationships between dependent and independent variables can at times be unrealistic. For example, age has a curvilinear relationship with volunteering rates (Einolf & Chambré, 2011). Polynomial regression analysis allows for estimating nonlinear relationships and can thus help to explain additional variance (Edwards & Parry, 1993).

Hypothesis 1 requires that we model age as a function of the interplay between volunteer contributions and organization inducements. We use a hierarchical procedure and fit a series of increasingly complex polynomial regression models until no additional variance can be significantly explained (see Edwards & Parry, 1993, for a detailed discussion). In particular, we start by estimating a first-order (linear) regression model in Equation 1, with Z denoting age, and X and Y representing promised volunteer contributions and promised organization inducements, respectively. We also add two control variables: tenure (C_1) and whether or not someone was active as a paid employee in another organization (C_2). Our model is not meant to "predict" age, but rather forms an application of the general linear model in which we relate variance in age to variance in balance, as measured by the interplay between volunteer and organization obligations. Subsequently, we estimate a second-order (nonlinear) model (Equation 2), by adding the quadratic terms of X and Y as well as their interaction term. Independent variables were scale centred before creating higher order terms.

In line with previous studies (see Devloo, Anseel, & De Beuckelaer, 2011), we follow a similar hierarchical procedure to test Hypothesis 2, treating age as a continuous moderator in our analyses. We start by estimating a (linear) first-order model, regressing intention to leave the NPO on the same two control variables (C_1 and C_2), the main effect of age (M), promised volunteer contributions (X), and promised organization inducements (Y) (Equation 3). Next, we add the interaction terms between age on the one hand and volunteer contributions and organization inducements on the other hand to the model (Equation 4) and examined whether this addition significantly explained more variance in intention to leave the NPO. Finally, we examined whether a nonlinear model without (Equation 5) and with interaction terms (Equation 6) explained more variance in the outcome compared to the linear models.

$$Z_{(age)} = b_0 + b_1 C_1 + b_2 C_2 + b_3 X + b_4 Y + e \quad (1)$$

$$Z_{(age)} = b_0 + b_1 C_1 + b_2 C_2 + b_3 X + b_4 Y + \\ b_5 X^2 + b_6 XY + b_7 Y^2 + e \quad (2)$$

$$Z_{(ITL)} = b_0 + b_1 C_1 + b_2 C_2 + b_3 M + b_4 X + b_5 Y + e \quad (3)$$

$$Z_{(ITL)} = b_0 + b_1 C_1 + b_2 C_2 + b_3 M + b_4 X + b_5 Y \\ + b_9 MX + b_{10} MY + e \quad (4)$$

$$Z_{(ITL)} = b_0 + b_1 C_1 + b_2 C_2 + b_3 M + b_4 X + b_5 Y \\ + b_6 X^2 + b_7 XY + b_8 Y^2 + e \quad (5)$$

$$Z_{(ITL)} = b_0 + b_1 C_1 + b_2 C_2 + b_3 M + b_4 X + \\ b_5 Y + b_6 X^2 + b_7 XY + b_8 Y^2 + b_9 MX + \\ b_{10} MY + b_{11} MX^2 + b_{12} MXY + b_{13} MY^2 + e \quad (6)$$

To interpret the effects of these polynomial regressions, we display them graphically using three-dimensional response surfaces. To further ease the interpretation, we plot the response surface along the line of imbalance (X = –Y; see Figure 2). Substantively, this line depicts how the dependent variable (age or intention to leave the NPO) varies when moving along the imbalance continuum from organization overobligation to organization underobligation.

We have clustered data with volunteers nested in NPOs, and the ICC values of our dependent variables age (.62) and intention to leave the NPO (.10) indicated that this hierarchical structure needed to be taken into account (Byrne, 2011). We therefore estimated the polynomial regressions using path analysis (see Montes & Irving, 2008, for a prior example) in Mplus version 6, which allowed us to take the hierarchical structure of the data into account to correct the standard errors of estimated parameters.

RESULTS

Simple correlation analyses (Table 1) revealed that age correlated negatively with organization inducements and intention to leave the NPO. Organization inducements and volunteer contributions correlated positively, indicating that as volunteers perceived more organization inducements had been promised, they also perceived to owe more contributions to the organization, which is in line with the reciprocity norm. Finally, neither organization inducements nor volunteer contributions correlated with intention to leave the NPO, suggesting that no significant linear relationships exist between intention to leave and these variables.

Our first hypothesis stated that age increases when moving from organization over- to organization underobligation. Table 2 shows the results of the first-order and second-order models regressing age on volunteer contributions and organization inducements. Although the first-order model significantly explained 33.9% of the variance in age, $Z = 7.81$, $p < .001$, the second-order model did not

TABLE 1
Descriptive statistics, correlations, and internal reliability scores

	α	M	SD	1	2	3	4	5	6	7	8
1. Age		45.58	17.18								
2. Tenure		6.67	6.31	.23***							
3. Paid employment		0.47	0.50	−.42***	.12*						
4. Gender		0.58	0.49	−.11*	−.11*	−.06					
5. Educational degree		4.00	1.39	−.11*	.01	.25***	−.02				
6. Organization obligations	.90	2.87	0.91	−.31***	−.01	.17***	−.01	−.02			
7. Volunteer obligations	.86	4.13	0.83	.01	.03	−.10	−.02	−.12*	.54***		
8. Intentions to leave the NPO	.71	2.02	1.20	−.15**	−.08	.00	−.01	.00	.06	−.05	

$N = 401$. *$p < .05$, **$p < .01$, ***$p < .001$.

TABLE 2
Results from regressions explaining variance in age by
volunteer and organization obligations

		Age	
		First-order model	Second-order model
Intercept	b_0	42.73***	43.23***
Tenure	b_1	0.78***	0.75***
Paid employment	b_2	−13.70***	−13.33***
Volunteer obligations (X)	b_3	2.88*	−0.15
Organization obligations (Y)	b_4	−6.02***	−4.87
X^2	b_5		1.51
$X \times Y$	b_6		−1.00
Y^2	b_7		.57
R^2		.34***	.34***
ΔR^2			.00

$N = 398$. *$p < .05$, ***$p < .001$.

significantly improve upon the first-order model, $F(3, 394) = 0.98$, ns, as it explained 34.4% of the variance in age, $Z = 4.83$, $p < .001$.

Hence, we used the first-order model parameter estimates to plot a response surface (Figure 3, top). As can be observed in Figure 3, the highest age coincided with perceiving organization underobligation, whereas lower age coincided with perceiving organization overobligation. To further ease the interpretation of this response surface, we plotted the line of imbalance and inspected its slope and curvature (Figure 3, middle). The slope and curvature can be obtained by substituting Y by –X in the first-order equation, which yields: $Z = b_0 + (b_3 - b_4)X$. Hence, the slope is calculated by $b_3 - b_4$ using the parameter estimates from the first-order model (Edwards & Parry, 1993). The line of imbalance in Figure 4 has a significant positive slope, $\beta = 9.93$, $t = 4.48$, $p < .001$, meaning that age increases as we move from organization overobligation (left) to organization underobligation (right). Hence, this finding lends support for Hypothesis 1. Although not the focus of Hypothesis 1, we also plotted the

shape of the response surface along the line of balance for illustrative purposes (Figure 3, bottom). As can be observed from this line, age increases as we move from mutual-low obligations (left) to mutual-high obligations (right).

Our second hypothesis stated that age moderates the relationship between the degree of imbalance in volunteers' PCs and their intentions to leave the NPO. To this end, we estimated regression models with intention to leave the NPO as the dependent variable and age as the moderator (Table 3). We first estimated linear first-order regression without interaction terms (Model A) and with interaction terms (Model B). It is, however, possible that the relationship between the degree of balance and intention to leave the NPO is nonlinear. Hence, we subsequently estimated nonlinear second-order regression models without interaction terms (Model C) and with interaction terms (Model D). We compared the change in explained variance to ascertain whether age moderated the effect of PC balance on intention to leave the NPO. Model A significantly explained 4% variance in intention to leave the NPO, $Z = 2.03$, $p < .05$; Model B significantly explained 4.4% variance in intention to leave the NPO, $Z = 1.96$, $p < .05$; Model C significantly explained 4.1% variance in intention to leave the NPO, $Z = 2.07$, $p < .05$; and Model D significantly explained 6.3% of the variance in intention to leave the NPO, $Z = 2.59$, $p < .01$. Comparing these models indicated that Models A, B, and C did not differ significantly regarding the amount of variance explained in the dependent variable: Model B versus Model A, $F(2, 386) = 0.81$, ns; Model C versus Model B, $F(3, 385) = 0.13$, ns. However, Model D significantly explained 2.3% additional variance when compared to the second-order polynomial model without moderator (Model C), $F(5, 380) = 1.87$, $p < .05$. Hence, we can conclude that age moderates the effect of PC balance on intention to leave the NPO if we take nonlinear effects of PC balance into consideration.

Regressing age on volunteer contributions and organization inducements

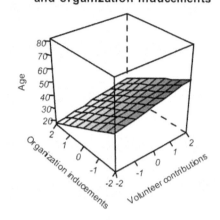

Response surface along the line of imbalance

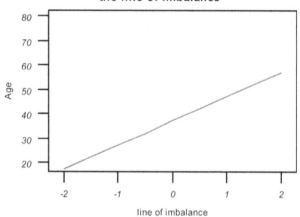

Response surface along the line of balance

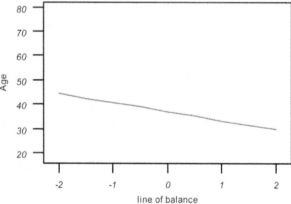

Figure 3. Response surface of the first-order polynomial model regressing age on volunteer contributions and organization inducements (top) with corresponding shape along the line of imbalance (middle) and the line of balance (bottom).

To interpret this moderating role of age, we followed Aiken and West's (1991) recommendations for probing interaction effects and plotted three response surfaces using the parameter estimates from Model D and replacing the moderator (M)

with three theoretically relevant values (Figure 4, top row – interested readers may consult the supplementary online video which illustrates this moderating effect for all values of age in the sample [see Video S1, which is available via the supplementary tab on the article's online page at http://dx.doi.org/10.1080/1359432X.2012.721354]). These chosen values coincide with distinct work roles in people's life spans (Super, 1980): 25 years (establishment phase), 45 years (maintenance phase), and 65 years (decline phase). Subsequently, we investigated the slope and curvature of the lines of imbalance for each of these three response surfaces (Figure 4, middle row). We substituted Y by –X in the second-order model with moderator terms (Model D), yielding: $Z = (b_0 + b_1C_1 + b_2C_2 + b_8M) + (b_3 - b_4 + b_9M - b_{10}M)X + (b_5 - b_6 + b_7 + b_{11}M - b_{12}M + b_{13}M)X^2$. Hence, the slope can be calculated by $b_3 - b_4 + b_9M - b_{10}M$ and the curvature by $b_5 - b_6 + b_7 + b_{11}M - b_{12}M + b_{13}M$.

For the younger age (establishment phase) response surface, the line of imbalance's slope was positive and significant, $\beta = 1.26$, $t = 7.42$, $p < .001$, while its curvature was negative and significant, $\beta = -0.48$, $t = -2.08$, $p < .05$. This positive slope implies that young volunteers have a lower intention to leave their NPO in situations of organization overobligation than in situations of organization underobligation, whereas the negative curvature implies a ∩-shaped curve. When inspecting Figure 4, one notices that intention to leave the organization even drops to a minimum as the line of imbalance approaches the left side of the figure (i.e., organization overobligation). For the middle age (maintenance phase) response surface, both the slope, $\beta = 0.08$, $t = 0.10$, ns, and the curvature, $\beta = -0.04$, $t = -0.07$, ns, of the line of imbalance did not significantly differ from zero. This implies that these volunteers have a similar intention to leave the NPO in situations of organization under- and overobligation. For the older age (decline phase) response surface, the line of imbalance's slope was negative and significant, $\beta = -1.10$, $t = -2.04$, $p < .05$, whereas its curvature was not significant, $\beta = 0.40$, $t = 0.52$, ns. This negative slope implies that older volunteers have a higher intention to leave their NPO when faced with organization overobligation than with organization underobligation. In sum, these findings lend support for our second hypothesis. Once again, although not the focus of our second hypothesis, we also plotted the line of balance of the three response surfaces for illustrative purposes (Figure 4, bottom row).

DISCUSSION

The objective of this study was to investigate whether age-related differences exist in volunteers' perceptions

TABLE 3
Results from regressions explaining variance in intention to leave the NPO by volunteer and organization obligations, including age as a moderator

		Age			
		Model A	Model B	Model C	Model D
Intercept	b_0	2.75***	2.42***	2.79***	1.73***
Tenure	b_1	−0.01	−0.01	−0.01	0.001
Paid employment	b_2	−0.16	−0.18	−0.16	0.001*
Age (M)	b_3	−0.01*	−0.003	−0.01*	0.01
Volunteer obligations (X)	b_4	−0.10	0.21	−0.18	1.25**
Organization obligations (Y)	b_5	0.11	−0.10	0.18	−0.73
X^2	b_6			0.03	−0.53**
$X \times Y$	b_7			−0.06	0.46
Y^2	b_8			0.02	0.20
$M \times X$	b_9		−0.01		−0.03***
$M \times Y$	b_{10}		0.004		0.02
$M \times X^2$	b_{11}				0.01**
$M \times X \times Y$	b_{12}				−0.01
$M \times Y^2$	b_{13}				−0.003
R^2		.04*	.04*	.04*	.06*
ΔR^2			.00	.00	.02*

$N = 398$. *$p < .05$, **$p < .01$, ***$p < .001$. Model A: (linear) first-order model without interaction terms. Model B: (linear) first-order model with interaction terms. Model C: (nonlinear) second-order model without interaction terms. Model D: (nonlinear) second-order model with interaction terms.

of the degree of balance in their PC and in their reactions to imbalanced PCs in terms of intention to leave their NPO. First, we hypothesized that age increases as one moves along the imbalance continuum from organization over- to organization underobligation. Our data supported this hypothesis, meaning that older volunteers tend to report organization underobligation whereas younger volunteers tend to report organization overobligation. Based on socioemotional selectivity theory (Carstensen, 1992), generativity theory (McAdams et al., 1993), and Kanfer and Ackerman's (2004) life-span view on changes in work motivation, we argued that as people age they focus on different goals, motives, and values in life and hence seek out a matching degree of PC balance in exchange agreements (Clary et al., 1998; De Cooman et al., 2009; Schneider, 1987). For example, older volunteers may seek out exchange agreements characterized by organization underobligation because this allows them to feel prosocial and hence to fulfil value-related motives. An alternative explanation for our findings may be that younger and older people get selected into different volunteer tasks, for example because of ageism stereotypes (Minichiello, Browne, & Kendig, 2000), meaning that older volunteers have no alternative but to engage in exchange agreements characterized by organization underobligation. In contrast, younger individuals may be offered several inducements as a means of attracting and retaining new volunteers. In view of Schneider's (1987) ASA framework, the former original explanation of our findings fits into the attraction stage, whereas the latter alternative explanation fits into the selection stage. However, it is probable that age-related differences in volunteers' PCs emerge due to all three stages of the framework, as volunteers seek out exchange agreements in line with their age-specific needs (attraction), are recruited into distinct exchange agreements based on their age (selection), and quit exchange agreements if these do not fit their age-specific needs (attrition). Further research is needed to fully understand the interplay between these stages in the coming about of age-related differences in perceptions of the degree of balance in the PC.

Our second hypothesis stated that age moderates the relationship between the degree of imbalance in the PC and intention to leave the NPO. Social exchange theory (Blau, 1964) and equity theory (Adams, 1963) suggest that PC imbalance—both in the form of organization over- and underobligation—has negative consequences for the individual and the organization. However, empirical studies disagree as to which type of PC imbalance—organization over- or underobligation—has the most adverse effects (De Cuyper et al., 2008; Shore & Barksdale, 1998). We argue that the effect of PC imbalance on outcomes depends upon age-related differences, as people will remain in an NPO if the (im)balance in the exchange agreement aligns with the goals, motives, and values that they prioritize at their particular age. We expected that older volunteers would be less inclined to leave their NPO in case of organization underobligation, whereas younger volunteers would have a lower intention to quit their NPO when experiencing organization overobligation. The results of our

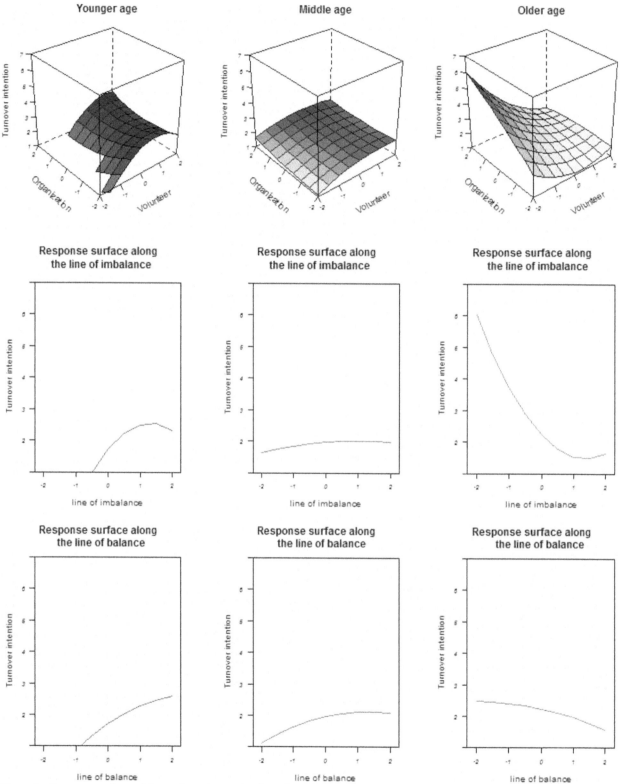

Figure 4. Response surfaces of the moderated second-order polynomial models regressing turnover intentions on volunteer contributions and organization inducements for younger age (first column), middle age (second column), and older age (third column), with corresponding shapes along the lines of imbalance (middle row) and balance (bottom row).

moderated polynomial regression analysis supported our second hypothesis and, thus, our argument that age moderates the effects of PC imbalance on intention to leave the NPO. However, the explained variance of this model was rather low, albeit significant. This might be due to the fact that age is only a proxy for the underlying cause of these age-related differences in reactions to PC imbalance, such as future time perspective (Bal et al., 2010) or regulatory focus (de Lange et al., 2011).

It is important to note that, although we demonstrate differences between younger and older volunteers' perceptions of and reactions to the degree of balance in the PC, we cannot pinpoint the exact source of these differences. It is possible that perceptions of and reactions to PC balance evolve as people age, but an alternative explanation for our findings might be that generational differences, functional age, psychosocial age, or age relative to covolunteers' ages—as opposed to chronological age—influence perceptions of the PC (Caldwell et al., 2008; Schalk et al., 2010). In addition, it might be that certain life events are important in determining perceptions of and reactions to the degree of balance in the PC. For example, retirement may have a profound effect as retirees have more time available and may wish to replace certain inducements they previously derived from paid employment by volunteering (Wilson, 2000). Although we controlled for effects of tenure and paid employment by adding them as covariates to our models, we believe that research into the specific role of life-events in the PC is an important avenue for future research.

Despite these remaining questions, the general implication of our findings is clear: Age-related differences exist in the perception of and reactions to the degree of balance in the PC of volunteers. Combined, these findings seem to support our assumption that people choose to volunteer in an exchange agreement in line with the specific motives, needs, and values related to their age. If the degree of balance in this exchange agreement turns out not to match these motives, needs, and values, they report a higher intention to leave their NPO.

Limitations

We believe our study makes noteworthy contributions to the literature; however, we have to point out a number of limitations. First, in line with the majority of prior studies, we focused on promise-based balance (e.g., De Cuyper et al., 2008; Payne et al., 2008). However, as de Jong et al. (2009) demonstrated, fulfilment-based balance—the balance between delivered inducements and delivered contributions—can also be important to explain individuals' attitudes and behaviours. Ideally, future studies should include all four elements of the PC, to simultaneously assess promise-based balance, fulfilment-based balance, employer breach-fulfilment, and employee breach-fulfilment (Lambert, 2011). Second, we can only describe whether age-related differences in perceptions of and reactions to PC balance exist due to the cross-sectional nature of our data. We cannot pinpoint the underlying causes—e.g., ageing, cohort, or time effects—of these age-related differences. However, we believe that exploratory cross-sectional studies, such as ours, are warranted in case of novel research topics. Once age-related differences can be empirically discerned, more elaborate studies—for example, using a cross-sequential design (Farrington, 1991)—can be undertaken to try to explain these differences. Moreover, future studies ought to include variables—for example, future time perspective (de Lange et al., 2011) or motives to volunteer (Clary et al., 1998)—to explain why age-related differences in the degree of balance in the PC exist. Third, we used only one dependent variable, namely volunteers' intention to leave their NPO, to assess age-related differences in the effects of PC imbalance. Hence, additional research that considers other outcomes, such as satisfaction or the amount of time that people donate to their NPO as a volunteer, is warranted. Finally, we opted to use the widely adopted PCI measure by Rousseau (2000) to assess the degree of balance in the PC as this measure has been recommended for PC research (Freese & Schalk, 2008) and captures various types of inducements and contributions. Nevertheless, it is possible that this measure ignores certain types of inducements and contributions that are unique to volunteering. For example, the PCI does not include the ideological PC type, which involves inducements and contributions that relate to the mission, values, and principles of the organization (Thompson & Bunderson, 2003). This PC type appears promising in PC and volunteering research (Bal & Vink, 2011; Scheel & Mohr, 2012; Vantilborgh et al., 2011a; Vantilborgh, Bidee, Pepermans, Willems, Huybrechts, & Jegers, 2011b). In view of age-related differences, one might expect that older volunteers attach more importance to ideological PCs as this would be in line with their value-driven motives (Omoto et al., 2000). Future studies could benefit from including the ideological PC measure by Bal and Vink (2011) or by Scheel and Mohr (2012) in research on PC balance.

Implications for future research and practice

Our article demonstrates that future studies could benefit from taking individual differences into consideration when studying the PC. Previous studies have already indicated that certain individual factors, such as future time perspective and personality (Bal et al., 2010; Orvis, Dudley, & Cortina, 2008), moderate the relation between PC breach/fulfilment and attitudinal or behavioural outcomes. Exploring these moderators can help us to better understand and predict individual behaviour. Our study strengthens previous arguments that age should not just be treated as a control variable in PC research (Bal et al., 2008), as age-related differences also matter in perceptions of and reactions to the degree of balance in the PC. We believe that an important next step in research is to unravel the exact process by which age-related differences influence the PC. For example, cross-sequential studies could examine whether age-related differences are due to ageing processes, such as a diminishing future-time perspective, due to cohort effects, e.g., certain shared life events such as economic crises, or both. From a methodological perspective, we introduce the polynomial regression and response surface methodology to this line of research, as PC balance essentially is a matter of congruence. The benefits of this methodology have been extensively documented (e.g., Edwards, 2002; Edwards & Parry, 1993) and its application in PC breach and fulfilment research is growing steadily (e.g., Lambert, Edwards, & Cable, 2003; Montes & Irving, 2008). We demonstrate that this methodology is not merely limited to PC breach and fulfilment, but can also be applied to PC balance.

For NPO managers, the topic of volunteer age is likely becoming increasingly important, given that demographic changes imply they have to manage a growing age-diverse voluntary workforce (Einolf, 2008). We demonstrate that considerable age-related differences exist in volunteers' perceptions of mutual obligations. Hence, NPO management ought to recognize these individual differences by offering PCs tailored to the specific needs of the volunteer. In particular, this means that NPO managers should attempt to become aware of the distinct needs of their volunteers and match the content and the degree of balance in the PC accordingly. For example, they may motivate younger volunteers by focusing on providing several inducements that satisfy their knowledge- and career-related motives, whereas they can satisfy older people's prosocial needs by emphasizing the societal impact of their contributions. In general, our results indicate that a "one-size-fits-all" approach to volunteer management is unlikely to succeed in age-diverse NPOs.

REFERENCES

Adams, J. S. (1963). Towards an understanding of inequity. *Journal of Abnormal and Social Psychology, 67*, 422–436.

Aiken, L. S., & West, S. G. (1991). *Multiple regression: Testing and interpreting interactions.* Newbury Park, CA: Sage.

Bal, P. M., De Lange, A., Jansen, P., & Van Der Velde, M. (2008). Psychological contract breach and job attitudes: A meta-analysis of age as a moderator. *Journal of Vocational Behavior, 72*, 143–158.

Bal, P. M., Jansen, P., van der Velde, M. E., de Lange, A. H., & Rousseau, D. M. (2010). The role of future time perspective in psychological contracts: A study among older workers. *Journal of Vocational Behavior, 76*, 474–486.

Bal, P. M., & Vink, R. (2011). Ideological currency in psychological contracts: The role of team relationships in a reciprocity perspective. *International Journal of Human Resource Management, 22*, 2794–2817.

Blau, P. (1964). *Exchange and power in social life.* New York, NY: Wiley.

Byrne, B. (2011). *Structural equation modeling with Mplus: Basic concepts, applications, and programming.* New York, NY: Routledge.

Caldwell, S., Farmer, S., & Fedor, D. (2008). The influence of age on volunteer contributions in a nonprofit organization. *Journal of Organizational Behavior, 29*, 311–333.

Cammann, C., Fichman, M., Jenkins, D., & Klesh, J. (1979). *The Michigan Organization Assessment Questionnaire.* Ann Arbor, MI: University of Michigan.

Carstensen, L. L. (1992). Social and emotional patterns in adulthood: Support for socioemotional selectivity theory. *Psychology and Aging, 7*, 331–338.

Carstensen, L. L., & Löckenhoff, C. E. (2004). Socioemotional selectivity theory, aging, and health: The increasingly delicate balance between regulating emotions and making tough choices. *Journal of Personality, 72*, 1395–1424.

Clary, E., Snyder, M., Ridge, R., Copeland, J., Stukas, A., Haugen, J., & Miene, P. (1998). Understanding and assessing the motivations of volunteers: A functional approach. *Journal of Personality and Social Psychology, 74*, 1516–1530.

De Cooman, R., De Gieter, S., Pepermans, R., Hermans, S., Du Bois, C., Caers, R., & Jegers, M. (2009). Person-organization fit: Testing socialization and attraction-selection-attrition hypotheses. *Journal of Vocational Behavior, 74*, 102–107.

De Cuyper, N., Rigotti, T., De Witte, H., & Mohr, G. (2008). Balancing psychological contracts: Validation of a typology. *International Journal of Human Resource Management, 19*, 543–561.

de Jong, J., Schalk, R., & De Cuyper, N. (2009). Balanced versus unbalanced psychological contracts in temporary and permanent employment: Associations with employee attitudes. *Management and Organization Review, 5*, 329–351.

de Lange, A., Bal, P., & Van der Heijden, B. (2011). When I'm 64: Psychological contract breach, work motivation and the moderating roles of future time perspective and regulatory focus. *Work and Stress, 25*, 338–354.

Devloo, T., Anseel, F., & De Beuckelaer, A. (2011). Do managers use feedback seeking as a strategy to regulate demands-abilities misfit? The moderating role of implicit person theory. *Journal of Business Psychology, 26*, 453–465.

Edwards, J. (2002). Alternatives to difference scores: Polynomial regression analysis and response surface methodology. In F. Drasgow & N. Schmitt (Eds.), *Measuring and analyzing behavior in organizations: Advances in measurement and data analysis.* San Fransisco, CA: Jossey-Bass.

Edwards, J., & Parry, M. (1993). On the use of polynomial regression equations as an alternative to difference scores in organizational research. *Academy of Management Journal, 36*, 1577–1613.

Einolf, C., & Chambré, S. M. (2011). Who volunteers? Constructing a hybrid theory. *International Journal of Nonprofit and Voluntary Sector Marketing, 16*, 298–310.

Einolf, C. J. (2008). Will the boomers volunteer during retirement? Comparing the baby boom, silent, and long civic cohorts. *Nonprofit and Voluntary Sector Quarterly, 38*, 181–199.

European Union. (2011). *European Year of Volunteering 2011.* Retrieved from http://europa.eu/press_room/pdf/eyv2011_figures_en.pdf

Farmer, S. M., & Fedor, D. B. (1999). Volunteer participation and withdrawal. *Nonprofit Management and Leadership, 9*, 349–368.

Farrington, D. P. (1991). Longitudinal research strategies: Advantages, problems, and prospects. *Journal of the American Academy of Child and Adolescent Psychiatry, 30*, 369–374.

Freese, C., & Schalk, R. (2008). How to measure the psychological contract? A critical criteria-based review of measures. *South African Journal of Psychology, 38*, 269–286.

Gouldner, A. W. (1960). The norm of reciprocity: A preliminary statement. *American Sociological Review, 25,* 161–178.

Grant, A. M., & Wade-Benzoni, K. A. (2009). The hot and cool of death awareness at work: Mortality cues, aging, and self-protective and prosocial motivations. *Academy of Management Review, 34,* 600–622.

Kanfer, R., & Ackerman, P. (2004). Aging, adult development, and work motivation. *Academy of Management Review, 29,* 440–458.

Kooij, D., De Lange, A., Jansen, P., Kanfer, R., & Dikkers, J. (2011). Age and work-related motives: Results of a meta-analysis. *Journal of Organizational Behavior, 32,* 197–225.

Lambert, L. S. (2011). Promised and delivered inducements and contributions: An integrated view of psychological contract appraisal. *Journal of Applied Psychology, 96,* 695–712.

Lambert, L. S., Edwards, J., & Cable, D. (2003). Breach and fulfillment of the psychological contract: A comparison of traditional and expanded views. *Personnel Psychology, 56,* 895–934.

Liao-Troth, M. A. (2001). Attitude differences between paid workers and volunteers. *Nonprofit Management and Leadership, 11,* 423–442.

MacCallum, R., Zhang, S., Preacher, K., & Rucker, D. (2002). On the practice of dichotomization of quantitative variables. *Psychological Methods, 7,* 19–40.

McAdams, D., de St Aubin, E., & Logan, R. (1993). Generativity among young, midlife, and older adults. *Psychology and Aging, 8,* 221–230.

Minichiello, V., Browne, J., & Kendig, H. (2000). Perceptions and consequences of ageism: Views of older people. *Ageing and Society, 20,* 253–278.

Montes, S. D., & Irving, P. G. (2008). Disentangling the effects of promised and delivered inducements: Relational and transactional contract elements and the mediating role of trust. *Journal of Applied Psychology, 93,* 1367–1381.

Ng, T. W. H., & Feldman, D. C. (2009). Age, work experience, and the psychological contract. *Journal of Organizational Behavior, 30,* 1053–1075.

Nichols, G., & Ojala, E. (2009). Understanding the management of sports events volunteers through psychological contract theory. *VOLUNTAS: International Journal of Voluntary and Nonprofit Organizations, 20,* 369–387.

Okun, M., & Schultz, A. (2003). Age and motives for volunteering: Testing hypotheses derived from socioemotional selectivity theory. *Psychology and Aging, 18,* 231–239.

Omoto, A. M., Snyder, M., & Martino, S. C. (2000). Volunteerism and the life course: Investigating age-related agendas for action. *Basic and Applied Social Psychology, 22,* 181–197.

Orvis, K., Dudley, N. M., & Cortina, J. M. (2008). Conscientiousness and reactions to psychological contract breach: A longitudinal field study. *Journal of Applied Psychology, 93,* 1183–1193.

Payne, S., Culbertson, S., Boswell, W., & Barger, E. (2008). Newcomer psychological contracts and employee socialization activities: Does perceived balance in obligations matter? *Journal of Vocational Behavior, 73,* 465–472.

Raja, U., Johns, G., & Ntalianis, F. (2004). The impact of personality on psychological contracts. *Academy of Management Journal, 47,* 350–367.

Rousseau, D. M. (1989). Psychological and implied contracts in organizations. *Employee Responsibilities and Rights Journal, 2,* 121–139.

Rousseau, D. M. (2000). *Psychological Contract Inventory: Technical report.* Pittsburgh, PA: Carnegie Mellon University.

Rousseau, D. M. (2001). Schema, promise and mutuality: The building blocks of the psychological contract. *Journal of Occupational and Organizational Psychology, 74,* 511–541.

Salamon, L., Sokolowski, S., & Haddock, M. (2011). Measuring the economic value of volunteer work globally: Concepts, estimates, and a roadmap to the future. *Annals of Public and Cooperative Economics, 82,* 217–252.

Schalk, R., van Veldhoven, M., de Lange, A.H., De Witte, H., Kraus, K., Stamov-Roßnagel, C., et al. (2010). Moving European research agenda on work and ageing forward: Overview and agenda. *European Journal of Work and Organizational Psychology, 19,* 76–101.

Scheel, T., & Mohr, G. (2012). The third dimension: Value-oriented contents in psychological contracts. *European Journal of Work and Organizational Psychology.* Advance online publication. doi: 10.1080/1359432X.2012.665229

Schneider, B. (1987). The people make the place. *Personnel Psychology, 40,* 437–453.

Shore, L., & Barksdale, K. (1998). Examining degree of balance and level of obligation in the employment relationship: A social exchange approach. *Journal of Organizational Behavior, 19,* 731–744.

Starnes, B. (2007). An analysis of psychological contracts in volunteerism and the effect of contract breach on volunteer contributions to the organization. *International Journal of Volunteer Administration, 24,* 31–41.

Super, D. (1980). A life-span, life-space approach to career development. *Journal of Vocational Behavior, 16,* 282–298.

Taylor, T., Darcy, S., Hoye, R., & Cuskelly, G. (2006). Using psychological contract theory to explore issues in effective volunteer management. *European Sport Management Quarterly, 6,* 123–147.

Thompson, J. A., & Bunderson, J. S. (2003). Violations of principle: Ideological currency in the psychological contract. *Academy of Management Review, 28,* 571–586.

Tsui, A., Pearce, J., Porter, L., & Tripoli, A. (1997). Alternative approaches to the employee-organization relationship: Does investment in employees pay off? *Academy of Management Journal, 40,* 1089–1121.

Vantilborgh, T., Bidee, J., Pepermans, R., Willems, J., Huybrechts, G., & Jegers, M. (2011a). Volunteers' psychological contracts: Extending traditional views. *Nonprofit And Voluntary Sector Quarterly.* Advance online publication.

Vantilborgh, T., Bidee, J., Pepermans, R., Willems, J., Huybrechts, G., & Jegers, M. (2011b). A new deal for NPO governance and management: Implications for volunteers using psychological contract theory. *VOLUNTAS: International Journal of Voluntary and Nonprofit Organizations, 22,* 639–657.

Wilson, J. (2000). Volunteering. *Annual Review of Sociology, 26,* 215–240.

Ziemek, S. (2006). Economic analysis of volunteers' motivations: A cross-country study. *Journal of Socio-Economics, 35,* 532–555.

Differential effects of task variety and skill variety on burnout and turnover intentions for older and younger workers

Sara Zaniboni[1], Donald M. Truxillo[2], and Franco Fraccaroli[1]

[1]Department of Psychology and Cognitive Sciences, University of Trento, Rovereto, Italy
[2]Department of Psychology, Portland State University, Portland, OR, USA

The purpose of the present studies was to compare the effects of two job characteristics, task variety and skill variety, on the burnout and turnover intentions of older and younger workers. Based on socioemotional selectivity theory and selective optimization with compensation theory, we hypothesized that task variety would lead to more positive outcomes for younger workers, whereas skill variety would lead to more positive outcomes for older workers. Across two samples using time-lagged designs, we found that increased task variety led to less work-related burnout and turnover intentions for younger workers compared to older workers. On the other hand, increased skill variety led to lower turnover intentions for older workers than for younger workers. We discuss the implications for lifespan ageing theories and for organizational practices regarding older and younger workers.

Industrialized societies face challenges to keep older employees at work in a healthy way and to productively manage the increased age diversity of the modern workforce (Zaniboni, Sarchielli, & Fraccaroli, 2010). This is due to the rapid ageing of the workforce and recent policies that raise the mandatory retirement age (National Institute on Aging, 2007). One way to address these challenges is through a better understanding of work characteristics to help with the redesign of jobs for workers at different life stages. In particular, understanding the job characteristics that benefit workers at different points in their work lives is important but has received relatively little scrutiny. Specifically, how certain job characteristics differentially affect the well-being of older and younger workers has only recently begun to be raised as a research question (Truxillo, Cadiz, & Rineer, 2012; Truxillo, Cadiz, Rineer, Zaniboni, & Fraccaroli, 2012).

Research has shown that the enrichment of job characteristics can lead to positive outcomes for employees, such as satisfaction and organizational commitment, but may also lead to negative outcomes, such as turnover and burnout (e.g., Hochwarter, Zellars, Perrewé, & Harrison, 1999; Karsh, Booske, & Sainfort, 2005; Slattery, Selvarajan, Anderson, & Sardessai, 2010; Spector & Jex, 1991). Research has also shown that

job characteristics can affect work stress (e.g., Karasek & Theorell, 1990; LePine, Podsakoff, & Lepine, 2005). However, although many researchers point to a need for studies about the role of individual differences such as age in job design (e.g., Grant, Fried, & Juillerat, 2010; Morgeson & Humphrey, 2006), only a few studies have examined differential age effects of job characteristics (e.g., de Lange et al., 2010; Shultz, Wang, Crimmins, & Fisher, 2010; Zacher & Frese, 2011; Zaniboni, Truxillo, Fraccaroli, McCune, & Bertolino, 2011). In other words, although enrichment may benefit workers of all ages, lifespan ageing theories (Baltes & Baltes, 1990; Carstensen, 1991) suggest that different job characteristics will differentially benefit workers of different ages.

To address these issues, we conducted two studies to examine whether age differentially moderates the effects of two job characteristics, task variety and skill variety. We examine these two characteristics—performing more tasks versus using more skills—because they are job characteristics which should be of differential value to older and younger workers (e.g., Truxillo et al., 2012; Truxillo, Cadiz, Rineer, et al., 2012). In particular, we believed that task variety would be more useful to younger workers for whom it provides the opportunity to accumulate the increased job skills that they need to advance in their careers (Truxillo et al., 2012; Truxillo,

Cadiz, Rineer, et al., 2012). On the other hand, older workers would not benefit as much from task variety, as they do not need to be doing more tasks, but would benefit from applying a range of their accumulated skills (Truxilloet al., 2012; Truxillo, Cadiz, Rineer, et al., 2012). Moreover, in contrast to other job characteristics, task and skill variety have received relatively less attention in the job design research (Morgeson & Humphrey, 2008), such that they deserve some increased study. Across these two studies, we examine two different outcome variables, burnout and turnover intentions, chosen because both are important to an ageing workforce; and because, although they are different types of outcomes—a well-being measure and a behavioural intention—they are both hypothesized to be similarly affected by task variety and skill variety in the context of worker age. Specifically, in the first study, we examine how age interacts with task variety and skill variety to affect a well-being outcome, work-related burnout. In the second study, we examine the moderating effects of age in the relationship between task variety and skill variety and a negative behavioural intention, turnover intentions. We base our hypotheses on two lifespan ageing theories, Socioemotional Selectivity Theory (SST; Carstensen, 1991) and Selective Optimization with Compensation Theory (SOC; Baltes & Baltes, 1990). Specifically, these theories suggest that older workers would benefit most from increased skill variety, whereas younger workers would benefit most from increased task variety.

LIFESPAN THEORIES: SELECTIVE OPTIMIZATION WITH COMPENSATION AND SOCIOEMOTIONAL SELECTIVITY

Selective Optimization with Compensation Theory (SOC; Baltes & Baltes, 1990) suggests that people use three interrelated strategies to successfully adapt to the ageing process. *Selection strategies* refer to developing goals and outcomes and making decisions about how to pursue them. Throughout the life span, there is a decline in some available resources, and people select specific goals and outcomes to pursue that successfully match their needs, resources, and environmental demands. To achieve the selected goals and outcomes, people can use *optimization strategies* to better use the time available to them, allocate efforts and the resources to perform, and achieve the desired results. Moreover, to cope with losses and maintain positive functioning, people can use *compensation strategies*. If previously established resources or means no longer lead to desired results, people may discover and use other ways that can serve to get the same results. Thus, older workers can use these strategies to adapt to the workplace and continue to work successfully (Baltes & Dickson, 2001). For example, older workers might select job domains that give them the opportunity to use the wide variety of skills that they already have accumulated, allowing them to optimize

their efforts to maintain good performance and achieve desired results. Meanwhile, they can compensate for any decline in other domains (e.g., cognitive declines) through their accumulated work experience. In contrast, older workers might not select job domains characterized by high task variety. Performing more tasks requires efforts and energy and might not be a good way to optimize resources. Instead, such task variety may be more beneficial to younger workers who can use these tasks to gain needed experience and skills.

A second lifespan ageing theory, Socioemotional Selectivity Theory (SST; Carstensen, 1991), is more specifically focused on the selection process as adaptive behaviour related to people's perception of time. During the ageing process, people become progressively more selective, and they prefer to maximize their positive emotional and social experiences and minimize their social and emotional risks (Carstensen, Isaacowitz, & Charles, 1999). According to this theory, young adults are more likely to perceive time as open-ended and thus tend to prioritize future-oriented goals with knowledge-acquisition purposes (e.g., to be engaged in activities for gaining new knowledge). Relevant to the workplace, this means that younger adults will be interested in performing a variety of job tasks that allow them to accumulate the skills and experiences they need at work. In contrast, older adults will perceive time as limited and will tend to prioritize present-oriented goals with emotion-regulation purposes (e.g., to be engaged in activities focused on pursuing emotionally gratifying experiences). Thus, older and younger workers are likely to be interested in different job design features. For example, the job characteristics that increase work-related knowledge important for future career development, such as task variety (i.e., the performance of many different and new tasks), should be more attractive to younger workers. In contrast, older workers will not value the performance of more job tasks, because they have already accumulated the necessary skills and experience, and because they are also less focused on further advancement of their careers. Rather, older workers should benefit from a job that allows them to increase work-related emotional-regulation goals, which give them the opportunity to maximize gratifying experiences in the present. Thus, skill variety (i.e., the use of a wide range of skills to complete the work), should be more attractive to older workers, giving them the possibility to use the already accumulated knowledge and skills.

Age as moderator of the relationship between job characteristics and work outcomes

In their meta-analysis of the job design literature, Humphrey, Nahrgang, and Morgeson (2007) documented the relationship between many job characteristics and well-being (e.g., burnout) and behavioural outcomes (e.g., turnover intentions). It has been noted that there could be moderators in the relationship between job characteristics and worker outcomes (Grant et al., 2010), but only a few studies to date have examined this issue. In particular, only a few recent empirical studies have examined the interaction between job characteristics and age (e.g., de Lange et al., 2010; Shultz et al., 2010; Zacher & Frese, 2009, 2011; Zacher, Heusner, Schmitz, Zwierzanska, & Frese, 2010). More recently, Truxillo, Cadiz, and Rineer, et al. (2012) used lifespan ageing theories to posit that different job characteristics should have differential occupational health benefits to older and younger workers.

The goal of the two present studies was to use a time-lagged design to examine the moderating effect of age in the relationships between task variety and skill variety and two work outcomes, job burnout and turnover intentions. We believed that lifespan ageing theories such as SOC and SST (Baltes & Baltes, 1990; Carstensen, 1991) suggest that each of these job characteristics would be differentially beneficial to older and younger workers. Further, although these two outcomes are qualitatively different (i.e., a well-being outcome and a behavioural intention), we chose to examine them because we believed that both outcomes would be similarly affected by the interaction between task variety, skill variety, and age, and because of the importance of understanding how to keep older workers performing their jobs in a healthy way. We made our hypotheses using both SOC and SST (Baltes & Baltes, 1990; Carstensen, 1991). In the first study we examined job burnout (i.e., a well-being-related outcome), and in the second study we examined turnover intentions (i.e., a behaviour-related outcome).

Task variety. Task variety is defined as the degree to which the job requires that the employee perform a wide range of tasks (Morgeson & Humphrey, 2006; Sims, Szilagyi, & Keller, 1976). Task variety is similar to the concept of task enlargement (Lawler, 1969; Morgeson & Humphrey, 2006). Results from a meta-analytic study showed that task variety is positively related to job satisfaction and perceived performance, but also to job overload (Humphrey et al., 2007). We posit that task variety may have greater value for younger worker than for older workers. In fact, according to SST (Carstensen, 1991), younger workers should be more interested in performing more tasks to gain experience and to increase the opportunity of learning and acquiring knowledge. In contrast, older workers should be less interested in doing a large number of tasks. Furthermore, needing to perform a high number of different tasks requires a high level of effort and coping with frequently changing activities. Indeed, according to SOC Theory (Baltes & Baltes, 1990), older workers should prefer to select specific domains to invest in, optimizing their resources without a waste of time and efforts. This gives them an opportunity to compensate and cope with weaker domains, rather than investing in the performance of a wider range of tasks. This is aligned with the ideas posited by Truxillo, Cadiz, and Rineer, et al. (2012) regarding the relative occupational health benefits of task variety for older versus younger workers. These authors further noted that whereas task variety may be beneficial to younger workers, very high levels of task variety may actually be detrimental to older workers.

Skill variety. Skill variety is an aspect of the knowledge characteristics of work and is defined as the extent to which the job requires the use of a wide range of skills to complete the work (Morgeson & Humphrey, 2006). Meta-analytic results showed that skill variety is positively related to satisfaction, motivation, and involvement (Humphrey et al., 2007). Indeed, increased skill variety can lead employees to experience a higher chance of performing a challenging and interesting job that can positively affect their satisfaction (Hackman & Oldham, 1976). Moreover, a job with low skill variety can affect early retirement intentions (Schmitt, Coyle, Rauschenberger, & White, 1979), especially for older workers who feel that their work is less interesting. Thus, it seems that the opportunity to use different skills can be especially helpful in keeping older workers engaged in their work. Considering SST (Carstensen, 1991) and SOC theory (Baltes & Baltes, 1990), older workers should benefit from using their accumulated skills, with an increased gratification and ability to compensate for domains in which they are weak. Indeed, older workers should be more interested in selecting and investing in domains of well-established expertise, that give them the possibility to use accumulated knowledge and skill and accomplish their work demands. In contrast, younger workers are probably at the beginning of their career when they still need to develop knowledge and experience. For that reason, performing a job that requires the use a wide range of experience and knowledge can bring higher frustration. This is aligned with Truxillo, Cadiz, and Rineer, et al.'s (2012) suggestion that older workers should benefit more from skill variety than their younger counterparts because it allows them to draw on their accumulated skills, leading to more positive occupational health outcomes.

STUDY 1

Burnout is a well-established construct and recognized as an important well-being-related outcome (Maslach & Leiter, 1997; Maslach, Schaufeli, & Leiter, 2001). Originally burnout was considered to occur only in the human service occupations (e.g., Maslach & Schaufeli, 1993), but subsequent research explored a broader facet of burnout that can encompass social and nonsocial aspects of occupational accomplishments, such as job demands (e.g., Schaufeli & Bakker, 2004). Kristensen,

Borritz, Villadsen, and Christensen (2005) define work-related burnout as "the degree of physical and psychological fatigue and exhaustion that is perceived by the person as related to his/her work" (p. 197).

As already postulated, according to SST (Carstensen, 1991) and SOC theory (Baltes & Baltes, 1990), we expected that an older worker who performs a job characterized by a high variety of tasks may feel a diminished interest in the job and perceive his or her condition as more emotionally exhausting and frustrating. On the other hand, because a younger worker should feel that increased task variety will lead to greater opportunity to gain needed knowledge, experience, and resources, task variety should be invigorating for younger workers. Thus, we expected that age would moderate the relationship between task variety and job burnout (H1), such that task variety would be more negatively related to job burnout for younger than for older workers.

Moreover, according to SST (Carstensen, 1991) and SOC theory (Baltes & Baltes, 1990), we expected that an older worker who performs a job that gives them the opportunity to use their accumulated skills may feel less fatigue and exhaustion, a higher sense of personal accomplishment, and an increasing interest in the job, as compared to a younger worker. An older worker who experiences more skill variety may in fact feel more invigorated by their work. Thus, we expected that age would moderate the relationship between skill variety and job burnout (H2) such that skill variety would be more negatively related to job burnout for older than for younger workers.

Method

Participants and procedure
Participants were 388 Italian workers from a publishing house located in northwest Italy. Of these, 117 completed both Time 1 and Time 2 surveys (final response rate of 30.15%). Attrition analysis was performed using independent-sample t-tests and chi-squared tests to determine differences in baseline characteristics between participants and drop-outs; no significant differences were found in terms of gender, age, educational level, and organizational tenure. The final sample was 54.7% female ($n = 64$), and the average age was 39.03 ($SD = 7.76$; range: 23–59 years). More specifically, the age distribution by decade was as follows: 14 participants (12%) were between 23 and 30 years, 54 (46.2%) were between 31 and 40 years, 40 (34.2%) were between 41 and 50 years, and 9 (7.7%) were between 51 and 59 years. In addition, 16.2% of the participants ($n = 19$) had a secondary-level education, 49.6% ($n = 58$) completed high school, and 33.3% ($n = 39$) attained a university-level education. Regarding the current type of job held by participants, 80.3% ($n = 94$) were office/clerical workers, and 19.7% ($n = 23$) were managers. The average organizational tenure was 9.81 years ($SD = 7.00$),

and the average work experience was 16.9 years ($SD = 7.84$); 85.5% of the participants ($n = 100$) had previous work experience. Respondents voluntarily participated in the surveys.

Data were collected at two time points to reduce common method variance (Edwards, 2008; Podsakoff, MacKenzie, Lee, & Podsakoff, 2003). At Time 1, participants provided demographic and work characteristics information (i.e., task variety, skill variety, and demographic information). At Time 2 (2–3 weeks later) they completed a questionnaire that assessed their work-related burnout and occupational self-efficacy (control variable). Time 1 and Time 2 surveys were matched via a code chosen by participants.

Measures
When needed, the items were translated into Italian using Brislin's (1970) classic backtranslation approach and are available by contacting the first author.

Task variety. We used the four-item scale from the Work Design Questionnaire (Morgeson & Humphrey, 2006) to assess the degree to which a job requires workers to perform a wide range of tasks on the job. A sample item is "The job requires the performance of a wide range of tasks." Items are on a 5-point Likert scale ranging from 1 ("strongly disagree") to 5 ("strongly agree"). Coefficient alpha in the present study was .93.

Skill variety. We used the four-item scale from the Work Design Questionnaire (Morgeson & Humphrey, 2006) to assess the degree to which a job requires workers to use a wide range of skills to perform the job. A sample item is "The job requires a variety of skills." Items are on a 5-point Likert scale ranging from 1 ("strongly disagree") to 5 ("strongly agree"). Coefficient alpha in the present study was .85.

Work-related burnout. Seven items developed by Kristensen et al. (2005) were used to assess the employee experience of physical and psychological fatigue and exhaustion related to the work. A sample item is "Does your work frustrate you?" Items are on a 5-point Likert scale ranging from 1 ("never/almost never") to 5 ("always"). Coefficient alpha in the present study was .90.

Demographic information. The demographic section of the questionnaire asked questions about the participants' chronological age, gender, education level, job type, and organizational tenure.

Control variables. Self-efficacy was used as a control variable because of its negative association with both burnout and turnover (e.g., Perrewé et al., 2002; Schwarzer & Hallum, 2008). We used eight items (Rigotti, Schyns, & Mohr, 2008; Schyns & Von Collani, 2002; Tani, Lazzaretti, Maggino, Smorti, & Giannini,

2009) to assess occupational self-efficacy, which refers to the perceived self-efficacy related to the work domain. A sample item is "No matter what comes my way in my job, I'm usually able to handle it." Items are on a 6-point Likert scale ranging from 1 ("completely true") to 6 ("not at all true"). Coefficient alpha in the present study was .79. The participants' job type was used as a control given the issues associated with job design. Accordingly, Morgeson and Humphrey (2006) showed the association between the WDQ scales and the archival DOT and O*NET measures. We created dummy variables, which were used as control variables in the regression analyses. Organizational tenure was also used as a control, as previous research shown that is strongly correlated to employees' age: .70 (Ng & Feldman, 2010a). Accordingly, Ng and Feldman (2010b) controlled for tenure in their meta-analysis of the effects of age on job attitudes.

Results

Means, standard deviations, intercorrelations, and alpha reliabilities of the variables of Study 1 are presented in Table 1. Regarding correlations among the primary study variables, we found that age had a small but statistically significant relationship with both task variety, $r = .26$, $p < .01$, and skill variety, $r = .22$, $p < .05$. In addition, age, task variety, and skill variety had nonsignificant zero-order correlations with burnout, $rs = -.01$ to .13, ns. Because of the significant correlation between task variety and skill variety, $r = .51$, $p < .01$, we performed a Confirmatory Factor Analysis, using the covariance matrix as input, and maximum likelihood as the estimation method. The CFA two-factor model (i.e., task variety and skill variety items load on two different latent variables), $\chi^2(19) = 31.42$, $p < .05$, RMSEA = .07, NNFI = .98, CFI = .99, was compared to the CFA one-factor model (i.e., task variety and skill variety items load on one latent variable), $\chi^2(20) = 176.23$, $p < .05$, RMSEA = .26, NNFI = .78, CFI = .84. The two-factor model showed better fit than the one-factor model. The chi-square difference test between the model with one factor and the model with two factors was significant, $\Delta\chi^2(1) = 144.81$, $p < .01$. Thus, the model with two

factors was preferred. Moreover, the confidence interval (±2 standard errors) around the correlation estimate between the two factors ($\varphi = .58$) did not include 1.0 ($.46 \leq \varphi \leq .70$). Thus, the two measures are related but are conceptually distinguishable.

We used moderated hierarchical regression to test our hypotheses. As recommended by Frazier, Tix, and Barron (2004), the main effects for the job characteristics variables and age were first standardized to centre them. In the first step, the control variables (i.e., occupational self-efficacy and job type) were entered.[1] In the second step, the main effects for age and the respective job characteristic (task variety or skill variety) were entered. In the third step, the product term was entered. Table 2 shows the results of the regression analyses.

According to Hypothesis 1, age would moderate the relationship between task variety and burnout such that there would be a more negative relationship between task variety and burnout for younger workers than for older workers. Results supported Hypothesis 1, as the addition of the interaction term on Step 3 significantly increased the R^2, $F(1, 110) = 8.55$, $p < .01$, $\Delta R^2 = .06$. As shown in Figure 1, for younger workers there was a stronger negative relationship between task variety and burnout than for older workers. In contrast, for older workers increased task variety appeared to be associated with increased burnout.

According to Hypothesis 2, age would moderate the relationship between skill variety and burnout, such that there would be a more negative relationship between skill variety and burnout for older workers than for younger workers. Results did not support Hypothesis 2, as there was no significant increase in R^2 with the addition of the interaction term on Step 3, $F(1, 110) = 1.72$, $p = .19$, $\Delta R^2 = .01$.

Study 1 provides some initial support for the idea that employees of different ages will react differently to job characteristics; however, the second hypothesis was not supported. Moreover, the results were limited to one organization with limited sample size. Therefore, Study 2 was performed examining the differential reaction of older and younger workers to task and skill variety using a sample that included a broader range of jobs and a broader age distribution. Further, we examined the effects

TABLE 1
Means, standard deviations, and intercorrelations among Study 1 variables

	M	SD	1	2	3	4	5	6
1. Organizational tenure	9.81	7.00	—					
2. Occupational self-efficacy	4.62	0.60	.16	(.79)				
3. Age	39.03	7.76	.53**	.21*	—			
4. Task variety	3.78	0.85	.28**	.21*	.26**	(.93)		
5. Skill variety	3.98	0.61	.18*	.19*	.22*	.51**	(.85)	
6. Work-related burnout	2.53	0.72	.22*	−.20*	−.01	.02	.13	(.90)

Listwise $N = 117$. Task variety, skill variety, and work-related burnout were on 5-point Likert scales. Occupational self-efficacy was on a 6-point Likert scale. Cronbach's alpha is in brackets on the diagonal. *$p < .05$, **$p < .01$.

TABLE 2
Results of hierarchical moderated regression analyses of Study 1

Step/variable	R^2	ΔR^2	Work-related burnout				
			B	SE	β	t	p
Task variety							
Step 1 (control variables)	.12**						
Manager			0.22	0.18	.12	1.23	.22
Organizational tenure			0.24	0.07	.34	3.34	.00
Occupational self-efficacy			−0.20	0.06	−.28	−3.13	.00
Step 2	.15**	.03					
Task variety			0.01	0.07	.02	0.20	.84
Age			−0.11	0.08	−.15	−1.29	.20
Step 3	.21**	.06**					
Task variety × Age			0.19	0.06	.26	2.92	.00
Skill variety							
Step 1 (control variables)	.12**						
Manager			0.20	0.19	.11	1.07	.28
Organizational tenure			0.21	0.08	.30	2.74	.01
Occupational self-efficacy			−0.19	0.06	−.27	−2.97	.00
Step 2	.16**	.04					
Skill variety			0.09	0.07	.13	1.34	.18
Age			−0.13	0.08	−.18	−1.56	.12
Step 3	.17**	.01					
Skill variety × Age			0.08	0.06	.12	1.31	.19

Values reported are for the final equation. The office/clerical worker variable was not entered in the regression (categorical variable with k levels was transformed into k–1 variables each with two levels). **$p < .01$.

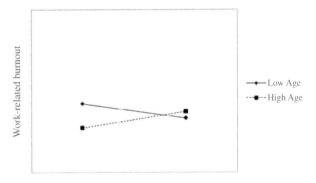

Figure 1. Workers' age and task variety interact to affect work-related burnout. Low age (younger workers): 1 standard deviation below the mean ($M - 1\ SD = 31.27$); high age (older workers): 1 standard deviation above the mean ($M + 1\ SD = 46.79$).

on a different type of outcome—turnover intentions—an important outcome in modern societies, which are striving to keep older workers (and younger workers as well) on the job. Rich evidence has suggested that the turnover process is more likely to occur for workers with a high degree of burnout in many professions (e.g., Cropanzano, Rupp, & Byrne, 2003; Huang, Chuang, & Lin, 2003; Iverson, Olekalns, & Erwin, 1998; Maslach et al., 2001).

STUDY 2

Turnover intentions can be described as the voluntarily inclination to leave an organization (Mobley, 1977; Mobley, Griffeth, Hand, & Meglino, 1979). Across a broad range of studies, turnover intentions were

reported to be highly correlated with actual turnover (e.g., Hom, Caranikas-Walker, Prussia, & Griffeth, 1992; Mobley, 1977). Moreover, job characteristics are important antecedents of turnover intentions (Hackman & Oldham, 1976; Morgeson & Humphrey, 2006).

Considering SST (Carstensen, 1991) and SOC theory (Baltes & Baltes, 1990), we developed hypotheses regarding turnover intentions for theoretical reasons similar to those for Study 1. Specifically, we expected that age would interact with task variety and skill variety to affect turnover intentions. As already mentioned, considering SST (Carstensen, 1991) and SOC theory (Baltes & Baltes, 1990), task variety should be a more interesting and useful job characteristic for younger workers, who need such variety in order to acquire needed skills and experience, and task variety can be a key job aspect for the retention of workers who are near the beginning of their career. In contrast, simply providing more tasks to older workers will not benefit them as much. Thus, we expected that task variety would be more negatively related to intention to quit for younger than for older workers (H3). In contrast, skill variety may have the greatest value to older workers, as this would allow them to apply their accumulated skills. As such, it should be an important aspect for keeping older workers on the job. In contrast, skill variety may be less attractive to younger workers who have not yet had the opportunity to gain these needed job skills. Thus, we expected that skill variety would be more negatively related to intention to quit for older than for younger workers (H4).

Method

Participants and procedure

Participants were 407 Italian workers from a number of different organizations located in north and northeast Italy. Of these, 242 completed Time 1 and Time 2 surveys (final response rate 59.46%). Attrition analysis was performed between participants and drop-outs, and no significant differences were found in terms of gender, age, educational level, and organizational tenure. The final sample was 51.7% male ($n = 125$), and the average age was 37.61 ($SD = 11.10$; range: 18–66 years). The age distribution by decade was: 76 participants (31.4%) were between 18 and 30 years, 83 (34.3%) were between 31 and 40 years, 40 (16.5%) were between 41 and 50 years, and 43 (17.8%) were between 51 and 66 years. Regarding educational level, 11.2% ($n = 27$) of the participants held a middle school certificate or less, 15.3% ($n = 37$) had a secondary-level education, 45.9% ($n = 111$) completed high school, and 27.7% ($n = 67$) attained a university-level education. In addition, 20.7% of the participants ($n = 50$) were labourers, 11.2% ($n = 27$) were service workers (e.g., shop assistants, waiters, and barmen), 57.9% ($n = 140$) were office/clerical workers, and 10.3% ($n = 25$) were managers. The average organizational tenure was 10.24 years ($SD = 9.64$) and work experience was 16.29 years ($SD = 11.39$); 82.6% of the participants ($n = 200$) had previous work experience.

Data were collected at two time points and surveys were matched via a code. At Time 1, participants provided demographic and work characteristics information (i.e., task variety and skill variety). At Time 2 (2–3 weeks later), they provided information about their intention to quit and occupational self-efficacy (control variable). Respondents voluntarily participated in the surveys.

Measures

We collected data on task variety, skill variety, demographic information, and control variables, as in Study 1. Alpha coefficients for the present study (all greater than .79) are given in Table 3.

Intentions to quit. Five items from Wayne, Shore, and Liden (1997) were used to assess workers' intentions to leave the organization. A sample item is "I am actively looking for a job outside my organization." Items are scored on a 7-point Likert scale ranging from 1 ("strongly disagree") to 7 ("strongly agree"). Coefficient alpha in the present study was .79.

Results

Means, standard deviations, intercorrelations, and alpha reliabilities for the variables in Study 2 are presented in Table 3. Regarding correlations among the primary study variables, we found that age had no relationship with either task variety, $r = -.12$, *ns*, or skill variety, $r = .02$, *ns*. In addition, age, $r = -.16$, $p < .05$, task variety, $r = -.19$, $p < .01$, and skill variety, $r = -.15$, $p < .05$, had small but significant zero-order correlations with burnout. We performed a CFA, using the covariance matrix as input and maximum likelihood as the estimation method, on task variety and skill variety due to the moderate correlation between these two variables, $r = .48$, $p < .01$. The CFA one-factor model, χ^2 (20) = 320.50, $p < .05$, RMSEA = .25, NNFI = .81, CFI = .87, was compared to the CFA two-factor model, $\chi^2(19) = 52.54$, $p < .05$, RMSEA = .08, NNFI = .98, CFI = .99. The chi-square difference test was significant, $\Delta\chi^2(1) = 267.96$, $p < .01$; thus, the model with two factors was preferred. Furthermore, the confidence interval (±2 standard errors) around the correlation estimate between the two factors ($\varphi = .53$) did not include 1.0 ($.41 \leq \varphi \leq .65$).

To test Hypotheses 3 and 4, regression equations were constructed in a manner similar to Study 1. Table 4 shows the results of the regression analyses. According to Hypothesis 3, age would moderate the relationship between task variety and intentions to quit, such that there would be a more negative relationship between task variety and intention to quit for younger workers than for older workers. Results supported Hypothesis 3, as the addition of the interaction term in Step 3 did significantly increase the R^2, $F(1, 233) = 3.93$, $p < .05$, $\Delta R^2 = .01$. As shown in Figure 2, for younger workers there was a stronger negative relationship between task variety and intention to quit than for older workers.

TABLE 3
Means, standard deviations, and intercorrelations among Study 2 variables

	M	SD	1	2	3	4	5	6
1. Organizational tenure	10.24	9.64	—					
2. Occupational self-efficacy	4.46	0.77	.12	(.90)				
3. Age	37.61	11.10	.74**	.18**	—			
4. Task variety	3.73	0.93	−.05	.30**	−.12	(.95)		
5. Skill variety	3.60	0.78	−.04	.32**	.02	.48**	(.89)	
6. Intention to quit	2.81	1.31	−.14*	−.16*	−.19**	−.15*	−.14*	(.79)

Listwise $N = 242$. Task variety and skill variety were on 5-point Likert scales. Occupational self-efficacy was on a 6-point Likert scale. Intention to quit was on a 7-point Likert scale. Cronbach's alpha is in brackets on the diagonal. *$p < .05$, **$p < .01$.

TABLE 4
Results of hierarchical moderated regression analyses of Study 2

Step/variable			Intention to quit				
	R^2	ΔR^2	B	SE	β	t	p
Task variety							
Step 1 (control variables)	.07**						
Labourer			−0.03	0.21	−.01	−0.13	.90
Service worker			0.24	0.27	.06	0.88	.38
Manager			−0.63	0.30	−.15	−2.13	.03
Organizational tenure			−0.05	0.12	−.04	−0.38	.70
Occupational self-efficacy			−0.09	0.09	−.07	−0.97	.33
Step 2	.09**	.02					
Task variety			−0.17	0.09	−.12	−1.82	.07
Age			−0.14	0.13	−.10	−1.04	.30
Step 3	.10**	.01*					
Task variety × Age			0.18	0.09	.13	1.98	.04
Skill variety							
Step 1 (control variables)	.07**						
Labourer			0.06	0.21	.02	0.27	.79
Service worker			0.25	0.27	.06	0.92	.36
Manager			−0.46	0.30	−.11	−1.55	.12
Organizational tenure			−0.03	0.12	−.02	−0.24	.81
Occupational self-efficacy			−0.09	0.09	−.07	−1.01	.32
Step 2	.08**	.01					
Skill variety			−0.11	0.09	−.08	−1.25	.21
Age			−0.15	0.13	−.12	−1.20	.23
Step 3	.10**	.01*					
Skill variety × Age			−0.18	0.09	−.13	−1.98	.04

Values reported are for the final equation. The office/clerical worker variable was not entered in the regression (categorical variable with k levels was transformed into $k–1$ variables each with two levels). *p <.05, **p <.01.

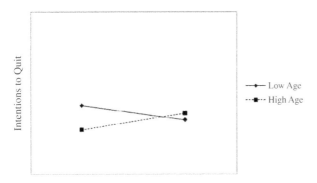

Figure 2. Workers' age and task variety interact to affect intention to quit. Low age (younger workers): 1 standard deviation below the mean ($M − 1\ SD = 26.51$); high age (older workers): 1 standard deviation above the mean ($M + 1\ SD = 48.71$).

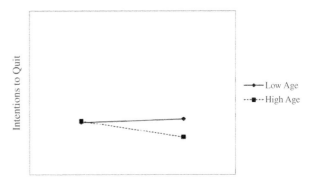

Figure 3. Workers' age and skill variety interact to affect intention to quit. Low age (younger workers): 1 standard deviation below the mean ($M − 1\ SD = 26.51$); high age (older workers): 1 standard deviation above the mean ($M + 1\ SD = 48.71$).

According to Hypothesis 4, age would moderate the relationship between skill variety and intention to quit, such that there would be a more negative relationship between skill variety and intention to quit for older workers than for younger workers. Results supported Hypothesis 4, as indicated by the significant increase in R^2 with the addition of the interaction term in Step 3, $F(1, 233) = 3.92$, $p < .05$, $\Delta R^2 = .01$. This interaction is shown graphically in Figure 3. Specifically, there was a stronger negative relationship between skill variety and intention to quit for older workers, but this relationship was weaker for younger workers.

GENERAL DISCUSSION

The purpose of these two studies was to address a gap in the literature by examining how age interacts with job characteristics, such as skill and task variety, to affect two different types of work outcomes that are both relevant to an ageing workforce in ways that would be specified by lifespan ageing theories such as SOC theory and SST. Specifically, in the first study, the goal was to understand the moderating effect of age on the relationship between task variety and skill variety and the well-being outcome of work-related burnout. In the second study, the goal was to understand the moderating effects of age in the relationship between task variety and skill variety and turnover intentions. Moreover, the second study overcomes certain sampling limitations encountered in the first study, namely, it had a larger sample with a broader range of jobs and age distribution. In keeping with SST (Carstensen, 1991) and SOC Theory (Baltes & Baltes, 1990), our results suggest that younger workers tend to benefit from task variety, whereas older workers tend to benefit more from skill variety.

As hypothesized, in Study 1, we found that task variety was differentially related to work burnout for older and younger workers (H1). Our results illustrate that age moderated the relationship between task variety and burnout, such that task variety was more negatively related to burnout for younger workers than for older workers. This result is particularly interesting, because neither age nor task variety on their own were related to burnout, but the combined interactive effects on burnout were significant and as hypothesized. However, our Study 1 results did not support the hypothesis that skill variety was differentially related to burnout for older and younger workers (H2), although this may be due to lower statistical power. In Study 2, as hypothesized, we found that task variety and skill variety were differentially related to intentions to quit for older and younger workers. Our results illustrate that age moderated the relationship between task variety and intentions to quit, such that task variety was more negatively related to intention to quit for younger workers than for older workers (H3). Moreover, our results illustrate that age moderated the relationship between skill variety and intention to quit, such that skill variety was more negatively related to intention to quit for older workers than for younger workers (H4).

Theoretical implications

These findings further support the idea that the relationship between job characteristics, such as task and skill variety, and work outcomes, such as burnout and turnover intentions, may differ across the life span (e.g., Truxillo, Cadiz, & Rineer, et al., 2012). As suggested by SST (Carstensen, 1991), young adults, who perceive time as open-ended, seem to be more energized to perform a job with characteristics (task variety) that help them to achieve knowledge-acquisition goals and to gain needed work-related experience. In contrast, older adults, who prefer to achieve present-oriented goals with emotional-regulation purposes, may experience a job characterized by high task variety with a reduced sense of personal accomplishment because they have long known how to perform these job tasks and have been performing them for many years. Rather, performing a wide range of tasks may simply lead to an increased sense of perceived physical and psychological fatigue and exhaustion. Indeed, according to SOC theory

(Baltes & Baltes, 1990), to successfully adapt to the ageing process, older workers will select specific domains and consequently optimize the use of their resources (acquired job skills), and better compensate and cope with those domains that are in decline. The results of Study 2 support that idea, in that increased skill variety seemed to benefit older workers, especially compared with their younger counterparts.

According to previous research, the opportunity to use different skills may be helpful in keeping older workers at work (Schmitt et al., 1979). Indeed, as suggested by SST (Carstensen, 1991) and SOC theory (Baltes & Baltes, 1990), older workers can use their accumulated skill, leading to an increased sense of gratification, and thus have decreased intention to quit. This is consistent with the results of the present study and with those of Zacher and Frese (2011) and Zacher et al. (2010), who found that job complexity leads to improved outcomes for older workers in terms of perceived opportunities at work, which suggests that organizations can sustain older workers by providing them with the opportunity to use and share their range of accumulated skills. In contrast, younger workers can benefit from greater task variety. A job with greater task variety gives them the opportunity to accumulate knowledge and experience through performing a wide range of job tasks and prepares them for the challenges and opportunities that lie ahead. High task variety should also lead to decreased intention to quit compared to older workers, because the job is providing younger workers with the developmental opportunities they need (cf. Zache & Frese, 2011; Zacher et al., 2010). This possibility is consistent with recent discussions of age and job design (Truxillo, Cadiz, & Rineer, et al., 2012) and is supported by a previous study that has shown that task variety has a more positive relationship with job satisfaction and engagement of younger workers than older workers (Zaniboni et al., 2011).

Practical implications

If these findings are borne out in other samples and contexts, they may have important implications for organizations. One of the principal purposes of job design literature is to maximize workers' resources through enrichment of the job. However, much of the recent job design literature has emphasized the average worker (e.g., Morgeson & Humphrey, 2006). Although focusing on the average worker may have practical value, we argue that it is also important to understand the differential effects of different job characteristics on work outcomes considering individual differences such as age. Indeed, some characteristics may have more positive effects for younger workers (e.g., task variety) and others for older workers (e.g., skill variety). Moreover, the negative effects (economic and psychological) of burnout and turnover for organizations are well known. In short, to keep workers of all ages psychologically engaged at work in a healthy way, we need to understand which working conditions are the best for them. Furthermore, considering the increase in the ageing of the workforce, it is imperative for organizations to develop jobs that accommodate not just the "average" worker, but workers across their lifespan, to increase employees' well-being and retention.

Limitations

These studies also have some potential limitations. First, our second hypothesis was not confirmed. However, this may be due to a relatively small sample size and thus decreased statistical power. We suggest that future work examine this hypothesis using a larger sample, and across a range of different jobs requiring a wide range of skills. Second, and partially related to the first limitation, we found relatively small effect sizes for some interactions. However, it is difficult to detect interactions using moderated regression, especially in field settings (Aguinis, 1995; McClelland & Judd, 1993). Moreover, as suggested by Prentice and Miller (1992), small effects can be important because they show that an effect is highly pervasive even under a conservative test. Third, we used two convenience samples, and in particular, for the second study, the heterogeneity in terms of types of jobs was quite high. However, this heterogeneity allowed for the potential for generalizability and greater variability in our job characteristics, and similar job-diverse samples have been used in past job characteristics research (Morgeson & Humphrey, 2006). Moreover, to address this diversity in job types, we controlled for job type in our analyses. Future research should compare these effects among different job types. Fourth, we assessed only two job characteristics (i.e., task and skill variety), because of their differential relationship with age, but future work should examine the full set of job characteristics and more work outcomes (e.g., positive aspects of work-related well-being such as satisfaction, engagement, positive emotions) in conjunction with workers' age. Finally, although there was good age variance in the two studies, the sample of the first study had few late-career and early-career workers. Despite this, our results were generally as expected, and our second study confirmed them. Future data collections to retest our hypotheses are suggested.

Future research

We see a number of avenues for future research. First, research is needed into how best to implement these findings within organizations. For example, future research could examine organizational interventions to design jobs for workers at different life stages, or to support workers in crafting jobs to fit their needs. Second, other age variables besides chronological age, such as subjective age and social age, can be used to assess age in the work context (Cleveland & Shore, 1992; Shore, Cleveland, & Goldberg, 2003). Thus, future studies should also examine the role of subjective and relative age and their interaction with job characteristics. Third, other job characteristics (e.g., Morgeson & Humphrey's [2006] comprehensive job design features) and outcomes (e.g., job performance) can be considered in studying ageing at work (Truxillo et al., 2012; Truxillo, Cadiz, Rineer, et al., 2012). Fourth, other moderators may affect the relationships between job characteristics and work outcomes. For example, it might also be that personality variables (e.g., proactivity) and contextual characteristics (e.g., professional membership, organizational culture and climate, management styles) moderate the relationship between job characteristics and work outcomes. Thus, we suggest that future research examines other aspects that may affect the relationships between job characteristics, age, and work outcomes. For example, it might also be that doing more tasks might be beneficial only for certain younger workers, such as those with higher levels of proactive personality. Moreover, it is possible that certain jobs more than others may allow workers to craft their jobs as they age. Fifth, future research should also examine mediating mechanisms such as the psychological states (meaningfulness, responsibility, and knowledge of results) suggested by Hackman and Oldham (1975). Humphrey et al. (2007) showed meta-analytically that meaningfulness and responsibility may be particularly important mediators. Future research, therefore, should examine such mediating mechanisms in explaining the effects of the age–job characteristics interaction. Sixth, future studies should take into account the job–age stereotype (e.g., Perry, Kulik, & Bourhis, 1996) as it could affect how both the worker and their coworkers perceive the fit between the worker and their job. Seventh, we suggest that these hypotheses be replicated in other samples and settings. Finally, we suggest future studies that examine intraindividual differences over time, to explore the change in a person's preferred job characteristics. This is a particularly challenging research issue, but one that will allow for greater understanding of the relationship between age and desired job characteristics.

CONCLUSION

In conclusion, this study is an important contribution to address the gap in the research about the role of age in job design. Specifically, we found that age differentially moderated the relationship between two job characteristics, task variety and skill variety, and two key outcomes, burnout and turnover intention, consistent with lifespan ageing theories. Whereas task variety appeared to benefit younger workers, skill variety appeared to benefit older workers. We encourage future research in additional contexts on the interaction of age with other job characteristics in affecting employee well-being and behaviour.

REFERENCES

Aguinis, H. (1995). Statistical power problems with moderated multiple regression in management research. *Journal of Management*, *21*, 1141–1158.

Baltes, B. B., & Dickson, M. W. (2001). Using life-span models in industrial-organizational psychology: The theory of selective optimization with compensation. *Applied Developmental Science*, *5*, 51–62.

Baltes, P. B., & Baltes, M. M. (1990). Psychological perspectives on successful aging: The model of selective optimization with compensation. In P. B. Baltes & M. M. Baltes (Eds.), *Successful aging: Perspectives from the behavioral sciences* (pp. 1–34). New York, NY: Cambridge University Press.

Brislin, R. W. (1970). Back-translation for cross-cultural research. *Journal of Cross-Cultural Psychology*, *1*, 185–216.

Carstensen, L. L. (1991). Selectivity theory: Social activity in life-span context. In K. W. Schaie (Ed.), *Annual review of gerontology and geriatrics* (Vol. 11, pp. 195–217). New York, NY: Springer.

Carstensen, L. L., Isaacowitz, D. M., & Charles, S. T. (1999). Taking time seriously: A theory of socioemotional selectivity. *The American Psychologist*, *54*, 165–181.

Cleveland, J. N., & Shore, L. M. (1992). Self- and supervisory perspectives on age and work attitudes and performance. *Journal of Applied Psychology*, *77*, 469–484.

Cropanzano, R., Rupp, D. E., & Byrne, Z. S. (2003). The relationship of emotional exhaustion to work attitudes, job performance, and organizational citizenship behaviors. *Journal of Applied Psychology*, *88*, 160–169.

de Lange, A. H., Taris, T. W., Jansen, P., Kompier, M. A. J., Houtman, I. L. D., & Bongers, P. M. (2010). On the relationships among work characteristics and learning-related behavior: Does age matter? *Journal of Organizational Behavior*, *31*, 925–950.

Edwards, J. R. (2008). To prosper, organizational psychology should … overcome methodological barriers to progress. *Journal of Organizational Behavior*, *29*, 469–491.

Frazier, P. A., Tix, A. P., & Barron, K. E. (2004). Testing moderator and mediator effects in counseling psychology research. *Journal of Counseling Psychology*, *51*, 115–134.

Grant, A. M., Fried, Y., & Juillerat, T. (2010). Work matters: Job design in classic and contemporary perspectives. In S. Zedeck (Ed.), *APA handbook of industrial and organizational psychology* (Vol. 1, pp. 417–453). Washington, DC: American Psychological Association.

Hackman, J. R., & Oldham, G. R. (1975). Development of the Job Diagnostic Survey. *Journal of Applied Psychology*, *60*, 159–170.

Hackman, J. R., & Oldham, G. R. (1976). Motivation through the design of work: Test of a theory. *Organizational Behavior and Human Performance*, *16*, 250–279.

Hochwarter, W. A., Zellars, K. L., Perrewé, P. L., & Harrison, A. W. (1999). The interactive role of negative affectivity and job characteristics: Are high-NA employees destined to be unhappy at work? *Journal of Applied Social Psychology*, *29*, 2203–2218.

Hom, P. W., Caranikas-Walker, F., Prussia, G. E., & Griffeth, R. W. (1992). A meta-analytical structural equations analysis of a model of employee turnover. *Journal of Applied Psychology*, *77*, 890–909.

Huang, I.-C., Chuang, C.-H. J., & Lin, H.-C. (2003). The role of burnout in the relationship between perceptions of organizational politics and turnover intentions. *Public Personnel Management*, *32*, 519–531.

Humphrey, S. E., Nahrgang, J. D., & Morgeson, F. P. (2007). Integrating motivational, social, and contextual work design features: A meta-analytic summary and theoretical extension of the work design literature. *Journal of Applied Psychology*, *92*, 1332–1356.

Iverson, R. D., Olekalns, M., & Erwin, P. J. (1998). Affectivity, organizational stressors, and absenteeism: A causal model of burnout and its consequences. *Journal of Vocational Behavior*, *52*, 1–23.

Karasek, R. A., & Theorell, T. (1990). *Healthy work*. New York, NY: Basic Books.

Karsh, B., Booske, B. C., & Sainfort, F. (2005). Job and organizational determinants of nursing home employee commitment, job satisfaction and intent to turnover. *Ergonomics*, *48*, 1260–1281.

Kristensen, T. S., Borritz, M., Villadsen, E., & Christensen, K. B. (2005). The Copenhagen Burnout Inventory: A new tool for the assessment of burnout. *Work and Stress*, *19*, 192–207.

Lawler, E. E. (1969). Job design and employee motivation. *Personnel Psychology*, *22*, 426–435.

LePine, J. A., Podsakoff, N. P., & Lepine, M. A. (2005). A meta-analytic test of the challenge stressor-hindrance stressor framework: An explanation for inconsistent relationships among stressors and performance. *Academy of Management Journal*, *48*, 764–775.

Maslach, C., & Leiter, M. P. (1997). *The truth about burnout: How organizations cause personal stress and what to do about it*. San Francisco, CA: Jossey-Bass.

Maslach, C., & Schaufeli, W. B. (1993). Historical and conceptual development of burnout. In W. B. Schaufeli, C. Maslach, & T. Marek (Eds.), *Professional burnout: Recent developments in theory and research* (pp. 1–16). Philadelphia, PA: Taylor & Francis.

Maslach, C., Schaufeli, W. B., & Leiter, M. P. (2001). Job burnout. *Annual Review of Psychology*, *52*, 397–422.

McClelland, G. H., & Judd, C. M. (1993). Statistical difficulties of detecting interactions and moderator effects. *Psychological Bulletin*, *114*, 376–390.

Mobley, W. H. (1977). Intermediate linkages in the relationship between job satisfaction and employee turnover. *Journal of Applied Psychology*, *62*, 237–240.

Mobley, W. H., Griffeth, R. W., Hand, H. H., & Meglino, B. M. (1979). Review and conceptual analysis of the employee turnover process. *Psychological Bulletin*, *86*, 493.

Morgeson, F. P., & Humphrey, S. E. (2006). The Work Design Questionnaire (WDQ): Developing and validating a comprehensive measure for assessing job design and the nature of work. *Journal of Applied Psychology*, *91*, 1321–1339.

Morgeson, F. P., & Humphrey, S. E. (2008). Job and team design: Toward a more integrative conceptualization of work design. In J. J. Martocchio (Ed.), *Research in personnel and human resources management* (Vol. 27, pp. 39–91). Bingley: Emerald Group.

National Institute on Aging. (2007). *Why population aging matters: A global perspective*. Retrieved from http://www.nia.nih.gov/sites/default/files/WPAM.pdf

Ng, T. W. H., & Feldman, D. C. (2010a). Organizational tenure and job performance. *Journal of Management*, *36*, 1220–1250.

Ng, T. W. H., & Feldman, D. C. (2010b). The relationships of age with job attitudes: A meta-analysis. *Personnel Psychology*, *63*, 677–718.

Perrewé, P. L., Hochwarter, W. A., Rossi, A. M., Wallace, A., Maignan, I., Castro, S. L., … Van Deusen, C. A. (2002). Are work stress relationships universal? A nine-region examination of role stressors, general self-efficacy, and burnout. *Journal of International Management*, *8*, 163–187.

Perry, E. L., Kulik, C. T., & Bourhis, A. C. (1996). Moderating effects of personal and contextual factors in age discrimination. *Journal of Applied Psychology*, *81*, 628–647.

Podsakoff, P. M., MacKenzie, S. B., Lee, J. Y., & Podsakoff, N. P. (2003). Common method biases in behavioral research: A critical review of the literature and recommended remedies. *Journal of Applied Psychology*, *88*, 879–903.

Prentice, D. A., & Miller, D. T. (1992). When small effects are impressive. *Psychological Bulletin*, *112*, 160–164.

Rigotti, T., Schyns, B., & Mohr, G. (2008). A short version of the occupational self-efficacy scale: Structural and construct validity across five countries. *Journal of Career Assessment*, *16*, 238–255.

Schaufeli, W. B., & Bakker, A. B. (2004). Job demands, job resources, and their relationship with burnout and engagement: A multi-sample study. *Journal of Organizational Behavior*, *25*, 293–315.

Schmitt, N., Coyle, B. W., Rauschenberger, J., & White, J. K. (1979). Comparison of early retirees and nonretirees. *Personnel Psychology*, *32*, 327–340.

Schwarzer, R., & Hallum, S. (2008). Perceived teacher self-efficacy as a predictor of job stress and burnout. *Applied Psychology: An International Review, 57*, 152–171.

Schyns, B., & Von Collani, G. (2002). A new occupational self-efficacy scale and its relation to personality constructs and organizational variables. *European Journal of Work and Organizational Psychology, 11*, 219–241.

Shore, L. M., Cleveland, J. N., & Goldberg, C. B. (2003). Work attitudes and decisions as a function of manager age and employee age. *Journal of Applied Psychology, 88*, 529–537.

Shultz, K. S., Wang, M., Crimmins, E. M., & Fisher, G. G. (2010). Age differences in the demand-control model of work stress: An examination of data from 15 European countries. *Journal of Applied Gerontology, 29*, 21–47.

Sims, H. P., Szilagyi, A. D., & Keller, R. T. (1976). The measurement of job characteristics. *Academy of Management Journal, 19*, 195–212.

Slattery, J. P., Selvarajan, T. T., Anderson, J. E., & Sardessai, R. (2010). Relationship between job characteristics and attitudes: A study of temporary employees. *Journal of Applied Social Psychology, 40*, 1539–1565.

Spector, P. E., & Jex, S. M. (1991). Relations of job characteristics from multiple data sources with employee affect, absence, turnover intentions, and health. *Journal of Applied Psychology, 76*, 46–53.

Tani, F., Lazzaretti, R., Maggino, F., Smorti, M., & Giannini, M. (2009). Uno strumento per misurare l'autoefficacia occupazionale: L'adattamento Italiano della Occupational Self-Efficacy Scale (OCCSEFF). *Giornale Italiano di Psicologia, 36*, 657–671.

Truxillo, D. M., Cadiz, D. A., & Rineer, J. R. (2012). Designing jobs for an aging workforce: An opportunity for occupational health. In J. Houdmont, S. Leka, & R. R. Sinclair (Eds.), *Contemporary occupational health psychology: Global perspectives on research and practice* (Vol. 2, pp. 109–125). Oxford: Oxford University Press.

Truxillo, D. M., Cadiz, D. M., Rineer, J. R., Zaniboni, S., & Fraccaroli, F. (2012). A lifespan perspective on job design: Fitting the worker to the job to promote job satisfaction, engagement, and performance. *Organizational Psychology Review, 2*, 340–360.

Wayne, S. J., Shore, L. M., & Liden, R. C. (1997). Perceived organizational support and leader-member exchange: A social exchange perspective. *Academy of Management Journal, 40*, 82–111.

Zacher, H., & Frese, M. (2009). Remaining time and opportunities at work: Relationships between age, work characteristics, and occupational future time perspective. *Psychology and Aging, 24*, 487–493.

Zacher, H., & Frese, M. (2011). Maintaining a focus on opportunities at work: The interplay between age, job complexity, and the use of selection, optimization, and compensation strategies. *Journal of Organizational Behavior, 32*, 291–318.

Zacher, H., Heusner, S., Schmitz, M., Zwierzanska, M. M., & Frese, M. (2010). Focus on opportunities as a mediator of the relationships between age, job complexity, and work performance. *Journal of Vocational Behavior, 76*, 374–386.

Zaniboni, S., Sarchielli, G., & Fraccaroli, F. (2010). How are psychosocial factors related to retirement intentions? *International Journal of Manpower, 31*, 271–285.

Zaniboni, S., Truxillo, D. M., Fraccaroli, F., McCune, E. A., & Bertolino, M. (2011, April). *Age moderates the effects of WDQ factors on job attitudes.* Paper presented at the 26th annual conference of the Society for Industrial and Organizational Psychology, Chicago, IL.

Customer stressors in service organizations: The impact of age on stress management and burnout

S. J. Johnson[1], L. Holdsworth[1], H. Hoel[1], and D. Zapf[2]

[1]Manchester Business School, University of Manchester, Manchester, UK
[2]Johann Wolfgang Goethe-University, Frankfurt, Germany

This study examined the impact of age on stress management strategies and burnout as a response to customer stressors. Questionnaire data from 273 retail sector employees revealed that age is negatively related to customer stressors but no direct relationships were found with stress management strategies. Moderation analysis revealed no pattern of interaction between customer stressors and age on burnout, although the older retail employees were less likely to experience cynicism when exposed to disliked customers. A key finding of this study is that older employees' stress management strategies of emotion control and active coping had a more positive effect on emotional exhaustion and cynicism compared to younger employees. As with previous studies few significant results were found for professional efficacy. The stress management strategies of humour and downplay had limited interaction effects with age. Exploratory analyses of three-way interactions between humour and downplay, customer stressors, and age on burnout revealed systematic findings in the expected direction in high stress situations with younger employees less successfully using these strategies to reduce levels of emotional exhaustion and cynicism. This article shows the competencies of older employees and argues against the deficits of older workers. Practical implications for organizations and supervisors are discussed.

As life expectancy and the average age of the population increases, the composition of the working population changes. For example, in the European Union the number of younger adults has been decreasing since 2005, which means the working population is gradually ageing, and simultaneously the total working population (16–64 years) is forecast to shrink by 20.8 million by 2030 (Commission of the European Communities, 2005, as cited in Schalk et al., 2010). Similar patterns are evident in the US. This will create an increased reliance on older workers and a need for a greater understanding of age differences in the workplace (Schalk et al., 2010). This is of particular interest for the retail sector, which has a very young workforce and already faces serious labour shortages and skills gaps, although recruitment strategies targeting older workers are rising (McNair & Flynn, 2006). Increasing numbers of academic articles are looking specifically at age (e.g., DeLange et al., 2010; Kooij, DeLange, Jansen, Kanfer, & Dikkers, 2011; Shultz, Wang, Crimmins, & Fisher, 2010), although there is more focus on "older" (typically 50+ years) than "middle-aged" workers.

This greater dependency on ageing workers must be seen against a backdrop of discrimination and prejudices in the workplace, with ageing workers perceived to have poorer cognitive functioning, be less capable with new technology, and be more resistant to change (McGregor & Gray, 2002). Such stereotypes are disputed (Schalk et al., 2010). Furthermore, literature has overlooked social and emotional competences and attitudes and their potential positive impact, despite indications from nonwork-related (everyday-life) research that ageing employees may be more competent in these areas.

Much of retail industry employment focuses on customer service where social and emotional skills are necessary to cope successfully with job requirements. Service employees are expected to cope with the stress of demanding customers, to meet emotional work demands such as being friendly to customers, and exhibit positive attitudes to work, the organization, and customers. Service employees are expected to behave towards customers according to "display rules", for example to behave in a pleasant manner towards the customer (Morris & Feldman, 1996). By contrast, the customer does not have a similar duty to behave with good manners, which may introduce tension and create a stressful situation for the service employee (Rafaeli, 1989). This unequal relationship can contribute to poor health and well-being (Pugliesi, 1999; Wharton, 1993), and burnout (Dorman & Zapf, 2004; Hochschild, 1983) for service employees. Employees often have little opportunity to influence customers (Rafaeli & Sutton, 1987) and, in the absence of control, need to develop effective strategies to cope with the stressful situation, and to create opportunities to offer solutions and meet customer demands. Successfully managing service interactions should result in feelings of competence, achievement, and development in employees and positively influence health and well-being.

Research into everyday life implies that the older the employee the better the potential to cope well with stressful customer interactions, due to better personal coping strategies and greater life experiences, resulting in positive health outcomes (e.g., Blanchard-Fields, Stein, & Watson, 2004; Diehl, Coyle, & Labouvie-Vief, 1996). The purpose of this study is to investigate the potentials and capabilities of the older service employees in the retail sector during stressful employee–customer interactions and contribute to knowledge underpinning the use of constructive and healthy coping strategies. This article will investigate: the relationship between customer stressors and age; how stress management strategies differ across ages; and the effect of age in relation to customer stressors and burnout, and stress management and burnout within service interactions. In addressing these issues, we intend to contribute to the literature by creating a greater understanding of the relationship between age, coping, and burnout in the service industry, and by investigating age differences within a sample of young and middle-aged employees as opposed to the more common focus in the research literature on older workers.

AGE IN RETAIL

The UK retail sector is very large, employing 10% of the national workforce, and is expected to increase employment faster than any other sector (McNair & Flynn, 2006). Traditionally, the sector has employed a third of their workforce from the 16–24 age group and employs fewer individuals aged 25–49 and 50 plus than the all-industry average (Skillsmart Retail, 2010). The predicted increase in the number of older people and the shrinking of the working population suggests the retail sector will benefit from reviewing recruitment strategies (McNair & Flynn, 2006) and having a better understanding of how workers of different ages cope with customer interactions.

CUSTOMER STRESSORS AND AGE

Dormann and Zapf (2004) identified four customer stressors aligned to service interactions: customers' expectations becoming disproportionate, customers behaving in unpleasant ways, customers' expectations being unclear, and customers being verbally aggressive. As employees age they may experience fewer of these difficult situations for several reasons. There is evidence that as people grow older they use a more positive and constructive approach in social interactions. For example, individuals are generally less confrontational and contribute less to conflict development as they mature (Folkman, Lazarus, Pimeley, & Novacek, 1987). One of the requirements of service work is to display positive emotions (e.g., Zapf, Vogt, Seifert, Mertini, & Isic, 1999), which are positively related to customers' positive responses (Zimmermann, Dormann, & Dollard, 2011). Studies suggest that as adults age they may be better at controlling their emotions (e.g., Gross et al. 1997) and showing positive emotions (Zapf, 2002), which can enhance positive, and minimize negative, emotional experiences (Carstensen, 1986). Older employees may therefore contribute to more pleasant service interactions, resulting in fewer customer stressors. Also, because of their life experience, more mature employees are perceived as better at building trustful relationships (Zeithaml & Bitner, 2000). As credibility and trust are related to customer satisfaction (Swan, Bowers, & Richardson, 1999), the older employees may be less exposed to customer stressors, as conflicts will occur less frequently. Finally, studies on "wisdom" (e.g., Staudinger & Pasupathi, 2003) provide further support for these assumptions, as people tend to be wiser with age with regard to social sensitivity and perspective taking (Baltes, Staudinger, Maercker, & Smith, 1995). These abilities should lead to higher acceptance of and tolerance for customers' perspectives and of partially uncontrollable situations. This theory converges with results from stress and coping research discussed in the next section. Because of these reasons we hypothesize the following:

Hypothesis 1: Age is negatively related to the exposure of customer stressors.

STRESS MANAGEMENT STRATEGIES AND AGE

To cope successfully with stressful customer interactions, effective stress management strategies are required. That is, how the customer service employee handles possible or actual harm, losses, or risks, and the negative reactions that arise (John & Gross, 2007). Primary coping strategies can be divided into two higher order categories: "managing or altering the problem (problem-focused coping), or regulating the emotional response to the problem (emotion-focused coping)" (Lazarus & Folkman, 1984, p. 179). Problem-focused (active) coping includes taking steps to develop plans and engage in actions to directly tackle the problem, for example, seeking out information, confronting the problem, or planful problem solving. Emotion-focused strategies are argued to be diverse, ranging from proactive, appraisal-oriented approaches, such as cognitive restructuring (e.g., downplaying the events), or controlling emotions (e.g., withholding inappropriate emotions), to more passive approaches, such as denial, avoidance, and escape from the incident (Carver, Scheier, & Weintraub, 1989). There is a distinction between efforts focused on the problem itself and efforts focused on emotional responses to the problem (Oakland & Ostell, 1996).

Literature suggests age-related preferences in the selection of stress management strategies. Blanchard-Fields et al. (2004) proposed that in everyday life adults aged 40–64 prefer proactive emotion-focused strategies, such as confronting negative emotions in order to cope with them, and looking at the situation from the other's point of view. They argue this may partly be explained by adults in this age group being at their peak of personal control and power. By contrast, some studies propose that younger adults prefer problem-focused strategies, such as problem solving or seeking support (e.g., De Lange et al., 2010; Folkman et al., 1987). Moreover, in high emotional conflict situations younger adults are more inclined to try not to think of, or feel emotions about the situation (Blanchard-Fields et al., 2004). Diehl et al. (1996) described middle-aged adults as using more cognitive restructuring such as emotional control than younger adults, whereas younger adults use coping strategies that are more psychologically immature, such as blaming someone or something else. The latter may help to restore self-esteem, in line with self enhancement theory (Shrauger, 1975), but can also lead to conflict with others which can create problems in the workplace.

Despite some inconsistencies, the literature generally suggests that problem-focused coping is more successful in acting as a stress buffer than emotion-focused coping (Billings & Moos, 1984). In low-control situations though, emotional coping strategies such as positive reinterpretation as well as avoidance, denial, or "doing nothing", may actually be more useful (e.g., Begley, 1998; Lazarus & Folkman, 1984; Semmer, 2003). As service employees are often expected to adhere to explicit and implicit display rules, and customers have the potential to exert influence, service interactions are potentially low-control situations (Rafaeli, 1989) in which these strategies may be preferable.

Studies suggest that in everyday life as individuals get older they may be better at controlling which emotions they experience or express (e.g., Gross et al., 1997) and demonstrate more effective use of emotion-focused coping strategies (Lazarus & Folkman, 1984). Support for this view is provided by socioemotional selectivity theory (e.g., Carstensen, 1995), which stresses that with age comes the search for emotionally meaningful goals, even in conflictual relationships. This implies that, as individuals age, emotion control and other types of emotion-focused coping might be used to calm otherwise stressful situations with the aim of achieving a successful customer service interaction (Folkman et al., 1987).

Employees who are older may therefore have an advantage over younger employees in adopting more effective types of strategies as they increasingly favour emotional coping strategies (Diehl et al., 1996) which appear to be more suitable for the low control situation of the service sector. This could also intimate that the life experience that age brings to a customer service role may be as valuable as relevant job experience. Based on this line of reasoning the following hypothesis is tested:

Hypothesis 2: Age is related to strategies of stress management. In that employees who are older will utilize more emotion-focused coping than younger employees.

STRESS MANAGEMENT, BURNOUT, AND AGE

Where work is emotionally demanding, such as dealing with difficult customers, high stress levels can result in employees being susceptible to burnout (e.g., Bakker, Schaufeli, Sixma, Bosveld, & van Dierendonck, 2000; Dormann & Zapf, 2004). Burnout is most commonly experienced in service relationships and develops as a condition consisting of three distinct states in which employees feel emotionally drained (emotional exhaustion), develop detached and negative attitudes to others (cynicism), and experience a deterioration of efficacy at work (reduced professional efficacy) (Maslach & Jackson, 1981; Maslach, Schaufeli, & Leiter, 2001). Dormann and Zapf (2004) reported all four of their customer-related social stressors were related to burnout. In particular they reported an association between customer stressors and cynicism. Other research looking at the aggressive element of the employee–customer relationship also found that stress emerging from dealing with aggressive customers is positively related to the exhaustion and cynicism dimensions of burnout (Ben-Zur & Yagil, 2005).

Meta-analytical studies indicate a negative relationship between burnout and age (Brewer & Shapard, 2004). As detailed earlier, one explanation is that as employees age they may develop competencies that protect them from negative health outcomes, although it is debatable whether these successful employees remain in their jobs, whereas less skilled employees leave. How service employees cope with stressors in the workplace has been investigated in a number of studies, although the findings are unclear (Ben-Zur & Yagil, 2005). For example, negative coping strategies, such as negative interpretations of intrusive memories, rumination, suppression, and disassociation, have been linked to increased stress in ambulance service workers (Clohessy & Ehlers, 1999). Humour, proposed to be a positive coping strategy because it allows individuals to evaluate stressful events as being less intimidating (Dixon, 1980), was found to provide no cushioning effects in coping with stress (Healy & McKay, 2000). Other research reported that nurses who used coping strategies of escape/avoidance, or confronting, experienced high levels of burnout, whilst those using "planful" problem solving, positive reappraisal, and seeking social support, experienced low levels of burnout (Ceslowitz, 1989). Emotional control was used by both groups but to a greater extent by nurses with higher levels of burnout. By contrast, research in the service industry suggests that using specific coping strategies, such as emotional control, could be a successful way to reduce burnout (Pienaar & Willemse, 2008). There is no clear consensus on optimum coping mechanisms, and the situational context in which they are used is likely to be relevant to their success.

Exploration of the pathways between stressful interactions and health should further our understanding of health risks to service employees and the impact of different coping strategies on health. This may provide some understanding of not only why, as employees age, they typically report less stress and burnout, but also the mechanisms that underpin the relationship between stressful situations and negative health outcomes. Existing research implies that older employees may use different coping strategies to deal with stressful customer interactions, and certain coping strategies may be more effective within the service industry. We hypothesize the following:

Hypothesis 3: Age will moderate the relationship between customer stressors and employee burnout. The positive relationship between customer stressors and burnout will be weaker for the older employees.

Some authors (e.g., Rafaeli, 1989) describe the struggle for control between service employee and customer. Especially if customer orientation is high, then control is low for the service employee. In such situations, emotion-focused instead of problem-focused stress management strategies tend to be more effective (e.g., Begley, 1998). As the older employees use emotion-focused strategies more effectively (Lazarus & Folkman, 1984), we hypothesize the following:

Hypothesis 4: Age will moderate the relationship between stress management strategies and employee burnout. Emotion-focused strategies are more negatively related to burnout for the older employees compared to younger employees. The expected influence of age in the study (hypotheses 1 to 4) is shown in Figure 1.

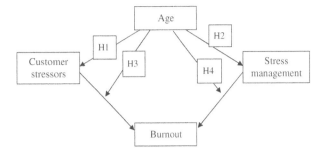

Figure 1. Hypothesized model.

METHOD

Participants and procedure

The participants were customer-facing employees working in a national retail organization in the UK. Three questionnaires were sent to each manager of 259 stores. Cover letters outlined the study, assured confidentiality and anonymity, and asked that completed questionnaires be returned directly to the researchers. Volunteers were invited to complete the questionnaires, with priority given to the oldest and youngest employees within each store. Of the 777 questionnaires distributed a total of 273 (35%) were returned. In the sample, 63% of respondents were female, and the mean age was 30.2 (SD = 10.5) years, which was representative of organizational demographics. The age profile of employees is younger than the general UK employee age profile but not unusual for the retail sector where the proportion of younger workers (16- to 24-year-olds) is more than double the UK all-industry average (Skillsmart Retail, 2010). It is recognized that this is a restricted range, with younger employees (–1 *SD*) having an approximate age of 20 years, and older (+1 *SD*) an approximate age of 40 years. This means that when discussing older employees in this sample this should not be interpreted as older employees as in the wider population, who are usually placed in the age brackets of over 40 or over 45 (e.g., DeLange et al., 2010; Shultz et al., 2010).

Measures

Scale means, standard deviations, and intercorrelations can be found in Table 1, with Cronbach's alphas on the diagonal.

Customer stressors. Customer stressors were assessed by the 15-item customer-related Social Stressor scale (Dormann & Zapf, 2004). Participants were asked how often they are exposed to: disproportionate customer expectations (five items, e.g., "who do not recognize when we are busy"), verbally aggressive customers (three items, e.g., "who often shout at us"), disliked customers (three items, e.g., "who are

TABLE 1

Customer stressors, stress management, and burnout correlations

Variable	M	SD	Age	1	2	3	4	5	6	7	8	9	10	11	12	13	14	15
Age	30.2	10.5																
1. Gender	1.4	0.48	.035															
2. Full/part-time work	1.3	0.47	-.110	-.230***														
3. Work experience	12.4	9.55	.876***	.063	-.188**													
4. Job age	3.6	3.36	.332***	-.002	-.097	.297***												
5. Disproportionate expectations	3.21	0.76	-.081	.114	-.103	-.049	.061	.81									
6. Aggressive customers	1.89	0.84	-.115	.068	-.019	-.086	-.015	.591***	.86								
7. Disliked customers	2.26	0.92	-.250***	.091	-.011	-.185**	-.065	.570***	.742***	.85							
8. Ambiguous expectations	2.24	0.89	-.237***	.165**	.026	-.182**	-.138*	.624***	.678***	.717***	.89						
9. Downplay	3.25	0.72	-.013	-.091	.034	.035	-.021	.183*	.244**	.171*	.119	.77					
10. Active coping	4.07	0.66	.118	-.068	-.051	.081	.139	.051	.067	-.019	-.129	.253**	.62				
11. Controlling emotions	4.28	0.82	.212**	.000	-.099	.151	.127	.033	.061	.005	-.098	.224**	.611***	.82			
12. Humour	3.07	1.01	-.165*	.087	.036	-.154	-.160	.067	.102	.054	.103	.368***	.115	.118	.78		
13. Emotional exhaustion	2.66	1.03	-.192***	.129*	-.179**	-.102	-.015	.330***	.409***	.391***	.365***	.070	-.067	-.117	.050	.92	
14. Cynicism	2.06	0.97	-.163**	.084	-.010	-.144*	-.037	.243***	.307***	.332***	.326***	.130	-.275**	-.310***	.125	.652***	.91
15. Reduced professional efficacy	1.67	0.53	-.007	.014	.147*	-.016	-.040	-.026	.095	.080	.146*	-.089	-.393***	-.322***	.021	.176**	.389***	.87

(n = 269) except overall customer stressors and ambiguous (n = 268); stress management strategy scales (n = 153); burnout scales (n = 272). Cronbach's alphas are shown on the diagonal. *p < .05, **p < .01, ***p < .001. Gender: 1 = female, 2 = male. Working hours: 1 = full-time, 2 = part-time.

unpleasant people"), and ambiguous customer expectations (four items, e.g., "whose requests are not clear"). Five-point scales were used, ranging from 1 = "several times an hour" to 5 = "rarely or never" (see Dudenhöffer & Dormann, in press).

Stress management. Respondents were asked whether they had experiences of uncomfortable customer situations within recent weeks. Only those who acknowledged experience of uncomfortable situations responded to a 14-item stress management scale ($n = 153$). Of these respondents, 59% were female, and mean age was 29.6 years, which was representative of organizational demographics.

Eleven items were used from the Stress Coping Questionnaire (Janke, Erdmann, & Kallus, 2002; Weyers, Ising, Reuter, & Janke, 2005). Subscales included: downplay (six items, e.g., "in the situations I try to talk myself into believing that it is not that important"); and emotional control (two items, e.g., "I told myself 'don't lose your self-control' "). Active coping, as an example of problem-focused coping, was included as literature perceives it to be the most useful overall (three items, e.g., "I took steps to remove the causes"). In addition, as a number of studies have highlighted the role of humour in the positive appraisal of stressful situations (e.g., McCrae & Costa, 1986), three items were developed to assess the degree to which individuals maintained a sense of humour in potentially stressful situations (e.g., "I tried to use humour in the situations"), and used humour as a means of coping with stress (e.g., "I tried to see the funny side of the situations" and "I tried to smile to myself about the situations"). Responses were made on a five-point scale ranging from 1 = "I totally agree" to 5 = "I totally disagree". Cronbach's alphas ranged from .77 to .82, with the exception of an active coping Cronbach's alpha of .62. However, the scale was accepted, as an interitem correlation was calculated (.451) and found to be within optimal levels (Briggs & Cheek, 1986).

Burnout. Burnout was measured by the Maslach Burnout Inventory–General Survey (Schaufeli, Leiter, Maslach, & Jackson, 1996). Subscales include: emotional exhaustion (five items, e.g., "I feel emotionally drained from my work"), cynicism (five items, e.g., "I have become less enthusiastic about my work"), and reduced professional efficacy (six items, e.g., "I just want to do my job and not be bothered"). Items were rated on five-point scale from "I totally agree" to 5 = "I totally disagree" (see Kim, Shin, & Umbreit, 2007).

Sociodemographic information. Respondents were asked to provide information on gender, age, working status (full/part-time), length of employment, and total years worked in their current job.

Age. We refer to biological age in this study and the focus is on the psychological implications of age and life experiences (Kooij et al., 2011), which may help individuals to cope with situations more successfully compared to individuals who lack such experiences. Biological age cannot be easily separated from length of overall work experience and in this study, as in many others, age and overall work experience are highly positively correlated. It is of little practical relevance that life experience and work experience are difficult to separate, the conclusion is the same, namely to focus on employee age. This is different for "job age", defined as the length of time working in the current job. If doing a job for a few years has the same effects as life experience, then it would not be possible to use the potential positive effects of life experience as an argument to employ older workers, since any positive benefits they would bring could also be offered by someone with a few years' work experience. In this study, we will use biological age as the key variable. We will also report overall work experience but we will not control for it; however, we will control for job age. In this way we can identify whether age (i.e., length of life experience including past work experience) or experience in the present job is more important in explaining the results of the present study.

RESULTS

Table 1 shows age to be negatively related to emotional exhaustion, $r = -.19$, $p < .01$, and cynicism, $r = -.16$, $p < .01$, although no relationship was found between age and reduced professional efficacy. This confirms existing research (e.g., Brewer & Shapard, 2004) and indicated that older employees were less likely to experience emotional exhaustion and feel cynical about the job than younger employees.

Our first hypothesis referred to a relationship between customer stressors and age. Responses were recoded with higher scores indicating increased exposure to customer stressors. Significant negative correlations were found with the subscales of disliked customers, $r = -.25$, $p < .001$, and ambiguous customer expectations, $r = -.24$, $p < .001$. Although nonsignificant, the direction of effect was the same for disproportionate customer expectations, $r = -.08$, $p > .05$, and verbally aggressive customers, $r = -.12$, $p > .05$. Hierarchical regression analysis with control variables (job age, full/part-time work, gender) and age revealed age to be significant for all customer stressor scales, suggesting that the inclusion of control variables allows the identification of significant associations not shown directly through correlation. Note that, for aggressive customers, the correlation of $r = .12$ just failed to reach the conventional significance level. In the case of disproportionate customer expectations, full-time employment masks the effect that older workers report less disproportionate

TABLE 2
Regression results for customer stressors and age (Hypothesis 1)

| | Customer stressor | | | | | | | |
| | Disproportionate customer expectations | | Verbally aggressive customers | | Disliked customers | | Ambiguous customer expectations | |
Variable	I	II	I	II	I	II	I	II
Job age	.05	.10	−.02	.03	−.07	.02	−.14*	−.06
Full/part-time work	−.09	−.10	−.01	−.02	.01	−.01	.06	.04
Gender	.11	.11	.06	.07	.10	.11	.19**	.19**
Age		−.14*		−.15*		−.27***		−.23***
R^2	.03	.04	.01	.03	.02	.08	.05	.10
R^2 change	.03	.02*	.01	.02*	.02	.07***	.05**	.05***

Entries are standardized regression coefficients. *$p < .05$, **$p < .01$, ***$p < .001$. Gender: 1 = female, 2 = male. Working hours: 1 = full-time, 2 = part-time.

customer expectations because full-time employees are older and at the same time report more disproportionate customer expectations. Hypothesis 1 was therefore supported, with older age associated with exposure to fewer customer stressors (see Table 2).

With regard to Hypothesis 2 responses were recoded with higher scores indicating use of a stress management strategy. An expected significant correlation was found with age and controlling emotions, $r = .21$, $p < .01$. However, downplay and active coping were not correlated with age, and humour was negatively related with age, $r = −.17$, $p < .05$. Control variables and age were again entered into a hierarchical regression analysis which revealed age to have no influence on any of the four stress management strategies. Hypothesis 2 was therefore not supported.

Hypotheses 3 and 4 were tested by moderated regression analyses. Predictor, moderator, and outcome variables were z-standardized (Cohen, Cohen, West, & Aiken, 2003). In the first step control variables were entered, in the second step the predictor and moderator variables were entered. Interaction effects were examined in the third and final step. Problems of low statistical power and the resulting increased chance of a Type II error (Lubinski & Humphreys, 1990) suggest a more liberal criterion for selecting moderator effects. We therefore accepted moderator effects if explained variance was at least 1% and the significance level 10% ($p < .10$) (Fairchild & MacKinnon, 2009; McClelland & Judd, 1993).

Hypothesis 3 proposed age to moderate the customer stressors–burnout relationship. Only the interaction term between age and disliked customers on cynicism was significant, explaining an additional 1% of the variance, $\beta = −.12$, $t (254) = −1.91$, $p < .1$. We calculated simple slopes of the disliked customer–cynicism relationship at a younger ($−1$ SD) and an older ($+1$ SD) age (Cohen et al., 2003), which revealed that the relationship between disliked customers with cynicism was positive

and stronger for younger employees than older employees: younger, $b = 0.418$, $t = 5.167$, $p < .001$; mean age, $b = 0.299$, $t = 5.058$, $p < .001$; older, $b = 0.180$, $t = 2.051$, $p < .05$. This indicated that younger employees were likely to feel more cynical towards their work when exposed to disliked customers than older employees. Analysis revealed only this one significant out of 12 possible interaction effects. It appears that whereas age influenced feelings of cynicism as a response to disliked customers, there was no influence of age on other aspects of burnout. So there is little evidence in support of Hypothesis 3.

In line with Hypothesis 4, we tested whether age influenced the relationship between stress management strategies and employee burnout. Analysis revealed six out of 12 significant interaction effects, suggesting partial support for Hypothesis 4 (see Table 3).

There was a particularly strong picture for emotional control and age with interaction effects on three subscales of burnout. To better interpret these interactions, we plotted them graphically (Aiken & West, 1991). Figure 2 shows the relationship between emotional control and emotional exhaustion was negative when employees were older, but positive for younger employees. Analyses of simple slopes revealed an effect for older employees just missing the 5% level, $b = −0.273$, $t = −1.919$, $p = .057$, suggesting that using emotional control as a stress management strategy was associated with significantly less emotional exhaustion for older employees.

Controlling emotions is linked to reduced cynicism for all employees but less so for younger than older. Significant simple slopes were found for mean age, $b = −0.297$, $t = −3.537$, $p = .001$, and older age, $b = −0.493$, $t = −3.398$, $p = .001$. Higher emotional control is also associated with decreased feelings of reduced professional efficacy for all employees, but more so for older employees than younger. Significant simple slopes were again found for mean age,

TABLE 3
Moderated regression results for stress management strategies and age on burnout (Hypothesis 4)

| Variable | Burnout | | | | | | | | |
| | Emotional exhaustion | | | Cynicism | | | Reduced professional efficacy | | |
	I	II	III	I	II	III	I	II	III
Emotional control									
Job age	−.02	.10	.12	−.02	.10	.12	−.10	−.08	−.06
Full/part-time work	−.06	−.15*	−.12	.01	−.07	−.04	.12	.11	.15*
Gender	.06	.05	.07	.06	.05	.07	.04	.04	.06*
Emotional control		−.05	−.11		−.25***	−.31****		−.28***	−.35****
Age		−.36****	−.31***		−.26***	−.21**		.05	.10
Emotional control × age			−.16*			−.18**			−.18*
R^2	.01	.12	.14	.00	.14	.17	.03	.11	.13
R^2 change	.01	.11****	.02*	.00	.14****	.03**	.03	.08***	.03*
Active coping									
Job age	−.02	.10	.14	−.02	.10	.13	−.10	−.06	−.05
Full/part-time work	−.06	−.15*	−.15*	.01	−.07	−.07	.12	.11	.11
Gender	.06	.05	.06	.06	.04	.05	.04	.01	.02
Active coping		−.01	−.04		−.21**	−.24***		−.35****	−.36****
Age		−.37****	−.38****		−.29***	−.30***		.02	.02
Active coping × age			−.18**			−14*			−.07
R^2	.01	.12	.15	.00	.12	.14	.03	.14	.15
R^2 change	.01	.11****	.03**	.00	.12****	.02*	.03	.12****	.00
Humour									
Job age	−.02	.10	.10	−.02	.09	.09	−.10	−.10	−.10
Full/part-time work	−.06	−.15*	−.13	.01	−.06	−.06	.12	.12	.12
Gender	.06	.05	.08	.06	.05	.05	.04	.04	.03
Humour		.02	.02		.11	.11		.01	.01
Age		−.36****	−.34****		−.29***	−.29***		.00	−.01
Humour × age			.17**			−.00			−.05
R^2	.01	.12	.15	.00	.09	.09	.03	.03	.03
R^2 change	.01	.11****	.03**	.00	.09***	.00	.03	.00	.00
Downplay									
Job age	−.02	.10	.10	−.02	.08	.08	−.10	−.10	−.10
Full/part-time work	−.06	−.15*	−.15*	.01	−.07	−.07	.12	.12	.12
Gender	.06	.06	.07	.06	.08	.07	.04	.03	.02
Downplay		.11	.11		.16*	.16*		−.09	−.09
Age		−.37****	−.37****		−.31***	−.32***		.00	−.01
Downplay × age			.01			−.09			−.13
R^2	.01	.13	.13	.00	.11	.11	.03	.04	.05
R^2 change	.01	.12****	.00	.00	.10***	.01	.03	.01	.02

Entries are standardized regression coefficients. $*p < .10$, $**p < .05$, $***p < .01$, $****p < .001$. Gender: 1 = female, 2 = male. Working hours: 1 = full-time, 2 = part-time.

$b = −0.364$, $t = −4.008$, $p < .001$, and older age, $b = −0.541$, $t = −3.440$, $p = .001$.

Active coping and age had interaction effects on two subscales of burnout. A similar pattern to Figure 2 was found for the relationship between active coping and age on emotional exhaustion. Here, simple slopes were not significant. This, as in other nonsignificant simple slopes detailed later, is because one slope is positive and the other negative resulting in the slopes being significantly different from each other (significant interaction effect) and yet not being significantly different from zero (insignificant simple slopes). The results are still important in understanding potential age differences in the workplace as they show differences between employees of different ages. Active coping was also associated with decreased cynicism for all employees, but more so for older employees than younger. Significant simple slope analyses were reported for mean age, $b = −0.234$, $t = −2.822$, $p < .01$, and older age, $b = −0.365$, $t = −2.889$, $p < .01$.

There was just one interactive effect for humour and age. Simple slopes analysis revealed that the relationship between emotional exhaustion and humour was positive for older and negative for younger employees (see Figure 3). Using more humour as a stress management strategy was associated with more emotional exhaustion when older, but less when younger. Analyses of simple slopes revealed individual lines to be nonsignificant. There were no significant interaction effects for downplay and age.

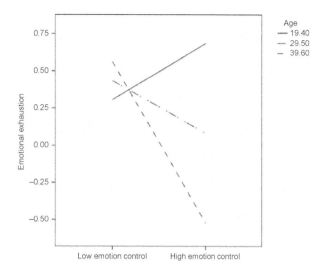

Figure 2. Emotional exhaustion, age, and emotion control.

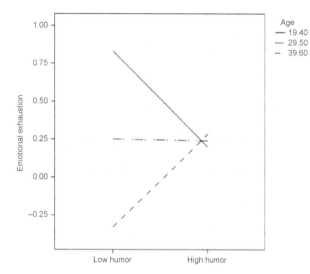

Figure 3. Emotional exhaustion, age, and humour.

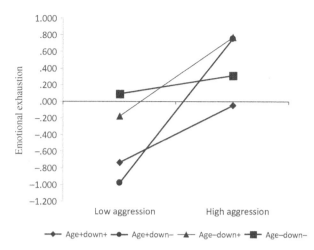

Figure 4. Interaction of aggression, age, and downplay on emotional exhaustion.

We were intrigued by the lack of findings regarding downplay and humour, so we conducted exploratory analyses of three-way interactions between customer stressors, age, and the stress management strategies downplay and humour.[1] Emotional exhaustion and cynicism as outcome variables were explored as the primary factors of burnout (Schaufeli et al., 1996). Three-way interactions are an appropriate analysis, despite the increased error associated with them, because the age variable can be considered to be an error-free measure; therefore, the risk of high error is reduced.

Nine out of 16 interactions were significant indicating that older workers are generally more effective in their use of these strategies in response to customer stressors suggesting age plays a significant role in using downplay and humour successfully. No interactions ran counter to

---

[0]Thank you to the anonymous reviewer who suggested the exploration of these three-way interactions.

expectations. Figure 4 shows the pattern of effect for the interaction of aggressive customers, age, and downplay on emotional exhaustion, $\beta = -.221$, $R^2 = .311$, $p < .05$. Older employees were more able to use successfully the stress management strategy of downplay than younger employees. Older workers using downplay show a weaker relationship between aggression and exhaustion compared to older workers not using downplay. This is the opposite for younger employees, where using downplay is associated with increased exhaustion.

A similar pattern to that shown in Figure 4 was reported for: aggression, age, and downplay on cynicism, $\beta = -.261$, $R^2 = .241$, $p < .05$; disliked customers, age, and downplay on exhaustion, $\beta = -.245$, $R^2 = .326$, $p < .01$; disliked customers, age, and downplay on cynicism, $\beta = -.183$, $R^2 = .246$, $p < .10$; ambiguous customers, age, and downplay on exhaustion, $\beta = -.284$, $R^2 = .318$, $p < .01$; ambiguous customers, age, and downplay on cynicism, $\beta = -.263$, $R^2 = .265$, $p < .01$; and disliked customers, age, and humour on cynicism, $\beta = -.167$, $R^2 = .238$, $p < .10$.

A slightly different pattern was found for the interactions with disproportionate customer expectations. Here, younger employees were similarly less able to use downplay successfully as a stress management strategy with their use of downplay associated with increased cynicism, $\beta = -.154$, $R^2 = .194$, $p < .10$. However, older employees use of downplay did not lower exhaustion in the way it did with the other customer stressors (i.e., the lines are parallel and not crossed). A similar pattern was reported for disproportionate customer expectations, age, and humour on cynicism, $\beta = -.160$, $R^2 = .171$, $p < .10$.

DISCUSSION

This study examined relations between age, customer stressors, stress management strategies, and burnout. In line with our first hypothesis, age was negatively related to each customer stressor in the expected direction, and older employees were less likely to experience negative customer behaviours than younger employees. It would seem, however, that a direct effect of coping strategies is not a possible explanation for this, as age was found to have no influence on stress management strategies (Hypothesis 2).

In Hypothesis 3, we assumed that age moderates the relation between customer stressors and burnout. Only for cynicism did age show a moderator effect in relation to one of the four customer stressors (disliked customers), with the older employees more able to keep their positive attitude towards work compared to the younger employees. Given the methodological difficulties in finding moderator effects (McClelland & Judd, 1993), the fact that this emerged for one out of four customer stressors is worth noting but offers minimal support for the hypothesis that age influences the relationship between customer stressors and burnout. That is, whilst customer stressors and burnout are linked (Dormann & Zapf, 2004), age is shown here to have a limited influence on this relationship. One explanation for this finding is that it is the way in which employees cope with stressors that is important, rather than age per se. This was explored in Hypothesis 4.

How employees cope with customer stressors is related to their health. This study indicates that older retail employee's use of the stress management strategies of emotion control and active coping generally had a more positive effect on emotional exhaustion and cynicism compared to younger employees. Hypothesis 4 assumed that emotion-focused coping strategies are helpful with regard to burnout for the older employees but less so for the younger employees. Results show that when the older employees respond to customer stressors by keeping their emotions under control they feel less emotionally exhausted and less cynical. However, when the younger employees use the same strategy it does not have the same positive impact on feelings of emotional exhaustion and cynicism. Maybe younger employees are not as competent at controlling their emotions to reduce the risk of experiencing burnout. This is in line with prior research which has shown that older people can more effectively control their emotions (e.g., Diehl et al., 1996; Lazarus & Folkman, 1984).

It was found that using active coping strategies led to increased exhaustion for the younger employees and decreased exhaustion for the older employees, and although active coping reduced cynicism for both groups this was significantly more so for the older employees than the younger. The results are in line with the literature on coping and health (e.g., Semmer, 2003) in that active coping in general is negatively related to emotional exhaustion and cynicism. Although a number of studies propose that younger adults prefer problem-focused strategies (e.g., De Lange et al., 2010; Folkman et al.,1987), they may not have the ability, or enough control over the situation, to use them effectively

at work in a service interaction and may try to actively solve problems inappropriately thus increasing their exhaustion. Also, they cannot use emotion control as effectively as older employees and so are less likely to successfully reduce exhaustion if they change their stress management strategy from active coping to emotion control. Again, lack of life experiences may be the explanation. Given the low control situation of the service employee, older employees may be more aware of their limitations in dealing with situations and, as a consequence, know when to stop trying to actively solve the situation (Diehl et al., 1996) and instead use more appropriate and successful emotion control strategies.

Age and the type of stress management strategy used had a limited relationship with reduced professional efficacy with only one interaction reported. This is in line with previous studies showing professional efficacy to be more dependent on resources than stressors (e.g., Schaufeli & Bakker, 2004), and may be linked to exhaustion and cynicism being the primary factors of burnout (Schaufeli et al., 1996). Whilst emotional exhaustion and cynicism are related to employee's age and choice of stress management strategy, feelings of reduced professional efficacy are less so.

The results regarding downplay and humour were less clear. Downplay was shown not to be moderated by age, and older employees used humour less often and were more emotionally exhausted when they did, whereas humour reduced exhaustion for the younger employees. However, only the interaction between age and humour on emotional exhaustion was found to be significant with no effects seen for cynicism or professional efficacy. There is some indication that the moderating effect of age may be more complex than we hypothesized with exploratory analysis of three-way interactions for each customer stressor revealing age to play a significant role in using downplay and humour successfully. Systematic findings in the expected direction showed that in high stress situations younger employees use these strategies less successfully to reduce levels of emotional exhaustion and cynicism. The effects are less clear when stressors are low; however, there is less need for stress management with low stressors and therefore this does not run against our findings. This may explain why two-way interactions were not always identified since the amount of stress people are exposed to affects the need for the use of stress management strategies. Finding interaction effects can be difficult (McClelland & Judd, 1993), and so these systematic findings and the fact that no interactions ran counter to expectations supports the importance of three-way interactions and suggests that the inclusion of three-way interactions when investigating age effects may be necessary.

Overall, the findings of this study are in the expected direction with no contrary effects. They thus fit well with and supplement existing literature revealing that older retail employees' coping strategies are used more successfully and generally have a more positive effect on burnout than younger employees. They are in line with studies on coping and stress demonstrating the positive effects of active coping (e.g., Semmer, 2003). However, we can show that under conditions of little control (e.g., Begley, 1998), emotion-focused strategies such as emotion control, which has previously been shown to be more successfully used by older people (e.g., Folkman et al. 1987), can have a positive effect as well. It should not be too surprising that we found less effects for professional efficacy as it has been shown that this component of burnout is more affected by resources and less so by stressors (e.g., Schaufeli & Bakker, 2004). The study is one of the first to show these effects in the workplace and supports and extends findings on age and coping (Blanchard-Fields et al., 2004; Folkman et al., 1987) from the nonworking world to working in the retail industry.

Stress management is an important social competence and the findings of this study show that older employees use stress management strategies more successfully. This is therefore one of few articles that show the benefits, and competencies, of older employees and thus argues against the perception of "deficits" of older workers, which can lead to discrimination and prejudice in the workplace (McGregor & Gray, 2002).

Limitations and future research

Although longitudinal data is preferable to allow investigation of any temporal order of variables, we argue cross-sectional designs are relevant. It is not justifiable to interpret sample differences as pure age effects in either longitudinal or cross-sectional studies, as generational effects are present in both (Baltes, 1968). Whether or not specific coping strategies are a factor of age or of generation-specific experiences cannot be declared absolutely using either method. The purpose of this research is to understand how employees of different ages cope in today's workplace, and not to identify how particular individuals change over time; therefore, a cross-sectional study is appropriate. Furthermore, as age cannot experience reverse causality, the cross-sectional design does not limit conclusions on causality (e.g., Zapf, Dormann, & Frese, 1996).

This study used self-report, and method artefacts therefore cannot be discounted, although Spector (2006) argues the problem of common method variance is often overstated. Since observation of coping strategies is impractical self-report is appropriate. Our study was anonymous, and study participants will know their age, meaning this variable should be little affected by the typical self-report measurement problems leading to common method variance (e.g., inflated correlations due to social desirability (Spector, 2006) or negative affect (Spector, Zapf, Chen, & Frese, 2000), etc.).

We have already explained the relevance of the study design. Nevertheless future research should gather longitudinal and multisource data (e.g., to show customer stressors, coping strategies, and burnout at different times) with which to further explore the interactions detailed here.

"Job age" as a control variable had no significant impact on our study results, supporting the proposal that life experience and not job experience is important. One of the criticisms of studies focusing on employee age is that of self-selection, where older workers who "survive" continue working, whereas less healthy individuals select out of the job, thus creating the impression that older workers are more skilled or more healthy than younger ones. With regard to health, we cannot exclude this interpretation. With regard to age and coping, as studies outside work (Blanchard-Fields et al., 2004; Folkman et al., 1987) reach similar conclusions, this suggests selection effects may contribute, but are not the sole explanation.

As common in the retail sector, the workforce in this organization was relatively young; therefore, age-related differences are limited to this restricted age range. Finding age differences in this limited age range is indicative of the importance of age as an influential factor in service interactions. Will differences across age groups persist, or get smaller or larger if comparing more disparate age groups? If competencies in service interactions continue to develop with age then older employees may be of significant value to employers. Future studies should include a wider age range and investigate age-related differences throughout the life span.

Finally, the study population was very homogenous and, although this reduces variance due to different occupational and customer demands, any generalization of the theory to other sectors should be treated with caution. Future studies should consider the influence of age on the experience of customer stressors, stress management strategies, and burnout within different service industries, and within different cultural contexts.

Practical implications

This research challenges preconceptions about older employees. Traditionally employer strategies focus on the health of older employees but younger employees require more support to reduce emotional exhaustion and cynicism and to use stress management strategies successfully. Additionally, this study suggests there are differences between younger and older employees with respect to customer interaction in the service sector. Our findings suggest that older employees make good service employees and represent an important resource, particularly in light of the ageing population.

From an organizational point of view this study suggests that encouraging employees to use particular coping strategies to limit burnout may be important for health outcomes, although a one size fits all approach to this issue will not be effective. Employees of different ages cope with customer stressors in different ways and as a result experience higher or lower levels of burnout. Managers and HR professionals should direct burnout prevention programmes to employees most in need. As younger employees appear to have a greater tendency to experience burnout and to be less successful in using stress management strategies, targeting this group with helping them to develop the most appropriate coping skills in response to customer stressors is a proactive measure for organizations. For example, providing training in handling customer stressors and ensuring supervisors are equipped to support young employees who are more likely to suffer from burnout. This is especially important as supervisory support is effective in minimizing burnout (Brewer & Shapard, 2004). Also, as older workers use stress management strategies more successfully, introducing mentoring programmes will allow older workers to provide support and advice to help younger workers develop these skills. Another practical suggestion is that organizations should emphasize that handling stressful customer interactions effectively are important for several reasons. A dissatisfied customer is bad for business, and a stressful encounter handled ineffectively is bad for the employee's health and, consequently, also bad for the organization. Employees should be encouraged to appreciate the benefits of successful stress management, both for customer satisfaction and their own.

CONCLUSION

The current study illustrates the important role of age within employee–customer interactions in the service sector. We found that older employees can bring a level of emotional maturity to service organizations, which, when compared to younger employees, could offer a more positive customer experience. We encourage organizations in the service sector to recognize the valuable contribution older workers can make to their business. Where younger workers are involved, we advise employers to be aware of the need to provide support to develop their emotional resources.

REFERENCES

Aiken, L. S., & West, S. G. (1991). *Multiple regression: Testing and interpreting interactions.* Newbury Park, CA: Sage.

Bakker, A. B., Schaufeli, W. B., Sixma, H. J., Bosveld, W., & van Dierendonck, D. (2000). Patient demands, lack of reciprocity and burnout: A five-year longitudinal study among general practitioners. *Journal of Organizational Behavior, 21*, 425–441.

Baltes, P. B. (1968). Longitudinal and cross-sectional sequences in the study of age and generation effects. *Human Development, 11*, 145–171.

Baltes, P. B., Staudinger, U. M., Maercker, A., & Smith, J. (1995). People nominated as wise: A comparative study of wisdom-related knowledge. *Psychology and Aging, 10*, 155–166.

Begley, T. M. (1998). Coping strategies as predictors of employee distress and turnover after an organizational consolidation: A longitudinal analysis. *Journal of Occupational and Organizational Psychology, 71*, 305–329.

Ben-Zur, H., & Yagil, D. (2005). The relationship between empowerment, aggressive behaviours of customers, coping, and burnout. *European Journal of Work and Organizational Psychology, 14*, 81–99.

Billings, A. G., & Moos, R. H. (1984). Coping, stress and social resources among adults with unipolar depression. *Journal of Personality and Social Psychology, 46*, 877–891.

Blanchard-Fields, F., Stein, R., & Watson, T. L. (2004). Age differences in emotion-regulation strategies in handling everyday problems. *Journal of Gerontology, 59B*, 261–269.

Brewer, E. W., & Shapard, L. (2004). Employee burnout: A meta-analysis of the relationship between age or years of experience. *Human Resource Development Review, 3*, 102–123.

Briggs, S. R., & Cheek, J. M. (1986). The role of factor analysis in the development and evaluation of personality scales. *Journal of Personality, 54*, 106–148.

Carstensen, L. L. (1986). Social support among the elderly: Limitations of behavioral interventions. *The Behavior Therapist, 6*, 111–113.

Carstensen, L. L. (1995). Evidence for a life-span theory of socioemotional selectivity. *Current Directions in Psychological Science, 4*, 151–156.

Carver, C. S., Scheier, M. F., & Weintraub, J. K. (1989). Assessing coping strategies: A theoretical based approach. *Journal of Personality and Social Psychology, 56*, 267–283.

Ceslowitz, S. B. (1989). Burnout and coping strategies among hospital staff nurses. *Journal of Advanced Nursing, 14*, 553–557.

Clohessy, S., & Ehlers, A. (1999). PTSD symptoms, response to intrusive memories and coping in ambulance service workers. *British Journal of Clinical Psychology, 38*, 251–265.

Cohen, J., Cohen, P., West, S., & Aiken, L. S. (2003). *Applied multiple regression/correlation analysis for the behavioral sciences* (3rd ed.). Mahwah, NJ: Lawrence Erlbaum Associates.

Commission of the European Communities. (2005). *Confronting demographic change: A new solidarity between generations* (EU Green Paper COM (2005) 94). Brussels: Author.

DeLange, A., Taris, T. W., Jansen, P., Kompier, M. A. J., Houtman, I. L. D., & Bongers, P. M. (2010). On the relationships among work characteristics and learning-related behavior: Does age matter? *Journal of Organizational Behaviour, 31*, 925–950.

Diehl, M., Coyle, N., & Labouvie-Vief, G. (1996). Age and sex differences in strategies of coping and defence across the life span. *Psychology and Aging, 11*, 127–139.

Dixon, N. F. (1980). Humor: A cognitive alternative to stress? In I. G. Sarason & C. D. Spielberger (Eds.), *Stress and anxiety* (Vol. 7, pp. 281–289). Washington, DC: Hemisphere.

Dormann, C., & Zapf, D. (2004). Customer related social stressors and burnout. *Journal of Occupational Health Psychology, 9*, 61–82.

Dudenhöffer, S., & Dormann, C. (in press). Customer-related social stressors and service providers' affective reactions. *Journal of Organizational Behavior.*

Fairchild, A. J., & MacKinnon, D. P. (2009). A general model for testing mediation and moderation effects. *Prevention Science, 10*, 87–99.

Folkman, S., Lazarus, R. S., Pimeley, S., & Novacek, J. (1987). Age differences in stress and coping processes. *Psychology and Aging, 2*, 171–184.

Gross, J. J., Carstensen, L. L., Pasupathi, M., Tsai, J. L., Gottestam, K., & Hsu, A. Y. C. (1997). Emotion and aging: Changes in experience, expression, and control. *Psychology and Aging, 12*, 590–599.

Healy, C. M., & McKay, M. F. (2000). Nursing stress: The effects of coping strategies and job satisfaction in a sample of Australian nurses. *Journal of Advanced Nursing, 31*, 681–688.

Hochschild, A. R. (1983). *The managed heart: Commercialization of human feelings.* Berkeley: University of California Press.

Janke, W., Erdmann, G., & Kallus, K. W. (2002). *Stress Coping Questionnaire.* Göttingen: Hogrefe.

John, O. P., & Gross, J. J. (2007). Individual differences in emotion regulation. In J. J. Gross (Ed.), *Handbook of emotion regulation* (pp. 351–372). London: Guilford Press.

Kim, H. J., Shin, K. H., & Umbreit, T. W. (2007). Hotel job burnout: The role of personality characteristics. *International Journal of Hospitality Management, 26*, 421–434.

Kooij, D. T. A. M., DeLange, A. H., Jansen, P. G. W., Kanfer, R., & Dikkers, J. S. E. (2011). Age and work-related motives: Results of a meta-analysis. *Journal of Organizational Behavior, 32*, 197–225.

Lazarus, R. S., & Folkman, S. (1984). *Stress, appraisal, and coping.* New York, NY: Springer.

Lubinski, D., & Humphreys, L. G. (1990). Assessing spurious "moderator effects": Illustrated substantively with the hypothesized ("synergistic") relation between spatial and mathematical ability. *Psychological Bulletin, 107*, 385–393.

Maslach, C., & Jackson, S. E. (1981). The measurement of experienced burnout. *Journal of Occupational Behavior, 2*, 99–113.

Maslach, C., Schaufeli, W. B., & Leiter, M. P. (2001). Job burnout. *Annual Review of Psychology, 52*, 397–422.

McClelland, G. H., & Judd, C. M. (1993). Statistical difficulties of detecting interactions and moderator effects. *Psychological Bulletin, 114*, 376–390.

McCrae, R. R., & Costa, P. T. (1986). Personality, coping, and coping effectiveness in an adult sample. *Journal of Personality, 54*, 385–405.

McGregor, J., & Gray, L. (2002). Stereotypes and older workers: The New Zealand experience. *Social Policy Journal of New Zealand, 18*, 163–177.

McNair, S., & Flynn, M. (2006). *Managing an ageing workforce in the retail sector: A report for employers.* Department for Work and Pensions. Retrieved from http://statistics.dwp.gov.uk/asd/asd5/rports2005-2006/agepos8.pdf

Morris, J. A., & Feldman, D. C. (1996). The dimensions, antecedents, and consequences of emotional labor. *Academy of Management Journal, 21*, 986–1010.

Oakland, S., & Ostell, A. (1996). Measuring coping: A review and a critique. *Human Relations, 49*, 133–155.

Pienaar, J., & Willemse, S. A. (2008). Burnout, engagement, coping and general health of service employees in the hospitality industry. *Tourism Management, 29*, 1053–1063.

Pugliesi, K. (1999). The consequences of emotional labor: Effects on work stress, job satisfaction, and well-being. *Motivation and Emotion, 23*, 125–154.

Rafaeli, A. (1989). When cashiers meet customers: An analysis of the role of supermarket cashiers. *Academy of Management Journal, 32*, 245–273.

Rafaeli, A., & Sutton, R. I. (1987). Expression of emotion as part of the work role. *Academy of Management Review, 12*, 23–37.

Schalk, R., van Veldhoven, M., De Lange, A. H., De Witte, H., Kraus, K., Stamov-Robnagel, C., … Zacher, H. (2010). Moving European research on work and ageing forward: Overview and agenda. *European Journal of Work and Organizational Psychology, 19*, 76–101.

Schaufeli, W. B., & Bakker, A. B. (2004). Job demands, job resources, and their relationship with burnout and engagement: A multi-sample study. *Journal of Organizational Behavior, 25*, 293–315.

Schaufeli, W. B., Leiter, M. P., Maslach, C., & Jackson, S. E. (1996). Maslach Burnout Inventory–General Survey (MBI–GS). In C. Maslach, S. E. Jackson, & M. P. Leiter (Eds.), *Maslach Burnout Inventory manual* (3rd ed., pp. 22–26). Palo Alto, CA: Consulting Psychologists Press.

Semmer, N. K. (2003). Individual differences, work stress, and health. In M. J. Schabracq, J. A. Winnubst, & C. L. Cooper (Eds.), *Handbook of work and health psychology* (2nd ed., pp. 51–86). Chichester: Wiley.

Shrauger, J. S. (1975). Responses to evaluation as a function of initial self-perceptions. *Psychological Bulletin, 82*, 581–596.

Shultz, K. S., Wang, M., Crimmins, E. M., & Fisher, G. G. (2010). Age differences in the Demand-Control Model of work stress. *Journal of Applied Gerontology, 29*, 21–47.

Skillsmart Retail. (2010). *Skillsmart Retail analysis: The age of retail.* Retrieved from http://www.skillsmartretail.com/SiteCollection Documents/Research/Themed%20Research/workforce%20demographics/The%20Age%20of%20Retail.pdf

Spector, P. E. (2006). Method variance in organizational research. *Organizational Research Methods, 9*, 221–232.

Spector, P. E., Zapf, D., Chen, P. Y., & Frese, M. (2000). Why negative affectivity should not be controlled in job stress research: Don't throw out the baby with the bath water. *Journal of Organizational Behavior, 21*, 79–95.

Staudinger, U. M., & Pasupathi, M. (2003). Correlates of wisdom-related performance in adolescence and adulthood: Age-graded differences in "paths" toward desirable development. *Journal of Research on Adolescence, 13*, 239–268.

Swan, J. E., Bowers, M. R., & Richardson, L. D. (1999). Customer trust in the salesperson: An integrative review and meta-analysis of the empirical literature. *Journal of Business Research, 44*, 93–107.

Weyers, P., Ising, M., Reuter, M., & Janke, W. (2005). Comparing two approaches for the assessment of coping: Part I. psychometric properties and intercorrelations. *Journal of Individual Differences, 26*(4), 207–212.

Wharton, A. S. (1993). The affective consequences of service work: Managing emotions on the job. *Work and Occupations, 20*, 205–232.

Zapf, D. (2002). Emotion work and psychological well-being: A review of the literature and some conceptual considerations. *Human Resource Management Review, 12*, 237–268.

Zapf, D., Dormann, C., & Frese, M. (1996). Longitudinal studies in organizational stress research: A review of the literature with reference to methodological issues. *Journal of Occupational Health Psychology, 1*, 145–169.

Zapf, D., Vogt, C., Seifert, C., Mertini, H., & Isic, A. (1999). Emotion work as a source of stress: The concept and development of an instrument. *European Journal of Work and Organizational Psychology, 8*, 371–400.

Zeithaml, V., & Bitner, M. J. (2000). *Service marketing: Integrating customer focus across the firm* (2nd ed.). New York, NY: Irwin McGraw-Hill.

Zimmermann, B. K., Dormann, C., & Dollard, M. F. (2011). On the positive aspects of customers: Customer-initiated support and affective crossover in employee-customer dyads. *Journal of Occupational and Organizational Psychology, 84*, 31–57.

Ageism at work: The impact of intergenerational contact and organizational multi-age perspective

Caroline Iweins, Donatienne Desmette, Vincent Yzerbyt, and Florence Stinglhamber

Université catholique de Louvain, Belgium

Despite the prevalence of ageism in the workplace, little empirical effort has been devoted to analysing the contextual factors that may help reduce it. Building upon research on intergroup contact and multiculturalism, we examine in two studies how intergenerational contact and organizational multi-age perspective may contribute toward mitigating ageism and improving work attitudes through a dual identity process. In Study 1, SEM analyses confirm that workers' dual identity is a key mediator of the effects of context on both ageism and attitudes at work. Study 2 replicates and extends the results of Study 1, firstly by showing the mediational effects of perceived procedural justice, and secondly by investigating stereotypes more closely related to the population of older workers. As a set, our findings shed new light on ageism at work as well as on the protective role of two aspects of the social context.

What is the worst thing that could happen to you in your professional career? According to Rogerson (2003), the biggest fear of many people is to be over the age of 50. In line with this feeling, a large body of research reveals the prevalence of negative stereotypes about older people and discriminatory behaviours toward them (for meta-analyses, see Posthuma & Campion, 2009; for a review, see Finkelstein & Farrell, 2007).

Still, although ageism at work—i.e., stigmatization of and discrimination against people because they are old (Butler, 1969)—is a well-established phenomenon, and despite the fact that studies have shown its devastating effects on older people's attitudes at work (Gaillard & Desmette, 2010), little empirical effort has been made to analyse the way organizations attempt to reduce ageism in the workplace. Within the literature on intergroup relations (for a review, see Yzerbyt & Demoulin, 2010), two main approaches have been offered for the reduction of intergroup bias: the contact hypothesis (Allport, 1954) and the multicultural perspective (Richeson & Nussbaum, 2003; Wolsko, Park, & Judd, 2006). As a matter of fact, research has repeatedly shown that the quality of contact with an outgroup (e.g., Pettigrew & Tropp, 2006, 2008) and fostering a multicultural perspective, that is, a diversity perspective proposing that group differences and memberships should be considered and celebrated (e.g., Richeson & Nussbaum, 2003; Yinger, 1994), are the most influential factors for reducing intergroup bias. Traditionally, however, the literature on multiculturalism has focused on race rather than age. In addition, there is still no clear consensus as to how intergroup contact and fostering a multiculturalist perspective can improve intergroup relations and attitudes at work (Dovidio & Gaertner, 2010).

The aim of the present contribution is to build upon the research on the reduction of intergroup bias (e.g., Dovidio & Gaertner, 2010) and to examine the influence of both intergenerational contact and organizational multi-age perspective on ageism and attitudes at work. Moreover, in recent years, social identity theory (Tajfel, 1978) has led researchers to emphasize the role of social categorization in the reduction of intergroup bias (e.g., Gonzàlez & Brown, 2003). Therefore, an additional goal of the present endeavour is to investigate identity processes that can explain the impact of an organizational context related to age diversity (intergenerational contact and organizational multi-age perspective) on intergenerational bias and attitudes at work.

Intergroup contact and multicultural perspective

For over fifty years, contact between groups, i.e., actual face-to-face interaction between members of distinguishable and defined groups (Pettigrew, 1998), has been conceived as one of the most effective strategies for improving intergroup relations and fighting against group biases (Allport, 1954; for meta-analyses, see Pettigrew & Tropp, 2006, 2008). Contact studies range across a variety of groups. Regarding contact with the elderly in particular, Tam, Hewstone, Harwood, Voci, and Kenworthy (2006) examined the role of grandparent–grandchild communication in improving intergenerational attitudes. These authors showed that contact with one's grandparents was associated with more favourable explicit attitudes toward older adults. More generally, extensive research in diverse settings (Brouwer & Boros, 2010; Pettigrew, Tropp, & Oskamp, 2000; Voci & Hewstone, 2003) leads to the conclusion that the quality of contact (e.g., a pleasant social atmosphere surrounding contact and a high degree of cooperation) is a better predictor of intergroup attitudes than the quantity of contact (e.g., the frequency of contact, the number of persons involved). Moreover, quality of contact could also improve work attitudes. Indeed, it is well known that favourable co-worker relationships influence work attitudes (e.g., Hodson, 1997). For example, studies reveal that satisfaction with one's co-workers is significantly related to engagement (Avery, McKay, & Wilson, 2007) and that social support between co-workers is significantly related to lower intentions to quit (Pomaki, DeLongis, Frey, Short, & Woehrle, 2010). To date, however, the effects of contact on outcomes other than prejudice have seldom been addressed in the contact literature (Dixon, Durrheim, & Tredoux, 2005). In light of this, the present paper aims to examine the way in which high quality contact between age groups has an impact on intergroup relations and work attitudes.

Positive effects of contact can be triggered by several optimal conditions, such as authority support to contact (Allport, 1954; Pettigrew & Tropp, 2006). In a similar vein, there is growing empirical evidence that the reduction of intergroup bias and the creation of a positive diversity climate are promoted by fostering a multicultural perspective (e.g., Plaut, Thomas, & Goren, 2009; Richeson & Nussbaum, 2003; Wolsko, Park, Judd, & Wittenbrink, 2000). For example, in a study conducted in the Netherlands, Verkuyten (2005) found that the greater the number of Dutch participants who endorsed the ideology of multicultural recognition, the more likely they were to evaluate the Muslim Turkish outgroup positively. This multicultural perspective is closely related to the "integration and learning" organizational perspective put forth by Ely and Thomas (2001), which consists in encouraging all employees to value and express themselves as members of their racial identity groups. Examining the effects of the organizational perspective, Ely and Thomas (2001) showed that the "integration and learning" perspective provided the rationale and guidance needed to secure sustained benefits from diversity, and increasing innovation from and performance of workers. Building upon this message, we hypothesize that fostering an organizational multi-age perspective will likely reduce ageism, as well as improving attitudes at work.

Interesting as they may be, the available studies on multiculturalism have a major limitation in that evidence regarding the processes that mediate the effects of a multicultural perspective remains rather scarce. In a recent contribution, van der Noll, Poppe, and Verkuyten (2010) showed that the reduction of perceived symbolic threat (perceived group differences in values, norms and beliefs) and safety threat (perceived competition over material and economic group interests) explained the relationship between a multicultural perspective and political tolerance. In the same vein, Chang and Le (2010) showed that fostering a multicultural perspective increased ethno-cultural empathy, which in turn improved academic achievement for Hispanics. Unfortunately, these studies have not yet investigated those specific processes through which multiculturalism triggers the reduction of prejudice itself. In our view, research on identity processes in contact situations offers some useful ideas in this respect.

Dual identity processes

Several studies have investigated the social categorization processes that are likely to contribute toward reducing intergroup bias in contact situations. Among the different models inspired from social identity theory (Tajfel, 1978) that have been proposed (e.g., Gomez, Dovidio, Huici, Gaertner, & Cuadrado, 2008; Hornsey & Hogg, 2000), the dual identity model appears to be one of the most promising. This model posits that simultaneously maintaining the ingroup–outgroup distinction and building a superordinate identity in a cooperative encounter is conducive to more harmonious group relations

(Huo, Smith, Tyler, & Lind, 1996; Richter, West, Van Dick, & Dawson, 2006). According to Hornsey and Hogg (2000), a dual identity approach works because whenever two social categories intersect, the accentuation of perceived differences between the categories in one dimension (i.e., the group identity) is weakened by a countervailing accentuation of perceived similarities in the shared category dimension (i.e., the common identity). Most past studies on dual identity have relied on artificial groups (e.g., Dovidio, Gaertner, & Validzic, 1998; Gonzàlez & Brown, 2003), but the few studies which have been conducted in real settings have confirmed that dual identity is a powerful mediator for the link between intergroup contact and the reduction of intergroup bias (Eller & Abrams, 2003, 2004; Guerra et al., 2010). For example, a longitudinal study carried out by Eller and Abrams (2004) in a Mexican organization shows that a strong dual identity (i.e., the perception that Americans are another group and at the same time that Americans share a common identity with Mexicans) explains how high quality contact between American and Mexican co-workers can improve the attitudes of Mexicans toward Americans.

To date, however, no study has addressed the mediating role of dual identity in the larger context of multiculturalism. As Hornsey and Hogg (2000) and Wolsko et al. (2000) have suggested, a multiculturalist context should likely activate a dual identity, thereby providing cognitive mechanisms to reduce the exclusion of disadvantaged groups. In the same way, Dovidio, Gaertner, and Kawakami (2003) outlined the striking similarity between an acculturation strategy of integration (i.e., a multicultural perspective) and dual identity, an integration context implying both the activation of different social categories (the acknowledgement and celebration of social differences) and the activation of a superordinate category (the promotion of social cohesion). Our aim was therefore to extend previous research on multiculturalism by examining the mediational status of dual identity in the context of age-related diversity in the workplace.

Across two studies we hypothesized that dual identity would mediate the relationships between a favourable intergenerational context at work on the one hand (high quality contact between age groups and multi-age organizational perspective), and less ageism at work and lower intentions to quit on the other.

STUDY 1

Study 1 tested three hypotheses (see Figure 1). We predicted that participants' dual identity (high identification with both age group and the organization) would mediate the relationships between the quality of contact with older workers on the one hand and positive stereotypes about them and lower intentions to quit on the other (Hypothesis 1). We also hypothesized that participants' dual identity would mediate the relationships between organizational multi-age perspective and the same dependent variables as stated above (Hypothesis 2).

An additional aim of Study 1 was to investigate ageist attitudes at work by considering stereotypes of, behaviours toward, and emotions about older workers. According to the tripartite model of attitudes (Finkelstein & Farrell, 2007), ageist views, like any other intergroup bias, can be thought of as a constellation of three components: cognitive, affective, and behavioural. Along these lines and as an offshoot of the stereotype content model, which depicts groups in terms of competence and warmth

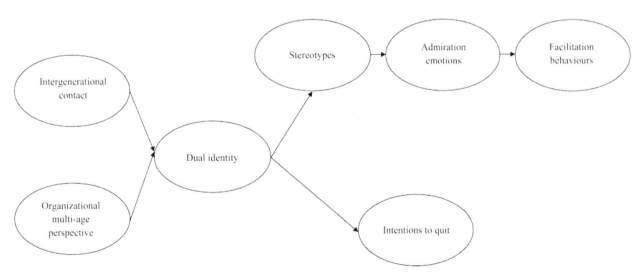

Figure 1. Hypothesized model (Study 1).

(Fiske, Cuddy, Xu, & Glick, 2002; Fiske, Xu, & Cuddy, 1999), the "behaviours from intergroup affect and stereotypes" map model (BIAS; Cuddy, Glick, & Fiske, 2007) predicts emotions about and behaviours toward members of a group as a function of people's perceptions of this group (Fiske et al., 2002). Specifically, several behavioural patterns are predicted by four affective states (admiration, contempt, pity, and envy), which are induced by stereotypes concerning competence and warmth (Fiske et al., 2002). For example, groups that are perceived as high in both warmth and competence would elicit feelings of admiration as well as (passive and active) facilitation behaviour. In line with the BIAS map model (Cuddy et al., 2007), our final hypothesis held that positive emotions (admiration) would mediate the link between positive stereotypes (perceptions of high competence and high warmth) and facilitation behaviour tendencies (Hypothesis 3).

Method

Participants and procedure

Data were collected in two financial companies on 496 French-speaking Belgian employees. We had a final sample of 129 employees aged less than fifty (mean age = 37.74, $SD = 7.68$, minimum = 21, maximum = 49, 80% of respondents being in the 30 to 49 age range) who completed the entire questionnaire (response rate = 26%). A majority of respondents were males (59%), worked full time (86%), were employees (55%), and had a college education (53%). Participants were invited to complete an open-ended questionnaire available on the internet and created with the DORIS software (UCL/PSP, version 1.5). The link to the questionnaire was included in an email sent by the researchers. This email indicated that the purpose of the study was to examine people's attitudes toward age diversity and intergenerational relationships at work.

Measures

At the beginning of the questionnaire, participants were informed that the group of older workers included workers of 50 years of age and above, and that the participants had to refer to themselves as members of the younger workers' generation at work (defined as workers of less than 50 years of age).[1]

Predictors. Intergenerational contact was measured by means of five items adapted from Voci and Hewstone (2003). On a seven-point scale ranging from 1 (*totally disagree*) to 7 (*totally agree*), respondents rated the degree to which their contact with older workers was *natural, positive, unpleasant, competitive,* and *involuntary*. The three last items were reverse coded so that higher scores indicated positive contact ($\alpha = .65$).[2]

The *organizational multi-age perspective* was measured with six items ($\alpha = .95$) adapted from the racial diversity scale by Wolsko et al. (2006). Participants were invited to rate on a seven-point scale ranging from 1 (*never*) to 7 (*always*) the extent to which they considered that their company supported a multi-age diversity perspective (e.g., "In its age management diversity, my organization considers that recognizing the specificity of each generation leads to harmony between workers").

Mediator. Participants' *dual identity* was measured by multiplying their age group (ingroup) identity with their organizational (common) identity (for a similar procedure, see Hofhuis, van der Zee, & Otten, 2012). Age group identity was measured with six items ($\alpha = .86$) adapted from Garstka, Schmitt, Branscombe, and Hummert (2004), and from Kessler and Mummendey (2002) (e.g., "You identify yourself as a member of your generation at work"). Organizational identity (common identity) was measured with the same six items ($\alpha = .91$) adapted to the organizational identity (e.g., "You identify yourself as a member of your organization"). Because each of the six identity scales ranged from 1 (*totally disagree*) to 7 (*totally agree*), participants' dual identity scores (age identity * organizational identity) ranged from 1 (lowest possible average score on both components) to 49 (highest possible average score on both components).

Criteria. The measure of ageism at work was adapted from Fiske et al. (2002) for stereotypes and from Cuddy et al. (2007) for emotions (admiration) and behaviours (facilitation) toward older workers as a group.

As far as *stereotypes* were concerned, participants used an eleven-point scale ranging from 1 (*0%*) to 11

---

[1]This age threshold was chosen on the basis of The Organisation for Economic Co-operation and Development (2006), which defines older workers as those who are 50 years of age and above, and also because it is commonly used in studies on ageism at work to distinguish between older workers and younger workers (Hassell & Perrewe, 1993).

[2]The rather low alpha of contact can be attributed to the last item of the scale (i.e., "contact with older workers is involuntary"). Confirmatory factor analyses revealed that this indicator had a lower (but acceptable) standardized loading (.50) than other indicators of contact. However, we did not remove this item for several reasons. Firstly, the whole scale adapted from Voci and Hewstone (2003) has been largely validated in the literature on intergroup contact. Secondly, we wanted to use similar scales in both Study 1 and Study 2 for replication aims, and the reliability score of the whole contact scale in Study 2 was good ($\alpha = .80$). Finally, DeVellis (1991) considers that an alpha of .65 is acceptable.

(*100%*) in order to indicate the extent to which they perceived older workers as being competent (e.g., "How competent are older workers?") and warmth (e.g., "How tolerant are older workers?"). Competence (four items, $\alpha = .77$) and warmth (four items, $\alpha = .81$) scales were multiplied so that the highest scores indicated that older workers were perceived as both warm and competent.

Admiration was measured with two items ($r = .37$, $p < .01$). Participants were invited to use a seven-point scale ranging from 1 (*totally disagree*) to 7 (*totally agree*) to rate the extent to which older workers elicited admiration (e.g., "You may feel admiration toward older workers").

Facilitation behavioural tendencies were measured with four items (two items for active facilitation, $r = .29$, $p < .001$; two items for passive facilitation, $r = .60$, $p < .001$). Participants were invited to use the same seven-point scale to rate the extent to which they thought that older workers elicited active facilitation (e.g., "You may want to help older workers") and passive facilitation (e.g., "You may want to cooperate with older workers"). As for stereotypes, the active facilitation scale and the passive facilitation scale were multiplied so that the highest scores indicated high active and passive facilitation.

Finally, *intentions to quit* were measured with four items ($\alpha = .86$) adapted from Price (1997) (e.g., "If I could, I would quit my organization today").

Personal and organizational variables.[3]. Age, gender, education, working time, and professional status were each measured using single items. With the exception of age, which was a continuous variable, the other variables were multiple choice questions.

Results

Preliminary analyses

The relationships between control variables and dependent measures were analysed in line with Becker's (2005) recommendations. We used one-way

analyses of variance (ANOVAs) for gender, working time, and professional status, and correlations for age. None of the control variables were related to the criterion variables. Therefore, none of the control variables were taken into account in the following analyses. Descriptive statistics and correlations among variables are presented in Table 1.

Our main data were analysed following a two-step procedure. First, using the LISREL software (LISREL, version 8.8), we assessed the measurement model through confirmatory factor analyses. Second, we constructed a structural equation model in order to test our hypotheses. Because of the small size of our sample, we decided to reduce the number of parameters to be estimated per factor, using the partial disaggregation method (Bagozzi & Edwards, 1998).[4] Based on Kline's (2011) recommendations, we examined the fit of the measurement and structural model by means of the chi-square (χ^2; e.g., Barrett, 2007), the Comparative Fit Index (CFI; Bentler, 1990), the standardized root mean square residual (SRMR; Hu & Bentler, 1999), and the root mean square error of approximation (RMSEA; Steiger & Lind, 1980).

Confirmatory factor analyses

In line with the hypothesized model, we specified seven latent constructs: intergenerational contact, organizational multi-age perspective, dual identity, stereotypes, admiration, facilitation behaviours, and intentions to quit. As expected, this model fitted the data very well: $\chi^2(98) = 111.37$, $p < .05$ (CFI = .98, SRMR = .05, RMSEA = .03). The standardized loadings were significant (all $t > 1.96$) and large, ranging from .50 to .95.

Next, following Bentler's (1990) recommendations, we compared this seven-factor model to a series of alternative measurement models to ensure that the predicted model best reflected the data structure. The fit indices of these alternative measurement models are presented in Table 2. The results indicated that our seven-factor model was significantly superior to all models that were more constrained.

Tests of hypotheses

The results indicated that the hypothesized model (see Figure 1) presented an adequate fit to the data: $\chi^2(112) = 143.86$, $p < .05$ (CFI = .96, SRMR = .09, RMSEA = .05). We then compared this model to alternative models containing additional paths that were theoretically plausible and suggested partial mediation instead of total mediation. The fit indices

---

[3]Age, gender, education, and professional status are generally controlled for studies on ageism at work (e.g., Redman & Snape, 2002), with several meta-analyses showing that these participant-level variables exert a significant impact on attitudes toward older workers (e.g., Gordon & Arvey, 2004). Working time is controlled less often in the literature on ageism at work. In the present context, this organizational variable was also considered along with the other variables mentioned above because they have been shown to be significant predictors of intentions to quit. In fact, studies showed that men (Chen & Francesco, 2000), employees with more education (Mathieu & Zajac, 1990), younger workers (Arnold & Feldman, 1982), and part-time employees (Burke & Greenglass, 2000) are less willing to quit than women, employees with less education, older workers, and full-time employees.

[4]Path analyses were also conducted for Study 1 and Study 2, and revealed similar results.

TABLE 1
Means, standard deviations and intercorrelations among the variables (Study 1)

Variable	M	SD	1	2	3	4	5	6
1. Intergenerational contact[1]	5.74	0.67						
2. Organizational multi-age perspective[1]	4.13	1.31	.14					
3. Dual identity[2]	43.50	7.74	.18*	.33***				
4. Stereotypes[3]	62.12	16.34	.19*	.22*	.29**			
5. Admiration[1]	3.94	1.10	.08	.19*	.25**	.21*		
6. Facilitation behaviours[2]	22.62	8.54	.30**	.26**	.22*	.21*	.40***	
7. Intentions to quit[1]	2.19	1.20	$-.17^{\dagger}$	$-.27$**	$-.37$***	$-.25$**	.03	$-.61$***

$N = 129.$ $^{\dagger}p < .10$, *$p < .05$, **$p < .01$, ***$p < .001$.

[1]ranges from 1 (=totally disagree) to 7 (=totally agree).

[2]ranges from 1 (=low dual identity, low facilitation behaviours) to 49 (=high dual identity, high facilitation behaviours).

[3]ranges from 1 (=low competence and warmth perceptions) to 121 (=high competence and warmth perceptions).

TABLE 2
Confirmatory factor analysis fit indices for measurement model (Study 1)

	Model	χ^2	df	$\Delta\chi^2$ (Δdf)	CFI	SRMR	RMSEA
1.	Seven-factor model	111.37	98	–	.98	.05	.03
2.	Six-factor model (CONT, MULTI = 1 factor)	206.06	104	94.69(6)***	.92	.09	.09
3.	Six-factor model (CONT, DI = 1 factor)	190.73	104	79.36 (6)***	.93	.08	.08
4.	Six-factor model (MULTI, DI = 1 factor)	364.81	104	253.44 (6)***	.80	.12	.14
5.	Six-factor model (STERE, ADM = 1 factor)	154.48	104	43.11(6)***	.95	.08	.06
6.	Six-factor model (STERE, FA = 1 factor)	191.12	104	79.75(6)***	.93	.09	.08
7.	Six-factor model (ADM, FA = 1 factor)	132.60	104	21.23 (6)**	.98	.06	.04
8.	Six-factor model (DI, STERE = 1 factor)	192.87	104	81.50(6)***	.91	.08	.08
9.	Six-factor model (DI, ADM = 1 factor)	153.54	104	42.17(6)***	.96	.07	.06
10.	Six-factor model (DI, FA = 1 factor)	184.22	104	72.85(6)***	.93	.09	.08
11.	Five-factor model (MULTI, CONT, DI = 1 factor)	465.99	109	354.52(11)***	.75	.14	.16
12.	Five-factor model (STERE, ADM, FA = 1 factor)	235.43	109	124.06(11)***	.92	.10	.10
13.	Four-factor model (MULTI, CONT = 1 factor; STERE, ADM, FA = 1 factor)	318.11	113	206.74(15)***	.86	.12	.12
14.	Three-factor model (MULTI, CONT, DI = 1 factor; STERE, ADM, FA = 1 factor)	567.55	116	456.18(18)***	.68	.16	.17
15.	Two-factor model (MULTI, CONT, DI = 1 factor; STERE, ADM, FA, IQ = 1 factor)	631.34	118	519.97(20)***	.60	.18	.18
16.	Two-factor model (MULTI, CONT = 1 factor; DI, STERE, ADM, FA, IQ = 1 factor)	442.81	118	331.44(20)***	.72	.14	.15
17.	One-factor model	764.57	119	653.02(21)***	.53	.17	.21

$N = 129.$ *$p < .05$, **$p < .01$, ***$p < .001$.

CONT, intergenerational contact; MULTI, "multi-age" diversity; DI, dual identity; STERE, stereotypes; ADM, admiration emotions; FA, facilitation behavioural tendencies; IQ, intentions to quit; CFI, Comparative Fit Index; SRMR, Standardized Root Mean Square Residual; RMSEA, Root Mean Square Error of Approximation.

of each alternative model are presented in Table 3. The alternative Model 9 (see Figure 2) had the lowest value of χ^2 and was the most parsimonious. In other words, a model with a direct link between intergenerational contact and behaviours, and between dual identity and admiration (i.e., suggesting partial mediation) showed a significantly superior fit ($\chi^2(110) = 130.09$, $p < .05$, CFI = .98, SRMR = .07, RMSEA = .04). Model 9 was thus retained as the best-fitting model.

Our first prediction (H1) was that dual identity mediates the link between intergenerational contact and both positive perceptions and lower intentions to quit. Inspection of the parameters revealed the presence of a marginally significant path between intergenerational contact and dual identity ($\gamma = .19$, $p < .10$), and significant paths between dual identity and both stereotypes ($\beta = .32$, $p < .001$) and intentions to quit ($\beta = -.43$, $p < .001$). The indirect effects between intergenerational contact and stereotypes (indirect effect = .04, $z' = 1.37$, $p < .05$, critical z-prime value for statistical significance = .97 in absolute value; see MacKinnon, Lockwood, Hoffman, West, & Sheets, 2002) and between intergenerational contact and intentions to quit (indirect effect = $-.06$, $z' = -1.55$, $p < .05$) were also significant. Moreover, intergenerational contact exerted a significant influence on facilitation behaviours ($\gamma = .36$, $p < .001$). In sum, our data suggest that dual identity partially mediates the link between intergenerational contact

TABLE 3
Fit indices for structural models (Study 1)

Model	χ^2	df	CFI	SRMR	RMSEA	$\Delta\chi^2$ (Δdf)	Model comparison
Hypothesized	143.86	112	.96	.09	.05	–	
Alternative 1	140.97	111	.97	.09	.05	2.89(1)	Hypothesized vs. Alternative 1
Alternative 2	141.47	111	.97	.08	.05	2.39(1)	Hypothesized vs. Alternative 2
Alternative 3	134.84	111	.97	.08	.04	9.02(1)**	Hypothesized vs. Alternative 3
Alternative 4	131.61	110	.97	.08	.04	3.23(1)	Alternative 3 vs. Alternative 4
Alternative 5	132.18	110	.97	.08	.04	2.66(1)	Alternative 3 vs. Alternative 5
Alternative 6	131.74	110	.98	.07	.04	3.10(1)	Alternative 3 vs. Alternative 6
Alternative 7	133.03	110	.97	.08	.04	1.81(1)	Alternative 3 vs. Alternative 7
Alternative 8	135.36	110	.97	.08	.04	0.52(1)	Alternative 3 vs. Alternative 8
Alternative 9	*130.09*	*110*	*.98*	*.07*	*.04*	*4.75(1)**	*Alternative 3 vs. Alternative 9*
Alternative 10	130.18	109	.98	.07	.04	0.09(1)	Alternative 9 vs. Alternative 10

$N = 129.$ $*p < .05$, $**p < .01$, $***p < .001$.

CONT, intergenerational contact; MULTI, "multi-age" diversity; DI, dual identity; STERE, stereotypes; ADM, admiration emotions; FA, facilitation behavioural tendencies; IQ, intentions to quit; CFI, Comparative Fit Index; SRMR, Standardized Root Mean Square Residual; RMSEA, Root Mean Square Error of Approximation.

Alternative 1: direct path between CONT and STERE; Alternative 2: direct path between CONT and ADM; Alternative 3: direct path between CONT and FA; Alternative 4: direct paths between CONT, FA and IQ; Alternative 5: direct paths between CONT and FA, and between MULTI and STERE; Alternative 6: direct paths between CONT and FA, and between MULTI and ADM; Alternative 7: direct paths between CONT and FA, and between MULTI and FA; Alternative 8: direct paths between CONT and FA, and between MULTI and IQ; Alternative 9: direct paths between CONT and FA, and between DI and ADM; Alternative 10: direct paths between CONT and FA, and between DI, ADM and FA.

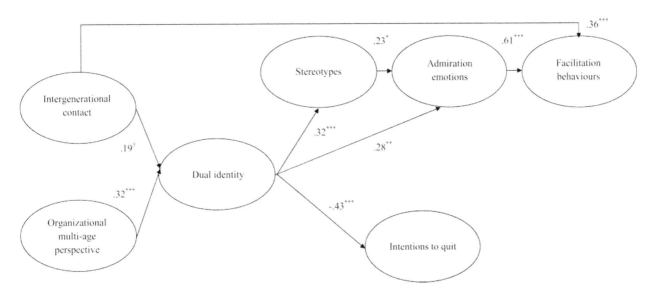

Figure 2. Alternative model 9 (Study 1): Final structural equation model showing relationships between intergenerational contact, organizational multi-age perspective, dual identity, stereotypes, admiration, facilitation behaviours and intentions to quit with standardized coefficients ($N = 129$). For the stake of clarity, only structural relationships are shown. $†p < .10$. $*p < .05$, $**p < .01$, $***p < .001$.

and stereotypes, and totally mediates the link between intergenerational contact and intentions to quit. In other words, our first hypothesis was supported for intentions to quit and received only partial support for stereotypes.

Our second prediction (H2) was that dual identity mediates the relationships between organizational multi-age perspective and both stereotypes and lower intentions to quit. In addition to the significant paths described above, we found a significant path between organizational multi-age perspective and dual identity ($\gamma = .32$, $p < .001$), and a significant indirect effect between organizational multi-age perspective and both stereotypes (indirect effect = .07, $z' = 1.81$, $p < .05$) and intentions to quit (indirect effect = $-.11$, $z' = -2.38$, $p < .05$). Our second hypothesis was thus clearly supported.

Finally, relying on the BIAS map model (Cuddy et al., 2007), our third hypothesis (H3) posited that admiration mediates the relationship between positive stereotypes and facilitation-behaviours tendencies. We found significant paths between stereotypes and emotions ($\beta = .23$, $p < .05$), and between emotions and behaviours ($\beta = .61$, $p < .001$). Moreover, the indirect effect between stereotypes and facilitation behaviours (indirect effect $= .09$, $z' = 1.12$, $p < .05$) was also significant, indicating that admiration fully mediates the link between stereotypes and facilitation behaviours. In sum, our third hypothesis was strongly supported. Moreover, the results indicated an unexpected direct link between dual identity and admiration ($\beta = .28$, $p < .01$).

Discussion

Extending the contact hypothesis (e.g., Pettigrew & Tropp, 2006) and the multicultural perspective (e.g., Plaut et al., 2009), this study suggests that dual identity is a relevant mediator regarding the effect of both intergenerational contact and organizational multi-age perspective on both stereotypes and intentions to quit, with the exception of the effect of contact on stereotypes, for which dual identity is a partial mediator. Moreover, building upon the tripartite model of attitudes (Finkelstein & Farrell, 2007) and in line with the BIAS map model, we showed that perceptions of high competence and warmth lead to facilitation behaviours through admiration emotions.

Innovative as Study 1 may be, it also has a number of limitations. First, the partial mediation indicates that mediators other than dual identity may account for the link between context and outcomes at work. Looking at the literature on diversity, organizational justice comes across as a prime candidate if one wishes to understand how a diversity programme at work may affect employees' attitudes. As a matter of fact, research has shown that procedural justice (i.e., the fairness of the decision-making process; see Richard & Kirby, 1998) is a powerful mediator of the relationships between diversity perspective and attitudes at work (Buttner, Lowe, & Billings-Harris, 2010; Crosby & Franco, 2003). In particular, procedural justice was shown to play a mediating role between both racial (Buttner et al., 2010) and gender (Gilson, 2001) diversity management and employee outcomes such as lower intentions to quit.

Clearly, the mediating role of procedural justice between diversity management and stereotypes has seldom been examined in the literature. Still, several studies have shown that diversity procedures like affirmative action result in positive general attitudes toward their beneficiaries when they are justified (Richard & Kirby, 1998, 1999; Roberson & Stevens, 2006). Based on these studies, we may expect that when employees perceive that their organization supports diversity, such as through an organizational multi-age perspective, they will tend to report higher levels of procedural justice (Triana & Garcia, 2009), which in turn may lead to positive outcomes at work

(Gilson, 2001) and lower intergroup bias (Crosby & Franco, 2003).

A second limitation of our study refers to a perception of older people's competence that could be more complex in the workplace than predicted by the stereotype content model. As a matter of fact, although several studies have confirmed the stereotype of older workers being incompetent (e.g., Rosen & Jerdee, 1976), some studies have shown that older employees may be seen as being at least as competent as, and sometimes even more than, younger employees (e.g., McCann & Giles, 2002). In light of this, Warr and Pennington (1993) showed that stereotypical beliefs about older workers are structured in two dimensions: work effectiveness (e.g., experience, reliability, interpersonal skills) and adaptability (e.g., ability to adapt to change, and to new technology). This factor structure was replicated in several studies which showed that, compared to younger workers, older workers were perceived positively in the work effectiveness dimension and negatively in the adaptability dimension (Chiu, Chan, Snape, & Redman, 2001; Redman & Snape, 2002). We thus decided to build on Warr and Pennington's (1993) findings to improve our analysis of the ageist perceptions as a function of the organizational context.

STUDY 2

The goal of Study 2 was threefold. Firstly, we wanted to replicate Study 1 in another organizational setting. Secondly, we hoped to test the role of perceived procedural justice as another mediator, in addition to dual identity. Finally, we intended to investigate stereotypes that were more closely related to the population of older workers. This time, we did not include emotions or behavioural tendencies. According to the BIAS map model (Cuddy et al., 2007), emotions and behavioural tendencies are predicted by both warmth and competence stereotypes. In Study 2, we decided to focus on the two factors of competence identified by Warr and Pennington (1993), preventing us from evidencing an impact of stereotypes on emotions and behavioural tendencies.

We predicted that dual identity would mediate the relationships between the quality of intergenerational contact on the one hand, and both more positive stereotypes toward older workers and lower intentions to quit on the other (Hypothesis 1). We also expected that dual identity would mediate the relationships between organizational multi-age perspective and the same dependent variables as stated above (Hypothesis 2). Finally, we hypothesized that perceived procedural justice would also mediate the relationships between organizational multi-age perspective and the same dependent variables as stated above (Hypothesis 3, see Figure 3).

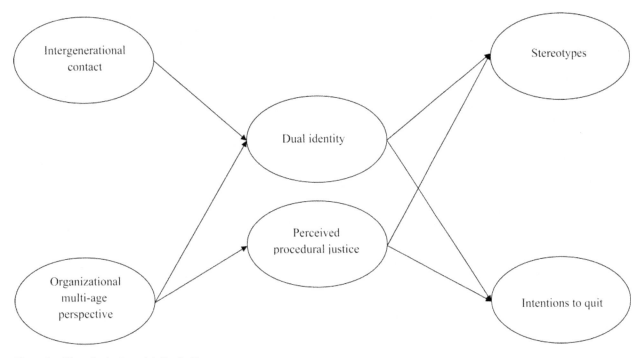

Figure 3. Hypothesized model (Study 2).

Method

Participants and procedure

Data were collected in a Belgian hospital on 534 French-speaking Belgian employees. We had a final sample of 187 employees aged less than fifty (mean age = 37.08, SD = 7.70, minimum = 20, maximum = 49, 80% of respondents being in the 30 to 49 age range) who completed the entire questionnaire (response rate = 35%). A majority of respondents were females (86%), worked full time (54%), were employees (89%), and had completed high school (63%).

Participants completed a paper questionnaire which was accompanied by a cover letter signed by the researchers and indicating that the purpose of the study was to examine people's attitudes toward age diversity and intergenerational relationships at work. An envelope was provided so that completed questionnaires could remain anonymous.

Measures

The measures were exactly the same as those used in Study 1 (all α > .85), except for perceived procedural justice and stereotypes.

Perceived procedural justice was measured with three items (α = .91) pertaining to a control-based view of perceived procedural justice adapted from Colquitt (2001), and Houlden, LaTour, Walker, and Thibaut (1978). Using a seven-point scale ranging from 1 (*totally disagree*) to 7 (*totally agree*), participants rated the extent to which they perceived

that their organization was fair about age diversity (e.g., "I have an influence on decisions concerning the management of age diversity in my organization").

The measure of *stereotypes* about older workers as a group (again defined as being workers of 50 years of age and above) was adapted from Warr and Pennington (1993), in Redman & Snape (2002). Work effectiveness was measured with six items (α = .87). Participants were invited to use an eleven-point scale ranging from 1 (=0%) to 11 (=100%) to rate the number of older workers who are for example *conscientious*. Adaptability was measured with six items (α = .89). Using the same eleven-point scale, participants rated the extent to which they think that older workers *learn quickly* for instance. Stereotype scales (work effectiveness and adaptability) were multiplied so that the highest scores indicated that older workers were perceived as both effective and adaptable in their work.

Results

Preliminary analyses

As in Study 1, we analysed the relationships between control variables and dependent measures with one-way ANOVAs using gender, working time and professional status as independent variables. None of these variables had a significant impact. Correlations between age and the dependent measures revealed no significant relationships. Therefore, none of the control variables were taken into account in the analyses. Table 4 presents descriptive statistics and correlations among variables. The data were

TABLE 4
Means, standard deviations and intercorrelations among the variables (Study 2)

Variable	M	SD	1	2	3	4	5
1. Intergenerational contact[1]	6.27	0.84					
2. Organizational multi-age perspective[1]	4.03	1.43	.23**				
3. Dual identity[2]	22.18	3.79	.24**	.38***			
4. Perceived procedural justice[1]	2.23	1.23	.02	.30***	.26***		
5. Stereotypes[3]	59.97	18.44	.23**	.24**	.19*	.18*	
6. Intentions to quit[1]	2.27	1.34	−.11	−.34***	−.47***	−.03	−.09

$N = 129$. *$p < .05$, **$p < .01$, ***$p < .001$.

[1]ranges from 1 (=totally disagree) to 7 (=totally agree).

[2]ranges from 1 (=low dual identity) to 49 (=high dual identity).

[3]ranges from 1 (=low effectiveness and adaptability perceptions) to 121 (=high effectiveness and adaptability perceptions).

analysed following the same two-step procedure and method as described in Study 1.

Confirmatory factor analyses

In line with the hypothesized model, we specified six latent constructs: intergenerational contact, organizational multi-age perspective, dual identity, perceived procedural justice, stereotypes, and intentions to quit. As expected, this model fitted the data very well, $\chi^2(89) = 109.54$, $p < .05$ (CFI = .99, SRMR = .03, RMSEA = .03). The standardized loadings were significant (all $t > 1.96$) and large, ranging from .67 to .95.

Next, we compared the six-factor model with a series of alternative measurement models to ensure that the hypothesized model best reflected the data structure (see Table 5). The results indicated that the six-factor model was significantly superior to all models that were more constrained.

Tests of hypotheses

We tested our hypotheses (see Figure 3) with a structural equation model. This model presented an adequate fit to the data, $\chi^2(96) = 147.58$, $p < .05$ (CFI = .98, SRMR = .07, RMSEA = .05). We then compared this model to alternative models to ensure that it best reflected the data structure. The fit indices for each structural model are presented in Table 6. The results indicated that the alternative Model 4 (see Figure 4) had the lowest value of χ^2 and was the most parsimonious. In other words, a model where direct links between intergenerational contact and stereotypes and between organizational multi-age perspective and intentions to quit were added (i.e., indicating partial mediations) showed a fit which was significantly superior ($\chi^2(94) = 117.01$, $p < .05$, CFI = .99, SRMR = .05, RMSEA = .04). We thus retained this model as the best-fitting one.

Our first hypothesis (H1) was that relationships between intergenerational contact on the one hand and stereotypes and work attitudes on the other are mediated by dual identity. The data revealed significant paths between intergenerational contact and dual identity ($\gamma = .18$, $p < .05$), and between dual identity and intentions to quit ($\beta = -.48$, $p < .001$), as well as a marginally significant link between dual identity and stereotypes ($\beta = .13$, $p < .10$). The indirect effects of intergenerational contact (all indirect effects were computed by a Sobel test for each mediator variable) were significant on intentions to quit (indirect effect = $-.30$, $z = -2.11$, $p < .05$) and marginally significant on stereotypes (indirect effect = .03, $z = 1.40$, $p < .10$). Moreover, the direct link between intergenerational contact and stereotypes is significant ($\gamma = .31$, $p < .001$). In other words, our first hypothesis was partially supported in that dual identity fully mediates the link between intergenerational contact and intentions to quit, and partially mediates the link between intergenerational contact and stereotypes.

Our second prediction (H2) was that dual identity mediates the relationships between organizational multi-age perspective and both perceptions and work attitudes. In addition to the significant and marginal (the relationship between contact and stereotype) paths described above, the results showed a significant path between organizational multi-age perspective and dual identity ($\gamma = .37$, $p < .001$), as well as a marginally significant indirect effect of organizational multi-age perspective on stereotypes (indirect effect = .06, $z = 1.10$, $p < .10$) on the one hand, and a significant indirect effect on intentions to quit on the other (indirect effect = $-.18$, $z = -3.98$, $p < .001$). Our second hypothesis was thus partially supported given that dual identity was a partial mediator of the relationship between organizational multi-age perspective and stereotypes, and a full mediator of the relationship between organizational multi-age perspective and intentions to quit.

Finally, our third hypothesis (H3) was that perceived procedural justice mediates the links between organizational multi-age perspective and

TABLE 5
Confirmatory factor analysis fit indices for measurement model (Study 2)

	Model	χ^2	df	$\Delta\chi^2$ (Δdf)	CFI	SRMR	RMSEA
1.	Six-factor model	109.54	89	–	.99	.03	.03
2.	Five-factor model (CONT, MULTI = 1 factor)	317.78	94	208.24(5)***	.91	.10	.11
3.	Five-factor model (MULTI, DI = 1 factor)	452.11	94	342.57(5)***	.86	.12	.14
4.	Five-factor model (CONT, DI = 1 factor)	316.14	94	206.60(5)***	.91	.10	.11
5.	Five-factor model (MULTI, JUST = 1 factor)	835.97	94	345.72(5)***	.92	.10	.09
6.	Five-factor model (CONT, JUST = 1 factor)	285.90	94	176.36(5)***	.89	.11	.10
7.	Five-factor model (JUST, DI = 1 factor)	264.72	94	155.18(5)***	.90	.09	.10
8.	Five-factor model (STERE, IQ = 1 factor)	300.60	94	191.06(5)***	.89	.13	.11
9.	Five-factor model (STERE, DI = 1 factor)	488.16	94	378.52(5)***	.81	.13	.15
10.	Five-factor model (IQ, DI = 1 factor)	230.60	94	121.06(5)***	.93	.06	.09
11.	Five-factor model (STERE, JUST = 1 factor)	493.66	94	348.12(5)***	.81	.14	.15
12.	Five-factor model (IQ, JUST = 1 factor)	304.12	94	194.58(5)***	.89	.13	.11
13.	Four-factor model (CONT, MULTI, DI = 1 factor)	665.03	98	555.49(9)***	.79	.15	.18
14.	Four-factor model (CONT, MULTI, JUST = 1 factor)	478.39	98	368.85(9)***	.80	.14	.14
15.	Four-factor model (DI, STERE, IQ = 1 factor)	606.249	98	586.70(9)***	.75	.14	.17
16.	Four-factor model (JUST, STERE, IQ = 1 factor)	696.85	98	587.31(9)***	.71	.18	.18
17.	Three-factor model (DI, JUST, STERE, IQ = 1 factor)	756.39	101	646.85(12)***	.67	.16	.19
18.	Three-factor model (MULTI, CONT = 1 factor; DI, JUST = 1 factor)	652.78	101	543.24(12)***	.74	.17	.17
19.	Two-factor model (MULTI, CONT, DI, JUST = 1 factor; STERE, IQ = 1 factor)	962.96	103	853.42(14)***	.63	.19	.21
20.	Two-factor model (MULTI, CONT = 1 factor; DI, JUST, STERE, IQ = 1 factor)	962.57	103	853.03(14)***	.60	.18	.21
21.	One-factor model	1324.60	104	1215.06(15)***	.47	.20	.25

$N = 187$. *$p < .05$, **$p < .01$, ***$p < .001$.

CONT, intergenerational contact; MULTI, "multi-age" diversity; DI, dual identity; JUST, perceived procedural justice; STERE, stereotypes; IQ, intentions to quit; CFI, Comparative Fit Index; SRMR, Standardized Root Mean Square Residual; RMSEA, Root Mean Square Error of Approximation.

TABLE 6
Fit indices for structural models (Study 2)

Model	χ^2	Df	CFI	SRMR	RMSEA	$\Delta\chi^2$ (Δdf)	Model comparison
Hypothesized	147.58	96	.98	.07	.05	–	
Alternative 1	122.36	95	.98	.06	.04	25.22(1)***	Hypothesized vs. Alternative 1
Alternative 2	122.41	94	.98	.06	.04	0.05(1)	Alternative 1 vs. Alternative 2
Alternative 3	120.51	94	.98	.05	.04	1.85(1)	Alternative 1 vs. Alternative 3
Alternative 4	117.01	94	.99	.05	.04	5.35(1)*	Alternative 1 vs. Alternative 4
Alternative 5	114.15	93	.99	.04	.03	2.86(1)	Alternative 4 vs. Alternative 5

$N = 187$. *$p < .05$, **$p < .01$, ***$p < .001$.

MULTI, "multi-age" diversity; DI, dual identity; JUST, perceived procedural justice; STERE, stereotypes; IQ, intentions to quit; CFI, Comparative Fit Index; SRMR, Standardized Root Mean Square Residual; RMSEA, Root Mean Square Error of Approximation.

Alternative 1: direct path between CONT and STERE; Alternative 2: direct paths between CONT, STERE and IQ; Alternative 3: direct paths between CONT and STERE, and between MULTI and STERE; Alternative 4: direct paths between CONT and STERE, and between MULTI and IQ; Alternative 5: Covariance between DI and JUST was added.

both positive stereotypes and work attitudes. The examination of the parameters indicated significant paths between organizational multi-age perspective and perceived procedural justice ($\gamma = .34$, $p < .001$), as well as between perceived procedural justice and both stereotypes ($\beta = .19$, $p < .05$) and intentions to quit ($\beta = -.17$, $p < .05$). These results indicated that perceived procedural justice mediates the link between organizational multi-age perspective and both positive stereotypes (indirect effect = .06, $z = 1.90$,

$p < .05$) and intentions to quit (indirect effect = $-.06$, $z = -2.08$, $p < .05$). Moreover, the direct link between organizational multi-age perspective and intentions to quit is significant ($\gamma = -.22$, $p < .01$). Our third hypothesis was thus partially supported, as perceived procedural justice fully mediated the link between organizational multi-age perspective and stereotypes, and partially mediated the link between organizational multi-age perspective and intentions to quit.

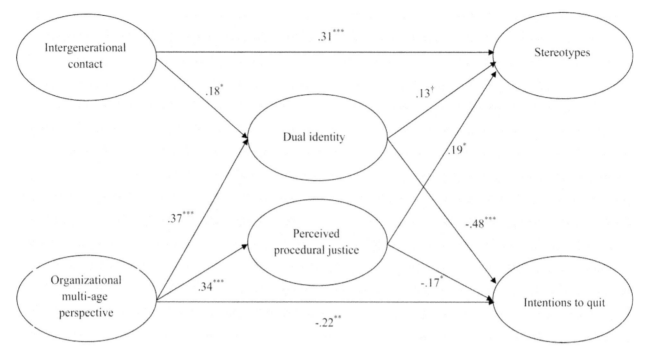

Figure 4. Alternative model 4 (Study 2): Final structural equation model showing relationships between intergenerational contact, organizational multi-age perspective, dual identity, perceived procedural justice, stereotypes and intentions to quit with standardized coefficients ($N = 187$). For the stake of clarity, only structural relationships are shown. $^{\dagger}p < .10$. $^{*}p < .05$, $^{**}p < .01$, $^{***}p < .001$.

Discussion

To sum up, just as in Study 1, Study 2 showed that dual identity is a partial mediator for the relationship between intergenerational contact and organizational multi-age perspective on stereotypes, and a full mediator for the relationship between this favourable context and intentions to quit. Moreover, perceived procedural justice appeared to be a complementary mediator in explaining the effects of a multi-age diversity on attitudes toward older workers and marginally on attitudes at work.

GENERAL DISCUSSION

Both high-quality intergroup interactions (Pettigrew & Tropp, 2006, 2008) and fostering a multicultural perspective (Richeson & Nussbaum, 2003) have proven to be effective strategies for reducing intergroup bias and improving work attitudes. On this basis, we designed two studies in order to investigate the impact of both contact between age groups and creating an organizational multi-age perspective on younger workers' age-related bias and attitudes in the workplace. Building upon research on identity dynamics in contact situations (Richter et al., 2006), we also aimed to analyse the role of dual identity as a potential mediator.

The present work shows that high-quality contact between age groups in the workplace is linked to positive perceptions of older workers: they are perceived as more sociable and competent in Study

1, and more effective and adaptable in their job in Study 2. In addition, supporting findings that co-worker relationships also influence employees' occupational attitudes (Avery et al., 2007), our studies demonstrate that high-quality intergenerational contact at work is linked negatively to intentions to quit. As such, our studies shed new light on the effects of contact on a series of variables that have often been neglected in the prejudice literature (Dixon et al., 2005).

In line with studies which have shown that dual identity is one of the most successful ways to reduce intergroup bias (e.g., Eller & Abrams, 2003, 2004), our studies indicate that dual identity is indeed a relevant mediator when it comes to the impact of intergenerational contact on stereotypes of older workers, as well as on intentions to quit. At the same time, we also observed direct links between contact and stereotypes in both studies, indicating that other variables may act as mediators of this relationship. In our opinion, the affective processes included in the contact situation, like empathy, could contribute toward modifying perceptions about outgroup members (e.g., Ensari & Miller, 2006).

Extending previous work on diversity (Homan, van Knippenberg, van Kleef, & de Dreu, 2007), our studies underline the role of organizational support of diversity in the still largely unexplored domain of age-related diversity at work. Indeed, in accordance with research on diversity showing that a multicultural perspective reduces race bias (e.g., Wolsko et al., 2000) and improves work attitudes (Plaut et al.,

2009), the present data confirm that fostering an organizational multi-age perspective is linked both to positive perceptions toward older workers and to a reduction of intentions to quit. As we predicted, dual identity was shown to mediate the effects of organizational support of diversity on perceptions about the outgroup as well as on intentions to quit. To the best of our knowledge, this is the first study that provides empirical support for the dual identity model proposed by Dovidio et al. (1998) in the context of multiculturalism.

Interestingly, perceived procedural justice was also shown to mediate the effects of organizational multi-age perspective on stereotypes and intentions to quit. These results are congruent with studies on diversity management which showed that the deleterious effects of procedures like affirmative action on perceptions toward beneficiaries can be reduced when the procedure is seen as fair (e.g., Crosby & Franco, 2003). They also dovetail nicely with work showing that perceived procedural justice is a powerful mediator of the relationship between diversity perspective and attitudes at work (Buttner et al., 2010). Here too, a direct link between organizational multi-age perspective and intentions to quit indicates that other variables, such as distributive justice, may mediate this relationship (Nadiri & Tanova, 2009).

Finally, the present research underlines that the effects of a favourable intergenerational context are linked not only to perceptions of older individuals but also to emotions about and behaviours toward them. In line with the BIAS map model (Cuddy et al., 2007), we found that perceptions of high competence and high sociability were linked to more admiration and facilitation behaviours (e.g., help, cooperation) in a favourable intergenerational context (high quality of intergenerational contact and organizational multi-age perspective). As such, this study fills a gap in the literature on ageism by examining more closely which emotions and behaviours can be expected according to the perceptual pattern related to age. As with stereotypes, the affective component, which is seldom examined and measured in the ageism literature (Finkelstein & Farrell, 2007), appeared both to be impacted by social context and to reinforce the likelihood of increasing favourable behaviours toward older individuals. Thus, our findings clearly offer new insights not only within the literature on ageism at work (Finkelstein & Farrell, 2007) but also for the broader literature pertaining to the tripartite model of attitudes (e.g., Cuddy et al., 2007).

Limitations and future research

Future work on these issues should take into account the limitations of the present set of studies. Firstly, the design used in our studies prevents us from drawing causal inferences about relationships between perceptions of the context (e.g., the quality of contact) and consequences. Indeed, structural analyses may well be suited to sanctioning those processes that derive from specific theoretical assumptions about a given causal process, but they do not allow the confirmation of which variables are either antecedents or consequences. In other words, future studies should aim at replicating findings of the present studies by using longitudinal or even experimental designs which are more constrained.

Secondly, the small size of our samples may represent a limitation of our statistical analyses. In fact, this limit led us to use the partial disaggregation method (Bagozzi & Edwards, 1998). This method allows researchers to perform meaningful tests of model fit despite a small sample size (von der Heidt & Scott, 2007) but it may also hide a more valid factor structure. Having said this, we note that our two studies yielded similar results, lending reasonable confidence regarding the reliability and generalization of our findings.

Thirdly, common method bias may have caused an inflation in the relationships among simultaneously measured variables using a self-report method. However, the concern over method bias may have been partially addressed by performing analyses for Study 1 and Study 2 showing that a single-factor solution provided an extremely poor fit of the data (i.e., Harman's single factor test; Podsakoff, MacKenzie, Lee, & Podsakoff, 2003).

Finally, in the present work, we were specifically interested in examining a reduction of ageism, which is defined as stigmatization of and discrimination against older people. From this perspective, focusing on younger people seemed relevant. However, future research should focus on the perceptions of both younger and older workers, to explore potential specific reactions to the organizational context related to age diversity. In fact, recent studies have shown that organizations promoting initiatives premised on a multicultural ideology are particularly attractive to minorities, because group identities such as race, ethnicity, and religious affiliation are retained and acknowledged (e.g., Wolsko et al., 2006). Our findings might be explained by the fact that the multi-age perspective is probably similar to both the "integration and learning perspective" (Ely and Thomas, 2001) and the "polyculturalist perspective" recently proposed by Rosenthal and Levy (2010), which encourages all employees to value and express themselves as members of their social group and to learn from each other. This kind of "all-inclusive" perspective could be better valued by majority groups than perspectives which only recognize specificities of the minority group without linking them to majority members' self-interests (Plaut, Garnett, Buffardi, & Sanchez-Burks, 2011). In other words, younger workers could also see themselves as beneficiaries of a multi-age diversity perspective.

CONCLUSION

The present research efforts show that high-quality intergenerational contact and the fostering of an organizational multi-age perspective are favourable both for the employees (more intergroup harmony within the organization) and the organization (more positive attitudes at work). Moreover, social categorization processes and perceived procedural justice have been highlighted as relevant and important mediational mechanisms through the way social context relates to intergenerational attitudes and attitudes at work. Finally, our findings complement the literature on ageism by measuring this bias with a proper consideration of its cognitive, affective, and behavioural components, according to the tripartite model of attitudes. Hopefully, the message emanating from our data will provide all parties involved in organizations with effective strategies for allowing further promotion of diversity and tolerance in the workplace.

REFERENCES

Allport, G. W. (1954). *The nature of prejudice*. Oxford: Addison-Wesley.

Arnold, H. J., & Feldman, D. C. (1982). A multivariate analysis of the determinants of job turnover. *Journal of Applied Psychology, 67*, 350–360.

Avery, D. R., McKay, P. F., & Wilson, D. C. (2007). Engaging the aging workforce: The relationship between perceived age similarity, satisfaction with coworkers, and employment engagement. *Journal of Applied Psychology, 92*, 1542–1556.

Bagozzi, R. P., & Edwards, J. R. (1998). A general approach for representing constructs in organizational research. *Organizational Research Methods, 1*, 45–87.

Barrett, P. (2007). Structural equation modelling: Adjudging model fit. *Personality and Individual Differences, 42*, 815–824.

Becker, T. E. (2005). Potential problems in the statistical control in variables in organization research: A qualitative analysis with recommendations. *Organizational Research Methods, 8*, 274–289.

Bentler, P. M. (1990). Comparative fit indexes in structural models. *Psychological Bulletin, 107*, 238–246.

Brouwer, M. A. R., & Boros, S. (2010). The influence of intergroup contact and ethnocultural empathy on employees' attitudes toward diversity. *Cognition, Brain, Behavior: An Interdisciplinary Journal, 14*, 243–260.

Burke, R. J., & Greenglass, E. R. (2000). Effects of hospital restructuring on full time and part time nursing staff in Ontario. *International Journal of Nursing Studies, 37*, 163–171.

Butler, R. N. (1969). Age-ism: Another form of bigotry. *The Gerontologist, 9*, 243–246.

Buttner, E. H., Lowe, K. B., & Billings-Harris, L. (2010). Diversity climate impact on employee of color outcomes: Does justice matter? *Career Development International, 15*, 239–258.

Chang, J., & Le, T. N. (2010). Multiculturalism as a dimension of school climate: The impact on the academic achievement of Asian American and Hispanic youth. *Cultural Diversity and Ethnic Minority Psychology, 16*, 485–492.

Chen, Z. X., & Francesco, A. M. (2000). Employee demography, organizational commitment, and turnover intentions in China: Do cultural differences matter? *Human Relations, 53*, 869–887.

Chiu, W. C. K., Chan, A. W., Snape, S., & Redman, T. (2001). Age stereotypes and discriminatory attitudes towards older workers: An east-west comparison. *Human Relations, 54*, 629–660.

Colquitt, J. A. (2001). On the dimensionality of organizational justice: A construct validation of a measure. *Journal of Applied Psychology, 86*, 386–400.

Crosby, F. J., & Franco, J. L. (2003). Connections between the ivory tower and the multicolored world: Linking abstract theories of social justice to the rough and tumble of affirmative action. *Personality and Social Psychology Review, 7*, 362–373.

Cuddy, A. J., Glick, P., & Fiske, S. T. (2007). The BIAS Map: Behaviors from intergroup affect and stereotypes. *Journal of Personality and Social Psychology, 92*, 631–648.

DeVellis, R. F. (1991). *Scale development: Theory and applications*. Newbury Park, CA: Sage.

Dovidio, J. F., & Gaertner, S. L. (2010). Intergroup bias. In S. T. Fiske, D. T. Gilbert, & G. Lindzey (Eds.), *Handbook of social psychology* (pp. 1084–1121). Hoboken, NJ: Wiley & Sons.

Dovidio, J. F., Gaertner, S. L., & Kawakami, K. (2003). Intergroup contact: The past, present, and the future. *Group Processes & Intergroup Relations, 6*, 5–21.

Dovidio, J. F., Gaertner, S. L., & Validzic, A. (1998). Intergroup bias: Status, differentiation, and a common in-group identity. *Journal of Personality and Social Psychology, 75*, 109–120.

Dixon, J., Durrheim, K., & Tredoux, C. (2005). Beyond the optimal contact strategy: A reality check for the contact hypothesis. *American Psychologist, 60*, 697–711.

Eller, A., & Abrams, D. (2003). "Gringos" in Mexico: Cross-sectional and longitudinal effects of language school-promoted contact on intergroup bias. *Group Processes & Intergroup Relations, 6*, 55–75.

Eller, A., & Abrams, D. (2004). Come together: Longitudinal comparisons of Pettigrew's reformulated intergroup contact model and the common ingroup identity model in Anglo-French and Mexican-American contexts. *European Journal of Social Psychology, 34*, 229–256.

Ely, R. J., & Thomas, D. A. (2001). Cultural diversity at work: The effect of diversity perspectives on work group processes and outcomes. *Administrative Science Quarterly, 46*, 229–273.

Ensari, N. K., & Miller, N. (2006). The application of the personalization model in diversity management. *Group Processes & Intergroup Relations, 9*, 589–607.

Finkelstein, L. M., & Farrell, S. K. (2007). An expanded view of age bias in the workplace. In K. S. Kenneth & G. A. Adams (Eds.), *Aging and work in the 21st century* (pp. 73–108). Mahwah, NJ: Erlbaum.

Fiske, S. T., Cuddy, A. J. C., Xu, J., & Glick, P. (2002). A model of (often mixed) stereotype content: Competence and warmth respectively follow from perceived status and competition. *Journal of Personality and Social Psychology, 82*, 878–902.

Fiske, S. T., Xu, J., & Cuddy, A. C. (1999). (Dis)respecting versus (dis)liking: Status and interdependence predict ambivalent stereotypes of competence and warmth. *Journal of Social Issues, 55*, 473–489.

Gaillard, M., & Desmette, D. (2010). (In)validating stereotypes about older workers influences their intentions to retire early and to learn and develop. *Basic and Applied Social Psychology, 32*, 86–95.

Garstka, T. A., Schmitt, M. T., Branscombe, N. R., & Hummert, M. L. (2004). How young and older adults differ in their responses to perceived age discrimination. *Psychology and Aging, 19*, 326–335.

Gilson, L. L. (2001). *The role of procedural justice in the relationship between demographic diversity, dissimilarity, work-related affective outcomes, and creative performance*. Ann Arbor, MI: ProQuest Information & Learning.

Gomez, A., Dovidio, J. F., Huici, C., Gaertner, S. L., & Cuadrado, I. (2008). The other side of we: When outgroup members express common identity. *Personality and Social Psychology Bulletin, 34*, 1613–1626.

Gonzàlez, R., & Brown, R. (2003). Generalization of positive attitude as a function of subgroup and superordinate group identification in intergroup contact. *European Journal of Social Psychology, 33*, 195–214.

Gordon, R. A., & Arvey, R. D. (2004). Age bias in laboratory and field settings: A meta-analytic investigation. *Journal of Applied Psychology, 34*, 468–492.

Guerra, R., Rebelo, M., Monteiro, M. B., Riek, B. M., Mania, E. W., Gaertner, S. L., & Dovidio, J. F. (2010). How should intergroup contact be structured to reduce bias among majority and minority group children? *Group Processes & Intergroup Relations, 13*, 445–460.

Hassell, B. L., & Perrewe, P. L. (1993). An examination of the relationship between older workers' perceptions of age discrimination and employee psychological states. *Journal of Managerial Issues, 5*, 109–120.

Hodson, R. (1997). Group relations at work. *Work and Occupations, 24*, 426–452.

Hofhuis, J., van der Zee, K. I., & Otten, S. (2012). Social identity patterns in culturally diverse organizations: The role of diversity climate. *Journal of Applied Social Psychology, 42*, 964–989.

Homan, A. C., van Knippenberg, D., van Kleef, G. A., & de Dreu, C. K. W. (2007). Bridging faultlines by valuing diversity: Diversity beliefs, information elaboration, and performance in diverse work groups. *Journal of Applied Psychology, 92*, 1189–1199.

Hornsey, M. J., & Hogg, M. A. (2000). Subgroup relations: A comparison of mutual intergroup differentiation and common ingroup identity models of prejudice reduction. *Personality and Social Psychology Bulletin, 26*, 242–256.

Houlden, P., LaTour, S., Walker, L., & Thibaut, J. (1978). Preference for modes of dispute resolution as a function of process and decision control. *Journal of Experimental Social Psychology, 14*, 13–30.

Hu, L., & Bentler, P. M. (1999). Cutoff criteria for fit indexes in covariance structure analysis: Conventional criteria versus new alternatives. *Structural Equation Modeling, 6*, 1–55.

Huo, Y. J., Smith, H. J., Tyler, T. R., & Lind, E. A. (1996). Superordinate identification, subgroup identification, and justice concern: Is separatism the problem; is assimilation the answer? *American Psychological Society, 7*, 40–45.

Kessler, T., & Mummendey, A. (2002). Sequential or parallel processes? A longitudinal field study concerning determinants of identity-management strategies. *Journal of Personality and Social Psychology, 82*, 75–88.

Kline, R. B. (2011). *Principles and practice of structural equation modeling* (3rd ed.). New York, NY: Guilford Press.

Mathieu, J. E., & Zajac, D. (1990). A review and meta-analysis of the antecedents, correlates, and consequences of organizational commitment. *Psychological Bulletin, 108*, 171–194.

McCann, R., & Giles, H. (2002). Ageism in the workplace: A communication perspective. In T. D. Nelson (Ed.), *Ageism: Stereotyping and prejudice against older persons* (pp. 163–199). Cambridge, MA: MIT Press.

MacKinnon, D. P., Lockwood, C. M., Hoffman, J. M., West, S. G., & Sheets, V. (2002). A comparison of methods to test mediation and other intervening variable effects. *Psychological Methods, 7*, 83–104.

Nadiri, H., & Tanova, C. (2009). An investigation of the role of justice in turnover intentions, job satisfaction, and organizational citizenship behavior in hospitality industry. *International Journal of Hospitality Management, 29*, 33–41.

Organisation for Economic Co-operation and Development (2006). *Ageing and employment policies – "Live longer, work longer"*. Paris: Author.

Pettigrew, T. F. (1998). Intergroup contact theory. *The Annual Review of Psychology, 49*, 65–85.

Pettigrew, T. F., & Tropp, L. R. (2000). Does intergroup contact reduce prejudice? Recent meta-analytic findings. In S. Oskamp (Ed.), *Reducing prejudice and discrimination* (pp. 93–114). Mahwah, NJ: Erlbaum.

Pettigrew, T. F., & Tropp, L. R. (2006). A meta-analytic test of intergroup contact theory. *Journal of Personality and Social Psychology, 90*, 751–783.

Pettigrew, T. F., & Tropp, L. R. (2008). How does intergroup contact reduce prejudice? Meta-analytic tests of three mediators. *European Journal of Social Psychology, 38*, 922–934.

Plaut, V. C., Garnett, F. G., Buffardi, L. E., & Sanchez-Burks, J. (2011). "What about me?" Perceptions of exclusion and whites' reactions to multiculturalism. *Journal of Personality and Social Psychology, 101*, 337–353.

Plaut, V. C., Thomas, K. M., & Goren, M. J. (2009). Is multiculturalism or color blindness better for minorities? *Psychological Science, 20*, 444–446.

Pomaki, G., DeLongis, A., Frey, D., Short, K., & Woehrle, T. (2010). When the going gets tough: Direct, buffering and indirect effects of social support on turnover intention. *Teaching and Teacher Education, 26*, 1340–1346.

Posthuma, R. A. & Campion, M. A. (2009). Age stereotypes in the workplace: Common stereotypes, moderators, and future research directions. *Journal of Management, 35*, 158–188.

Podsakoff, P. M., MacKenzie, S. B., Lee, J. Y., & Podsakoff, N. P. (2003). Common method biases in behavioural research: A critical review of the literature and recommended remedies. *Journal of Applied Psychology, 88*, 879–903.

Price, J. L. (1997). Handbook of organizational measurement. *International Journal of Manpower, 18*, 305–558.

Redman, T., & Snape, E. (2002). Ageism in teaching: Stereotypical beliefs and discriminatory attitudes towards the over-50s. *Work, Employment and Society, 16*, 355–371.

Richard, O. C., & Kirby, S. L. (1998). Women recruits' perception of workforce diversity program selection decisions: A procedural justice examination. *Journal of Applied Psychology, 28*, 183–188.

Richard, O. C., & Kirby, S. L. (1999). Organizational justice and the justification of work force diversity programs. *Journal of Business and Psychology, 14*, 109–118.

Richeson, J. A., & Nussbaum, R. J. (2003). The impact of multiculturalism versus color-blindness on racial bias. *Journal of Experimental Social Psychology, 40*, 417–423.

Richter, A. W., West, M. A., van Dick, R., & Dawson, J. F. (2006). Boundary spanners' identification, intergroup contact, and effective intergroup relations. *Academy of Management Journal, 49*, 1252–1269.

Roberson, Q. M., & Stevens, C. K. (2006). Making sense of diversity in the workplace: Organizational justice and language abstraction in employees' accounts of diversity-related incidents. *Journal of Applied Psychology, 91*, 379–391.

Rogerson, P. (2003, March 2). The great pensions panic. *Accounting and Business Magazine*. Retrieved from http://www2.accaglobal.com/members/publications/accounting_business/archive_by_topic/pensions/2003/912796

Rosen, B., & Jerdee, T. H. (1976). The influence of age stereotypes on managerial decisions. *Journal of Applied Psychology, 61,* 428–432.

Rosenthal, L., & Levy, S. R. (2010). The colorblind, multicultural, and polycultural ideological approaches to improving intergroup attitudes and relations. *Social Issues and Policy Review, 4,* 215–246.

Steiger, J. H., & Lind, J. C. (1980, May). *Statistical based tests for the number of common factors.* Paper presented at the Annual Spring Meeting of the Psychometric Society, Iowa City, IA.

Tajfel, H. (1978). *Differentiation between social groups: Studies in the social psychology of intergroup relations.* Oxford: Academic Press.

Tam, T., Hewstone, M., Harwood, J., Voci, A., & Kenworthy, J. (2006). Intergroup contact and grandparent-grandchild communication: The effects of self-disclosure on implicit and explicit biases against older people. *Group Processes & Intergroup Relations, 9,* 413–429.

Triana, M. D. C., & Garcia, M. F. (2009). Valuing diversity: A group value approach to understanding the importance of organizational efforts to support diversity. *Journal of Organizational Behavior, 30,* 941–962.

van der Noll, J., Poppe, E., & Verkuyten, M. (2010). Political tolerance and prejudice: Differential reactions toward Muslims in the Netherlands. *Basic and Applied Social Psychology, 32,* 46–56.

Verkuyten, M. (2005). Immigration discourses and their impact on multiculturalism: A discursive and experimental study. *British Journal of Social Psychology, 44,* 223–240.

Voci, A., & Hewstone, M. (2003). Intergroup contact and prejudice toward immigrants in Italy: The mediational role of anxiety and the moderational role of group salience. *Group Processes & Intergroup Relations, 6,* 37–54.

von der Heidt, T. & Scott, D. R. (2007, December). *Partial aggregation for complex structural equation modelling (SEM) and small sample sizes: An illustration using a multi-stakeholder model of cooperative interorganisational relationships (IORs) in product innovation.* Paper presented at the 21st ANZAM Conference, Sydney.

Warr, P., & Pennington, J. (1993). Views about age discrimination and older workers. In P. Taylor, A. Walker, B. Casey, H. Metcalf, J. Lakey, P. Warr, & J. Pennington (Eds.), *Age and employment: Policies and practices* (pp. 75–106). London: Institute of Personnel Management.

Wolsko, C., Park, B., & Judd, C. M. (2006). Considering the tower of Babel: Correlates of assimilation and multiculturalism among ethnic minority and majority groups in the United States. *Social Justice Research, 19,* 277–306.

Wolsko, C., Park, B., Judd, C. M., & Wittenbrink, B. (2000). Framing interethnic ideology: Effects of multicultural and color-blind perspectives on judgments of groups and individuals. *Journal of Personality and Social Psychology, 78,* 536–654.

Yinger, J. M. (1994). *Ethnicity: Source of strength? Source of conflict?* Albany, NY: State University of New York Press.

Yzerbyt, V., & Demoulin, S. (2010). Intergroup relations. In S. T. Fiske, D. T. Gilbert, & G. Lindzey (Eds.), *Handbook of social psychology* (pp. 1024–1083). Hoboken, NJ: Wiley & Sons.

Drivers of the expectation of remaining in the same job until retirement age: A working life span demands-resources model

Susanne C. Liebermann[1], Jürgen Wegge[1], and Andreas Müller[2]

[1]Institute of Work, Organizational and Social Psychology, Technical University Dresden, Dresden, Germany

[2]Institute for Occupational Medicine and Social Medicine, Medical Faculty, University of Düsseldorf, Düsseldorf, Germany

Many countries in Europe seek to increase labour force participation of older people. Previous literature regarding this issue has mainly focused on the last career stage to identify motivational forces affecting the retirement process. We propose that interventions to extend working life need to consider also young employees in order to be effective. We introduce a new construct, Expectation of Remaining in the Same Job until Retirement age (ERSJR), that is relevant for all age groups. Moreover, we suggest a Working Life Span Demands–Resources model to investigate the impact of perceived job demands and resources, as well as individual health on ERSJR. Our study is based on representative data from the German working population ($N = 1586$). Applying moderated multiple regression analysis we found that ERSJR is negatively related to job demands and positively to job resources and health. Resources and health interact with job demands. Analysing the model separately for different age and employment status groups we found that young blue-collar employees' expectation mainly depends on the job demands, whereas young white-collar employees only take the perceived job resources into account. Older blue-collar employees merely base their expectation on their health, whereas older white-collar employees are influenced by all three determinants. Therefore, interventions that seek to strengthen the expectation of remaining in the actual job until retirement should differentiate between blue-collar and white-collar jobs and provide different job conditions along the working life span.

Most industrialized countries are facing dramatic demographic changes. For example, projections for Europe and Central Asia forecast that the proportion of people over 50 years will rise from the current 28% to 40% in 2050 (World Bank, 2011). As a consequence, the proportion of retired people in comparison to the working population will grow enormously (Purcell, 2005). This development will unavoidably strain the existing mechanisms of the social security and pension systems (Bijak, Kupiszewska, Kupiszewski, Saczuk & Kicinger, 2007; Toossi, 2007). In order to relieve the drain on the social systems, people will inevitably have to work longer (Roth, Wegge, & Schmidt, 2007). In some industrialized countries, politicians have already established the preconditions for longer workforce participation by raising the official retirement age. This effort, however, falls short of expectations. The actual average retirement age is far lower than the official retirement age (Eurostat, 2008). In Germany, for example, the rate of full-time hired employees in the group older than 63 years is only 9% (Mascher, 2010). Moreover, the unemployment rate in this section of the population is higher than for any other age group. Additionally, a steadily growing number of people older than 50 years are employed in precarious forms of occupation (US Department of Labor, 2010). This situation is similar in many other industrial countries of the EU (Eurostat, 2008). Obviously, political actions aimed at encouraging later retirement on a macro level have so far failed to achieve the intended goals. There are still fewer older people in the labour force than are needed. The question arises whether all occupations are feasible for working over a longer period of time and until the official retirement age. In this article, we postulate that circumstances on the individual and organizational level help explain why employees retire earlier than the official retirement age. Research must urgently identify conditions on these levels that increase the *willingness* and *possibilities* of the older population to fully participate in the labour force until the official retirement age.

The present study helps to fill this void. Our contribution to the literature is threefold. First, we introduce the new construct, expectation of remaining in the same job until retirement age (ERSJR), to the retirement literature. ERSJR covers whether the individual can imagine staying in the same employment until the official retirement age. ERSJR enables us to identify conditions that foster early retirement *as well as* self-selection into age-adequate jobs along the working life span. Second, we develop the Working Life Span Demands–Resources model, integrating organizational and individual conditions for the expectation of remaining in the current job over the whole working life span. Third, we test this model separately for different age groups as well as for blue-collar and white-collar employees. In this way, we identify how drivers of ERSJR vary across age groups and in which way they are determined by employment status.

In sum, we suggest the Working Life Span Demands–Resources model (see Figure 1), based on the following propositions: the higher the perceived job demands, the weaker ERSJR; however, ERSJR rises with growing job resources, and a better health status. The influences of the latter two constructs interact with perceived job demands as will be described in more detail later. Hence, ERSJR

develops on the basis of a complex interplay of all three antecedents. We expect the drivers of ERSJR to differ between different age and employment status groups. We test these assumptions empirically with a large sample of the German work population ($N = 1586$) that is drawn representatively with regard to occupation and age to ensure the external validity and practical relevance of our findings.

CONCEPTUAL BACKGROUND AND HYPOTHESIS DEVELOPMENT

Antecedents of the retirement decision

As Wang and Shultz (2010) display in their review, retirement has been looked at from various perspectives. Some scholars analyse the adjustment during the transition to retiring (e.g., Wang, Zhan, Liu & Shultz, 2008), others shed light on retirement as a career development stage (e.g., Kim & Feldman, 2000) or as part of human resource management (e.g., Ferris et al., 1998). All of these different perspectives can help in finding answers to the question of how retirement decisions are made (see Adams, Prescher, Beehr, & Lepisto, 2002) and how to encourage longer workforce participation of older employees. Feldman (1994) summarizes that literature so far has identified external (e.g., social security system eligibility), organizational (e.g., organizational support), as well as individual factors (e.g., health, attitudes) as antecedents for the voluntary and involuntary decision to retire early. Previous studies have mainly considered employees who are in the last phase of their working life span (e.g., Adams, 1999; Shultz, Morton, & Weckerle, 1998), as, with increasing age, retirement plans become more concrete (Phua & McNally, 2008) and the will to deal with the retirement decision becomes stronger (Hershey, Henkens & van Dalen, 2007).

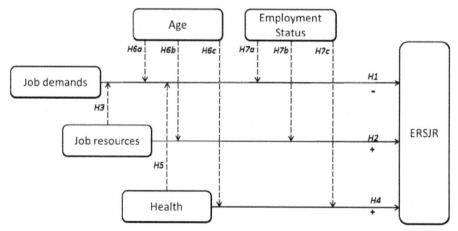

Figure 1. Conceptual model of this study. ERSJR = expectation of remaining in the same job until retirement age; H = hypothesis; dotted line = moderating effect.

However, if we want to identify job conditions that foster working until the official retirement age, we also have to consider employees at earlier career stages. As Ekerdt (2004) states, retirement is no longer a topic that is only relevant in the last career stage. Rather, retirement should be looked at as a result of career patterns over the lifetime (see Hayward, Friedman, & Chen, 1998). Decisions along the career are influenced by future time perspectives (Walker & Tracey, 2012). As some tasks and job characteristics are more suitable for specific career stages than others (see Hall & Mansfield, 1975; Jepsen & Dickson, 2003), employees at an early career stage (see Super, 1957) anticipate their job's age adequacy and change to more age-adequate jobs as they age. As a consequence, job conditions vary between different age groups (see Hedge, Borman, & Lammlein, 2006). Thus, examining only the last phase before retirement bears the risk of including only preselected organizational and individual conditions and disregarding the effect of job conditions at an earlier career stage on the employability at later career stages (see van der Heijden, 2002).

Expectation of remaining in the same job until retirement age

With the expectation of remaining in the *same* job until retirement age (ERSJR) we introduce a new construct that enables us to look at different age groups and include all career stages. It captures whether employees can picture themselves staying in their current job until the official retirement age. ERSJR broadens the perspective of hitherto applied concepts in retirement literature, such as retirement expectation (e.g., Elovainio et al., 2005) or intended early retirement (e.g., Siegrist, Wahrendorf, von dem Knesebeck, Jürges, & Börsch-Supan, 2006). These concepts give insights into whether employees can generally imagine staying in employment until the official retirement age, which is important information for the social security system.

However, these concepts disregard whether or not those employees stating that they will remain employed until the official retirement age actually picture themselves continuing to work in their *current* job or whether they have in mind that they will change into a more age-adequate job before the entry into retirement. In order to identify conditions on the organizational level that foster long-term workforce participation, we have to broaden our perspective. From a practical point of view, ERSJR helps organizations to identify job conditions that are not perceived as feasible for remaining long term. With this knowledge, human resources management can offer alternative career paths in these jobs, which might convince employees to stay in the company.

Compared to concepts like turnover intention (e.g., Tett & Meyer, 1993) or intention to leave (e.g., Loi, Hang-Yue & Foley, 2006) that are mainly focused on actual expectations, ERSJR indicates more distal expectations to leave or to stay within the organization. An employee might currently have no intentions at all to leave because he or she is satisfied with the job. At the same time he or she might expect not to be able to stay within the organization until retirement because the job incorporates age critical job demands that are harder to accomplish in higher age, like high physical workload. Furthermore, he/she might perceive his/her job to be adequate for staying in until an older age depending on the judgement about the job as possible promoter or risk for achieving their long-term personal career aspirations (see Defillipi & Arthur, 2006; Sullivan & Arthur, 2006) and about his/her future employability (see Fugate, Kinicki, & Ashforth, 2004; van der Heijde & van der Heijden, 2006; van der Heijden, 2002). As such, ERSJR is an early indicator of attitudes for leaving the job which can support the planning of preventive actions that are focused on the successful ageing of employees in organizations. ERSJR also adds a new perspective to the career literature. Career patterns change from the traditional unidirectional and stable to a more diverse, fragmented, and mobile pattern (Arnold, 1997a, 1997b; Biemann, Zacher, & Feldman, 2012). Dries, van Acker, and Verbruggen (2012) reveal that best performers rather follow the traditional career path. ERSJR gives further insight into job conditions that enable employees to follow this traditional career path.

To sum up, although there is a certain overlap between ERSJR and established constructs in the retirement, turnover, and career literature, we propose that the new construct of ERSJR will add valuable information to the literature because this construct can be assessed across the whole working life span and will be especially worthwhile for the long-term human resources planning in organizations.

Working life span adaptation of the Job Demands–Resources (JD-R) model

The conceptual framework of this study is an adaption and extension of the JD-R model (Demerouti, Bakker, Nachreiner, & Schaufeli, 2001). The JD-R model was developed as a follow-up of two of the most prominent stress models in occupational health psychology, the Demand–Control model (D-C model; Karasek, 1979) and the Effort–Reward-Imbalance model (E-R-I model; Siegrist, 1996). Both incorporate the idea that stressful work conditions (the combination of high job demands and low job control [Karasek, 1979], respectively an imbalance between effort and rewards [Siegrist, 1996]) lead to job stress and in turn to health impairments. Empirical research has already demonstrated that these models help to explain retirement plans. Elovainio et al. (2005) showed on the basis of the D-C model (Karasek, 1979) that stress-related factors at work increase thoughts of early retirement. Siegrist et al. (2006) applied the E-R-I model to explain intended early retirement. Using data from the Survey of Health, Ageing and Retirement in Europe (SHARE), they demonstrated that poor quality of work, operationalized as a high ratio of efforts to rewards, and health independently influence the intended early retirement.

Demerouti et al. (2001) propose two parallel processes in which job demands, on the one hand, and job resources, on the other hand, influence the perception of both job and work motivation. We postulate that applying the JD-R model improves the explanation of the retirement process, as it enables the explicit use of demands and resources that are especially relevant for the retirement process. It stands out as a research framework of high generality including various job demands and resources that have been shown to have an impact on various organizational and individual outcomes in diverse job settings (see Bakker & Demerouti, 2007). In the following, we will adapt and extend the JD-R model to holistically explain ERSJR.

Job demands

Job demands incite an exhausting effort to diminish the perceived strain, which can lead to health impairments (Bakker, Demerouti, & Euwema, 2005), absenteeism and turnover intentions (Bakker, Demerouti, De Boer, & Schaufeli, 2003). Job demands relate to physical as well as psychological work strain. Elovainio et al. (2005), Taylor and Shore (1995), as well as Siegrist et al. (2006), identified work strain as one of the main constraints for working until an advanced age. Accordingly, we expect that the perceived job demands will negatively relate to whether or not employees can picture themselves remaining in the same job until the official retirement age.

Hypothesis 1: The higher the perceived job demands, the lower ERSJR.

Job resources

The second psychological process of the JD-R model (Demerouti et al., 2001) describes how job resources strengthen intrinsic motives of growth, learning, and development. Resources also help to achieve extrinsically motivating goals and thus to fulfil the need for autonomy, competence, and relatedness. This in turn enhances engagement and leads to better performance and a less cynical perspective on work (Schaufeli & Bakker, 2004). Job resources are the characteristics of a job that ameliorate the fulfilment of the task while reducing the risk of stress-induced illnesses. According to Hackman and Oldham (1975), job resources bear a high motivational potential. As Bakker and Demerouti (2007) summarize in their review on the JD-R model, one of the strengths of this stress model is its generalizability and adaptability to diverse research contexts. Applying the JD-R model enables us to explicitly look into effects of *age-related* job resources that have been proved to be dominant indicators for the retirement decision. We postulate that the more easily employees can picture themselves remaining in the same job until the official retirement age, the more positively they judge the age-related job resources available.

Hypothesis 2: The more age-related job resources are available, the higher ERSJR.

The JD-R model proposes that resources buffer the negative effects of work demands on perceived job strain (see Bakker et al., 2005). Bakker et al. (2003) depict different mechanisms behind this buffer effect (see Cohan & Wills, 1985). Resources can help employees to cope with demands. For example, autonomy provides more opportunities for coping with stress (Jenkins, 1991) and social support helps employees to fulfil tasks with less stress. Additionally, resources can protect employees from the identified health-related consequences of stressful situations. Further, resources may help improve one's productivity and thus prevent negative effects of work load. We therefore propose that the more job resources are available, the less individuals take the level of job demands into account when judging whether or not they picture themselves remaining in the current job until the official retirement age.

Hypothesis 3: The relation of perceived job demands to ERSJR will be weaker the more job resources are available.

Health as an individual resource

So far the JD-R model has been applied to explain various health disorders as outcomes (e.g., Bakker et al., 2005). Reviews on the retirement decision confirm that health is one of the major antecedents of early retirement (e.g., Beehr, 1986; Shultz et al.,

1998). We introduce health as an additional individual resource to the JD-R model with regard to ERSJR. In doing so, we follow Bakker et al.'s (2003) call to enhance the JD-R model by including resources on the individual level. Age-related physical decline (see Baltes, Staudinger, & Lindenberger, 1999) and health impairments often cause employees to be unable to fulfil their work requirements, especially in highly demanding jobs (Warr, 1998). We hypothesize that the health status of an employee is positively related to ERSJR.

Hypothesis 4: The better the health status of an employee, the higher his/her expectation of remaining in the same job until retirement age.

With regard to the general performance of older employees, it has already been shown that there is an interaction between health, on the one hand, and work strain, on the other (Ilmarinen & Tempel, 2002). When judging their own anticipated productivity, employees take the work strain and their personal health status into account. Blekesaune and Solem (2005) show that early exits due to health problems occur mainly under work conditions that are physically wearing. In accordance with these findings, we suggest integrating health into the JD-R model as an individual resource that buffers the negative influences of work demands on ERSJR. We expect that the relationship between perceived job demands and the expectation of remaining in the same job until retirement will be stronger, the worse the health of an employee.

Hypothesis 5: The relation between perceived job demands and ERSJR is stronger, the weaker the health status of an employee.

Age and employment status as moderators

The construct of expectation of remaining in the *same* job until retirement age includes both exit options for a negative long-term expectation with regard to the current job—retiring early and changing into a more age-adequate job. As Adams and Beehr (1998) show, options on the job market decrease and turnover intentions become less strong with increasing age (see also Arnold & Feldman, 1982). Thus, we expect that younger employees that perceive their job as age-inadequate and cannot imagine remaining in the same job until retirement age will try to change into more age-adequate jobs, whereas older employees who do not perceive as many options for themselves on the job market will instead intend to retire early. Voluntary turnover into jobs that allow a better match between personal skills and job expectations

(Singh & Greenhaus, 2004) becomes less likely at a higher age (Ng & Feldman, 2009). As Zaniboni, Sarchielli, and Fraccaroli (2010) show, the identification as an older worker diminishes job mobility and also strengthens the retirement intention. Consequently, the turnover intention is expected to relate to ERSJR more strongly in the young age group. We test this assumption later, in the scale validation. As we expect that different age groups have different exit strategies in mind when judging their expectation of remaining in the same job until retirement age, we expect that the drivers for ERSJR will differ between different age groups.

Younger employees who do not perceive their job as feasible for long-term remaining will possibly strive towards a change into more age-adequate jobs. We expect that they will anticipate whether they will be able to counteract age-related changes taking the actual demands and resources of their job into account. Thus, we expect the relationship between job demands and ERSJR as well as between job resources and ERSJR to be stronger for the young age group.

The older age group will possibly not take job demands and resources as much into account as they can already assess consequences of these job conditions on their personal health. Borman and Motowidlo (1993) show that with increasing age employees judge their own workability in a more differentiated way and draw a closer connection between their capabilities and the necessity to retire. In line with these findings, we suggest that the older age group will take their actual health more into account than younger age groups when judging whether or not he/she will remain in the current job until the official retirement age.

Hypothesis 6: The drivers for ERSJR differ between different age groups.
Hypothesis 6a: The relation between perceived job demands and ERSJR is stronger in the young than in the old age group.
Hypothesis 6b: The relation between perceived job resources and ERSJR is stronger in the young than in the old age group.
Hypothesis 6c: The relation between health and ERSJR is stronger in the old than in the young age group.

As a further moderator variable, we introduce the employment status. Both, the retirement process (Stockes & Maddox, 1967) as well as career aspirations (Jacobs, Karen, & McClelland, 1991) have been shown to differ between blue-collar and white-collar employees. Furthermore, the employment status was proved to function as a moderator to the relationship between job demands as well as job resources and the intention to retire (Schreurs, van Emmerik, de Cuyper, Notelaers, & de Witte, 2011). We expect that differentiating between blue-collar and white-collar employees will also shed further light on antecedents of ERSJR.

Blue-collar and white-collar jobs bear different qualities of both job demands and job resources. Blue-collar job have been characterized mainly by high physical workload (see Schreurs et al., 2011). Joulain, Mullet, Lecomte, and Prévost (2000), as well as Joulain and Mullet (2001), found that the higher the *physical* work strain, the lower the perceived appropriate retirement age. We expect that this physical quality of job demands will influence ERSJR more strongly than job demands in white-collar jobs. On the other hand, white-collar jobs offer more challenges and more autonomy (Pelfrene et al., 2001) and the motivation to work in these jobs is driven more by intrinsically motivating aspects of the job (Centers & Bugental, 1966; Weaver, 1975). We therefore expect the relationship between ERSJR and job resources to be stronger for white-collar employees. Presumably, health impairments are more likely to reduce ERSJR in blue-collar jobs that are physically more strenuous than in white-collar jobs. Health impairments like back pain cannot be compensated as easily in physically demanding jobs (Sanderson, Todd, Holt, & Getty, 1995). Weis, Koch, Kruck, and Beck (1994) showed that blue-collar employees had to retire early more often after being diagnosed with cancer than white-collar employees. In line with these findings, we expect health to be more strongly related to ERSJR in blue-collar jobs.

Hypothesis 7: The drivers for ERSJR differ between different employment status groups (blue-collar and white-collar employees).
Hypothesis 7a: The relation between perceived job demands and ERSJR is stronger for blue-collar than for white-collar employees.
Hypothesis 7b: The relation between perceived job resources and ERSJR is stronger for white-collar than for blue-collar employees.
Hypothesis 7c: The relation between health and ERSJR is stronger for blue-collar than for white-collar employees.

METHOD

Sample

Our study is based on a representative survey, the "iga-Barometer 2010", which was carried out in cooperation with an alliance of German health and accident insurance companies for the investigation of workplace prevention and health promotion. To ensure representativeness, subjects were taken from a simple random sample of the German working population. In total, 2000 subjects answered questions on their work situation and health status via telephone interviews (32% participation rate). All participants with missing data on the relevant scales were not considered. The resulting sample consists of 1586 employees. Forty-three per cent of the subjects are male. The average age of the respondents is 45 years (Min = 17, Max = 71; $SD = 11.20$). Eleven per cent of the participants are younger than 30 years, 50% are between 30 and 50 years, and 39% are older than 50 years. The sample is representative with regard to age, gender, and the employment status. It consists of 23% blue-collar workers and 77% white-collar employees, which is very close to the official statistics on the workforce in Germany (Statistisches Bundesamt, 2006).

Measures

It was our intention to keep the questionnaire as short as possible to ensure high participation in the telephone interviews.

Job resources were measured by means of five 4-point rating scales assessing appreciation for one's work (Grube & Hertel, 2008), job variety (Fried, 1991; Fried & Ferris, 1987; Schmitt, Coyle, Rauschenberger, & White, 1979), and social support (Koslovski, Ekerdt, & DeVincy, 2001), as well as health-promoting aspects of the task and health promotion activities of the company (Rüdiger, 2009). A sample item is "In my job I get support from colleagues and supervisors". The internal consistency of the scale was Cronbach's $\alpha = .70$. Perceived job demands were measured by the question whether work is "too boring" (1), "just perfect" (2), or "too demanding" (3).

The respondents indicated their current health status on four items. First, participants had to rate their general health status on a 5-point rating scale (1 = "very bad" to 5 = "very good"). Next, they had to give the number of days within the last 4 weeks when they were not well because of physical and psychological impairments. Finally, they had to give the number of days within the last month when they were not able to accomplish their everyday activities. The internal consistency of the health indicator, made up of the mean of the four z-standardized items, is Cronbach's $\alpha = .73$.

To measure ERSJR, we asked the participants to state whether they could picture themselves remaining in the same job until the official retirement age by choosing one of the following options: "I cannot picture that" (1), "I can picture that with restrictions" (2), "I can picture that" (3).

Grouping variables

Definitions regarding the question of the age at which an employee is held to be young or old are inconsistent in the literature. According to Ilmarinen (2001), the term "ageing workforce" is applied to employees aged 45 or 50 years, based on workers' subjective and objective changes in work-related functioning. The German job agency supports older unemployed citizens from the age of 50 and up, offering special programmes to help them find new job opportunities (Bundesagentur für Arbeit, 2011). Accordingly, we set the cutoff for the older age group at the age of 50 years. The middle-aged subgroup consists of employees aged 30 to 49 years. Employees younger than 30 years are categorized into the young age group.

As a further grouping variable, we include the employment status, differentiating between blue-collar (0) and white-collar (1) employees in accordance with the categorization into manual workers and office workers (see Schreurs et al., 2011).

Control variables

To strengthen the validity of our findings, we consider positive and negative affectivity as control variables. According to the meta-analysis of Thoresen, Kaplan, Barsky, de Chermont, and Warren (2003), individuals high on negative affectivity typically report low job satisfaction and health, whereas individuals high on positive affectivity are generally more satisfied, having a positive outlook on life and fewer health complaints. Thus, controlling for both traits increases the amount of variance that is directly related to actual work conditions (personality differences partialled out). Positive and negative affectivity are measured by three selected items describing positive and negative mood states of the PANAS questionnaire (Watson, Clark, & Tellegen, 1988). On 5-point rating scale (1 = "not present" to 5 = "very strong"), participants were asked to rate how intensively they generally experience the moods anger, anxiety, bad temper (negative affectivity), joyful arousal, interest, and pride (positive affectivity). The internal consistency is Cronbach's $\alpha = .70$ for each affectivity scale.

Scale validation

Discriminant validity. The discriminant validity of our scales was tested applying an exploratory factor analysis with Varimax rotation including all indicators of the multiitem scales job resources, health, negative affectivity, and positive affectivity.

As expected, four factors with an Eigenvalue > 1 are extracted, with all items loading highest on the expected factor, explaining 60% of the variance.

Construct validity of ERSJR. In order to test the construct validity of ERSJR, we considered its nomological network by relating it to turnover intentions. As described earlier in the conceptual background section, we expect that the relationship will differ between the different age groups. We measured turnover intentions by a three-item scale asking participants whether or not they intended to change their job, their employer, or the job sector (Cronbach's $\alpha = .83$).

We find a weak negative correlation between ERSJR and turnover intention in the whole sample, $r = -.19$, $p = .000$. As expected, the association with turnover intentions is only significant for employees younger than 30 years, $r = -.32$, $p \leq .001$, and for the age group between 30 and 50, $r = -.27$, $p \leq .001$, whereas for employees older than 50 years, $r = -.03$, $p = .455$, there is no relation between ERSJR and the turnover intention.

Statistical analysis

In order to test our hypotheses, we conduct a moderated multiple regression analysis (Cohen, Cohen, West, & Aiken, 2003; Dawson & Richter, 2006). We incorporate several models that examine our conceptual model step by step. Model A only includes the perceived job demands as predictor of ERSJR (H1). Model B considers job resources and the interaction term of job resources and job demands (H2 and H3). Model C additionally includes health as well as the interaction term of health and job demands (H4 and H5). Before building the interaction terms, we z-standardized the predictors. We test the simple slopes for significance based on Aiken and West (1991) and Dawson and Richter (2006). Model D also takes into account the control variable positive and negative affectivity. In a next step, we conduct the multiple regression analyses separately for the three age groups as well as for blue- and white-collar employees.

Additionally, as a robustness check, we rerun Model D performing structural equation modelling (SEM). As the resources are measured formatively, we include this scale as a single-item sum construct into the model (see Kuester, Homburg, & Robertson, 1999). The interaction terms are also included with one indicator as applied by Cortina, Chen, and Dunlap (2001). We standardize the predictors for each group individually before calculating the interaction terms. We use AMOS 19.0 software (Arbuckle & Wothke, 1999) applying maximum likelihood estimation. The absolute model fit is determined by the χ^2-test. Values of .08 or less for the root mean square error of approximation (RMSEA; Hu & Bentler, 1999) and values of .90 or more for the goodness-of-fit-index (GFI; Jöreskog & Sörbom, 1982) are judged as adequate fit (e.g., Hair, Black, Babin, Anderson, & Tatham, 2006). The results of the separate analyses are also tested for robustness via multigroup SEM (MG-SEM). This analysis requires multiple runs. In a first step, we test a variant model without constraints permitting parameters to be freely estimated between the groups. In the second invariant model, all paths are restricted to be equal across all groups. The χ^2-difference test is used to compare the fit of the competing model with and without constraints (see Hoffmann & Müller, 2009, for a similar procedure).

RESULTS

The descriptive statistics and correlations are presented in Table 1. The descriptive statistics and correlations for the different age groups as well as for blue-collar and white-collar employees are depicted in Table 2.

Model test

The results of the moderated multiple regression analysis are displayed in Table 3. Model A corroborates Hypothesis 1. Job demands are negatively linked to ERSJR. Model B supports Hypothesis 2 as the job resources are identified as an important predictor of ERSJR. Job resources and perceived job demands interact in their influence on ERSJR. The slope test reveals that, in contrast to our Hypothesis 3, there is a weaker relation between job demands and ERSJR for the condition of low job resources than for the condition of high job resources: low job resources, $b = -0.18$, $SE = 0.05$, $t = 3.92$, $p = .000$; high job resources: $b = -0.24$, $SE = 0.05$, $t = 4.41$, $p = .000$. Model C demonstrates that, in accordance with Hypothesis 4, health is a central antecedent of ERSJR ($\Delta R^2_{adj} = .03$). The interaction term of

health and job demands is significant. The slope test reveals that the relation between job demands and ERSJR is stronger for employees with bad health than for employees with good health: bad health, $b = -0.24$, $SE = 0.04$, $t = 5.37$, $p = .000$; good health, $b = -0.18$, $SE = 0.05$, $t = 3.52$, $p = .000$. Our Hypothesis 5 is confirmed. Model C explains 11% of the variance in the dependent variable.

Model D shows that all previous findings remain stable when the control variables are included. Positive affectivity is significantly linked to ERSJR. The robustness test of Model D via SEM reveals an acceptable fit including the whole sample, $\chi^2(49) = 394.2$, GFI = .96, RMSEA = .07.

Group comparison

Age. Separate regression analyses for the three age groups show that the drivers of ERSJR differ between the age groups (see Table 4). As assumed in Hypothesis 6a, the direct influence of job demands is significantly stronger for the younger group than for the middle-aged, Fisher's $Z = -2.25$, $p = .012$, and older age group, Fisher's $Z = -1.7$, $p = .043$. In all age groups, resources have a positive influence on ERSJR. Also Hypothesis 6b is confirmed as the direct influence of job resources is significantly weaker for the older than for the middle-aged, Fisher's $Z = 2.49$, $p = .006$, and younger age group, Fisher's $Z = 1.6$, $p = .057$. As postulated in Hypothesis 6c, health only relates to ERSJR in the oldest group. For this age group, health is the major predictor for ERSJR. Including health into the model helps explain additional 12.6% of the variance of the dependent variable in this age group.

The MG-SEM analysis shows that the age groups differ significantly in their antecedent structure with regard to ERSJR. The χ^2-difference test comparing the model without constraints to the model with fixed parameters is statistically significant, χ^2-difference = 31.7, $df = 14$, $p \leq .05$.

TABLE 1
Descriptive statistics and intercorrelations

		M	SD	1	2	3	4	5	6
1.	ERSJR	2.15	0.88						
2.	Job demands	2.07	0.49	$-.10^{**}$					
3.	Age	44.87	11.07	$.06^*$	$.14^{**}$				
4.	Job resources	3.08	0.51	$.23^{**}$	$.10^{**}$	.03			
5.	Health status	-0.01	0.76	$.26^{**}$	$-.10^{**}$	$-.07^{**}$	$.24^{**}$		
6.	Neg. affectivity	4.42	0.63	$.15^{**}$	$-.12^{**}$	.00	$.22^{**}$	$.44^{**}$	
7.	Pos. affectivity	2.82	0.80	$-.02$	$-.34$	.02	$-.29^{**}$	$-.18^{**}$	$-.08^{**}$

ERSJR = expectation of remaining in the same job until retirement age. Level of significance: $^*p \leq .05$, $^{**}p \leq .01$.

TABLE 2
Descriptive statistics and intercorrelations for different subgroups

		M	SD	1	2	3	4	5
Younger than 30 years ($N = 181$)								
1.	ERSJR	2.07	0.88					
2.	Job demands	1.97	0.43	−.01				
3.	Job resources	3.09	0.53	.23**	.44**			
4.	Health status	0.12	0.66	.05	.24**	.27**		
5.	Neg. affectivity	4.53	0.57	−.13	−.06	.21**	.51**	
6.	Pos. affectivity	2.82	0.85	−.02	−.22**	−.40**	−.26**	−.05
Between 30 and 50 years ($N = 788$)								
1.	ERSJR	2.11	0.86					
2.	Job demands	2.04	0.48	−.03				
3.	Job resources	3.06	0.51	.26**	.18**			
4.	Health status	0.02	0.72	.16**	.00	.25**		
5.	Neg. affectivity	4.38	0.67	.21**	−.06	.25**	.52**	
6.	Pos. affectivity	2.80	0.80	−.02	.03	−.23**	−.22**	−.10**
Older than 50 years ($N = 617$)								
1.	ERSJR	2.22	0.89					
2.	Job demands	2.15	0.50	−.21**				
3.	Job resources	3.11	0.51	.19**	−.09*			
4.	Health status	−0.10	0.84	.43**	−.26**	.23**		
5.	Neg. affectivity	4.43	0.60	.15**	−.22**	.17**	.35**	
6.	Pos. affectivity	2.84	0.80	−.02	−.06	−.33**	−.11**	−.06
Blue-collar ($N = 366$)								
1.	ERSJR	1.96	0.89					
2.	Job demands	2.00	0.58	−.02				
3.	Job resources	2.96	0.59	.19**	.15**			
4.	Health status	−0.11	0.87	.07	.07	.09		
5.	Neg. affectivity	4.43	0.61	−.05	−.02	.15**	.50**	
6.	Pos. affectivity	2.98	0.84	−.16**	−.03	−.30**	−.30**	−.05
White-collar ($N = 1220$)								
1.	ERSJR	2.19	0.87					
2.	Job demands	2.09	0.46	−.14**				
3.	Job resources	3.12	0.48	.23**	.06*			
4.	Health status	0.01	0.73	.32**	.13**	.30**		
5.	Neg. affectivity	4.41	0.64	.21**	−.15**	.25**	.47**	
6.	Pos. affectivity	2.77	0.79	−.06*	.03	−.23**	−.22**	−.11**

ERSJR = expectation of remaining in the same job until retirement age. Level of significance: *$p \leq .05$, **$p \leq .01$.

TABLE 3
Predictors of ERSJR

	Model A		Model B		Model C		Model D	
	β	p	β	p	β	p	β	p
Job demands	−.10	.000	−.15	.000	−.11	.000	−.11	.000
Job resources			.23	.000	.18	.000	.20	.000
Job resources × Job demands			−.08	.004	−.09	.0021	−.08	.003
Health					.20	.000	.21	.000
Health × Job demands					.06	.013	.06	.015
Neg. affectivity							.00	.977
Pos. affectivity							.07	.004
R^2	.009		.072		.113		.118	
R^2_{adj}	.009		.071		.101		.114	

OLS-regression. ERSJR = expectation of remaining in the same job until retirement age. β = standardized regression coefficient. p = level of significance.

Employment status. The separate regression analyses for blue-collar and white-collar employees reveal that the direct influences of job demands and job resources do not differ significantly between the two groups (see Table 5). In both groups, resources have a positive influence on ERSJR, while job demands are related in a negative way. Thus, Hypotheses 7a and 7b cannot be confirmed. Health

TABLE 4
Predictors of ERSJR for different age groups

	Younger than 30 years (N = 181)		Between 30 and 50 years (N = 788)		Older than 50 years (N = 617)	
	β	p	β	p	β	p
Job demands	−.27	.003	−.09	.020	−.13	.003
Job resources	.24	.019	.24	.000	.11	.005
Job resources × Job demands	−.27	.011	−.08	.051	−.04	.365
Health	.15	.169	.07	.105	.40	.000
Health × Job demands	−.02	.843	.07	.060	−.03	.424
Neg. affectivity	−.36	.000	.11	.009	−.02	.590
Pos. affectivity	.14	.068	.07	.061	.04	.285
R^2	.168		.108		.205	
R^2_{adj}	.134		.100		.196	

OLS-regression. ERSJR = expectation of remaining in the same job until retirement age. β = standardized regression coefficient. p = level of significance.

TABLE 5
Predictors of ERSJR for blue-collar and white-collar employees

	Blue-collar (N = 366)		White-collar (N = 1220)	
	β	p	β	p
Job demands	−.14	.036	−.11	.000
Job resources	.22	.000	.17	.000
Job resources × Job demands	−.20	.004	−.02	.568
Health	.11	.045	.24	.000
Health × Job demands	.08	.151	.04	.236
Neg. affectivity	−.14	.011	.03	.269
Pos. affectivity	.23	.000	.04	.125
R^2	.132		.137	
R^2_{adj}	.114		.132	

OLS-regression. ERSJR = expectation of remaining in the same job until retirement age. β = standardized regression coefficient. p = level of significance.

relates to ERSJR in both groups. The finding that the direct influence of health is significantly stronger for white-collar employees, Fisher's $Z = -2.25$, $p = .012$, contradicts our expectations as postulated in Hypothesis 7c.

The MG-SEM analysis shows that the two groups differ significantly in their antecedent structure with regard to ERSJR. The χ^2-difference test comparing the model without constraints to the model with fixed parameters was statistically significant, χ^2-difference = 17.8, $df = 7$, $p \le .05$.

Age and employment status. In order to shed more light on the contraintuitive finding that health is related more strongly to ERSJR in white-collar jobs, we test Model D *separately* for the three age groups for both blue-collar and white-collar employees to

reveal whether our Hypotheses 7a–7c can be confirmed only for specific age groups. The results of the separate regression analyses are displayed in Table 6.

In the young age group, blue-collar employees' expectancy is based on job demands, while resources and health both moderate this relationship. Our model helps explain 45% of the variance in the dependent variable in this subgroup. The direct effects of job resources and health are insignificant. In the young white-collar employees group, only resources are related to ERSJR, explaining 7% of the variance. Thus, for the young age group our assumptions of Hypotheses 7a and 7b can be verified.

In the blue-collar middle-aged group, job demands and resources relate to ERSJR, whereas in the middle-age white-collar group, job resources and health are connected to ERSJR. Thus, in this age group, only Hypothesis 7a can be confirmed, as Hypotheses 7b and 7c are not valid in this age group.

In the older blue-collar employees group, only health relates to ERSJR. In this age group, health explains 19% of the variance in ERSJR. In accordance with Hypothesis 7c, we find a significantly stronger relationship between health and ERSJR for blue-collar employees than for the white-collar employees in the older age group, Fisher's $Z = 1.76$, $p = .039$. Only for white-collar employees, next to health, job demands, and job resources, relate to ERSJR in this age group. This corroborates Hypothesis 7b, but disconfirms Hypothesis 7a.

The χ^2-difference test in the MG-SEM analysis for the six groups, comparing the model without constraints to the model with fixed parameters, was statistically significant, χ^2-difference = 99.4, $df = 35$, $p \le .001$. Thus, the groups differ significantly in their antecedent structure with regard to ERSJR.

TABLE 6
Predictors of ERSJR for different age and employment status groups

	Blue-collar young (N = 48)		Blue-collar middle-aged (N = 185)		Blue-collar older (N = 133)		White-collar young (N = 133)		White-collar middle-aged (N = 603)		White-collar older (N = 484)	
	β	p	β	p	β	p	β	p	β	p	β	p
Job demands	−.52	.001	−.20	.043	−.17	.185	−.20	.091	−.08	.077	−.19	.000
Job resources	.30	.173	.30	.000	.09	.329	.28	.012	.18	.000	.11	.015
Job resources × Job demands	−.80	.000	−.20	.057	.09	.486	.05	.730	−.04	.339	.01	.847
Health	.19	.330	−.13	.130	.51	.000	.27	.053	.15	.002	.37	.000
Health × Job demands	−.38	.029	.03	.689	−.08	.460	−.01	.971	.07	.069	−.05	.286
Neg. affectivity	−.78	.000	−.05	.520	−.15	.071	−.29	.010	.14	.004	.00	.940
Pos. affectivity	−.65	.001	−.23	.002	−.15	.111	−.02	.818	−.04	.325	−.03	.502
R^2	.534		.172		.238		.115		.130		.218	
R^2_{adj}	.452		.139		.193		.065		.120		.207	

OLS-regression. ERSJR = expectation of remaining in the same job until retirement age. β = standardized regression coefficient. p = level of significance.

DISCUSSION

The main goal of this study is to identify conditions that not only enable employees to remain in the same job until the official retirement age but also foster their willingness to do so. We introduce ERSJR as a new construct into the retirement literature. Our validation of ERSJR shows that it can be used as a general measure for the long-term feasibility of different jobs. We consider the interplay between the organizational drivers, job demands, and resources, as well as the individual driver health status, to closely examine their complex influences. The study reveals that, from the employee's perspective, jobs with high *demands* are not suitable for remaining in the job until the official retirement age. This finding corroborates expectations based on previous research results (e.g., Ilmarinen & Tempel, 2002; Warr, 1998). As expected, we show that job *resources* relate positively to ERSJR. Job resources interact with job demands. However, job resources do not function as buffer against job demands. Our findings show that job demands relate more strongly to ERSJR in jobs offering more resources. The study proves that including health as an individual resource into the Working Life Span Demands–Resources model substantially improves the explanation of ERSJR. Health is obviously one of the most important predictors in the whole sample. Health buffers the negative effects of job demands. Our findings are in line with theories on the life-span development in motivation (e.g., Kanfer & Ackerman, 2004): An imbalance between available resources (e.g., job resources, health) on the one side and job demands

on the other side handicaps employees in doing their work well (Salonen, Arola, Nygård, Huhtala, & Koivisto, 2003; Tuomi, Huuhtanen, Nykyri, & Ilmarinen, 2001; Warr, 1998). This may reduce work motivation and increase the likelihood of withdrawal from the job (Kanfer & Ackerman, 2004).

These findings lay the ground for a deeper exploration of conditions that might determine the antecedent structure of ERSJR. To the best of our knowledge, this article is the first to investigate antecedents of ERSJR separately for different age groups and employment status groups building on a representative database. Our analyses suggest that there are different antecedents of ERSJR for different age groups in blue-collar and white-collar jobs. Blue-collar employees' expectation of remaining in the same job until retirement age is linked to the perceived job demands most strongly in the young, but also in the middle-aged group. Obviously, in terms of Kanfer and Ackerman (2004), young and middle-aged blue-collar employees do not judge the demands of their job as age-adequate. They don't expect that they will be able to effectively counteract age-related changes when they perceive high age-critical work demands. In contrast to this pattern, white-collar employees' expectation is independent of job demands in the young age group. Demands are not perceived as hazard to remaining in the same job until the official retirement age in white-collar jobs. The different quality of both job demands and job resources in white-collar and blue-collar jobs seems to determine the relationship between job demands as well as job resources and ERSJR. Young white-collar employees judge their long-term remaining in the same job based on job-enriching resources in the work context (see also Harris & Locke, 1974; Locke, 1973).

Both the younger white-collar and blue-collar employees judge their possible future employability depending on current job conditions. In contrast, older employees' ERSJR mainly relates to their current health. The older age group presumably do not take job conditions as much into account, as they can already assess the consequences of these conditions on their health. As postulated, in the old age group white-collar employees relate their own health less strongly to ERSJR than blue-collar employees. Remarkably, older white-collar employees also take job demands and job resources into account, whereas older blue-collar employees' health is revealed as the only predictor in our model, explaining 24% of the variance in ERSJR. This corroborates previous studies that show that in physically demanding jobs, health is the main reason for early retirement (Blekesaune & Solem, 2005).

The inclusion of age and employment status into the JD-R model reveals that the investigation of conditions for a longer working life should necessarily differentiate between different job qualities. Obviously, depending on the employment status, different job characteristics influence ERSJ along the working life span.

Limitations and directions for future research

Like all empirical examinations, our study is restricted in several ways. We therefore hope that future research will extend the scope of our findings in the following three directions. First, we carefully draw a representative sample of the German workforce to determine relationships across the span of all branches and occupations in different working teams. However, this sample is based on cross-sectional data. Hence, future studies should reanalyse our findings using a longitudinal design in order to give a better picture of self-selection into age-adequate jobs and the consequences for later retirement.

Second, to ensure a representative participation in the telephone interviews, we applied short scales. We operationalized the perceived job demands on a general level. Further studies may consider a set of (domain-)specific job demands. Additionally, we explicitly focused on job resources whose influence on the retirement process has already been proved in previous empirical studies. Future research should expand the set with additional organizational and individual resources and include validated scales for testing the JD-R model.

Third, and most importantly, this study introduces the construct of expectation of remaining in the same

job until retirement age (ERSJR) to the retirement literature. Hence, we lay the grounds for more research on working life span-related retirement decisions. ERSJR enables a long-term determination of age-adequate jobs. The results of our first construct validation support our claim that ERSJR broadens current concepts in retirement literature. As assumed, a negative expectation of remaining in the same job until retirement age increases the intention to switch into a job that is more adequate for long-term remaining in the same job. However, employees older than 50 years do not seem to have turnover intentions in mind when judging their expectation of remaining in the same job until retirement age. We suppose that this age group will rather have thoughts on early retirement as exit strategy (see Adams & Beehr, 1998). Future research efforts should explore the predictive validity of ERSJR with regard to retirement entry, instable transitions into retirement, anticipated future employability, and unemployment.

Practical implications

From a practical point of view, our study was motivated by the strong need to find answers to the dramatically increasing societal challenge in most industrialized countries to keep older people employed until the official retirement age. Our findings provide a set of recommendations that will hopefully help to master this challenge.

First of all, our results reveal that job designs have to be adapted differently in blue-collar and white-collar jobs in order to achieve the same goal that employees expect to remain until retirement age. Additionally, different requirements for different age groups have to be taken into consideration.

As we show, younger employees will instead have turnover intentions in mind when judging whether or not they will stay in the same job until their retirement. For younger employees in white-collar jobs, offering resources heightens the attractiveness of jobs for a longer work life. This study demonstrates that, in blue-collar jobs, job demands are the main driver for ERSJR for young and middle-aged employees. Designs for these jobs have to reduce the demands and offer more resources that actually help employees to cope with the demands of the task, starting from an early age. As it will not be possible to fully reduce job demands and create jobs that are suitable for all age groups in highly physically demanding jobs, we advocate job conditions that are adaptable to age-related changes and in this way enable compensations for age-related losses (see Brandtstädter & Greve, 1994; Heckhausen & Schulz, 1995). In jobs not feasible for long-term staying, employees should be given a long-term perspective. This can be achieved by integrating jobs that are not age-adequate into long-term career paths with early options of personnel development (see Frerichs, Lindley, Aleksandrowicz, Baldauf, & Galloway, 2012, for best practice examples). Human resources management has to deal with long-term career plans of younger employees and involve them in a discourse on their personal career plans over the whole life span.

If we intend to enable people to actually stay in highly demanding jobs, we cannot afford to ignore the risks of high demands to the health and employability of older people. As our Working Life Span Demands–Resources model reveals, in both blue-collar and white-collar jobs, older workers mainly take their personal health into account when judging whether they will stay in the current job until retirement. Healthy working conditions and health promotion should be fostered starting from the beginning of working life to ensure that employees are able to continue working until the official retirement age.

As we show in the validation of ERSJR, older employees do not seem to see alternatives to early retirement when they are stuck in a job they do not perceive as age-adequate. In the last career stage (Super, 1957), employees seem to have less ability, motivation, and opportunities (Hess & Jepsen, 2009) to work in the sense of the boundaryless or protean career model (Briscoe & Hall, 2006). Human resources management needs to open up new perspectives to employees in this career stage to foster their career adaptability competencies (see Brown, Bimrose, Barnes, & Hughes, 2012) and keep them motivated and able to remain in their job until retirement age.

REFERENCES

Adams, G. A. (1999). Career-related variables and planned retirement age: An extension of Beehr's model. *Journal of Vocational Behavior, 55*, 221–235.

Adams, G. A., & Beehr, T. A. (1998). Turnover and retirement: A comparison of their similarities and differences. *Personnel Psychology, 51*, 643–665.

Adams, G. A., Prescher, J., Beehr, T., A., & Lepisto, L. (2002). Applying work-role attachment theory to retirement decision-making. *International Journal of Aging and Human Development, 54*, 125–137.

Aiken, L. S., & West, S. G. (1991). *Multiple regression: Testing and interpreting interactions*. Newbury Park, CA: Sage.

Arbuckle, J. L., & Wothke, W. (1999). *Amos 4.0 user's guide*. Chicago, IL: SmallWaters.

Arnold, J. (1997a). *Managing careers into the 21st century*. London, UK: Chapman.

Arnold, J. (1997b). Nineteen propositions concerning the nature of effective thinking for career management in a turbulent world. *British Journal of Guidance and Counselling, 25*, 447–462.

Arnold, J., & Feldman, D. C. (1982). A multivariate analysis of the determinants of job turnover. *Journal of Applied Psychology, 67*, 350–360.

Bakker, A. B., & Demerouti, E. (2007). The job demands-resources model: State of the art. *Journal of Managerial Psychology, 22*, 309–328.

Bakker, A. B., Demerouti, E., De Boer, E., & Schaufeli, W. B. (2003). Job demands and job resources as predictors of absence duration and frequency. *Journal of Vocational Behavior, 62*, 341–356.

Bakker, A. B., Demerouti, E., & Euwema, M. C. (2005). Job resources buffer the impact of job demands on burnout. *Journal of Occupational Health Psychology, 10*, 170–180.

Baltes, P. B., Staudinger, U. M., & Lindenberger, U. (1999). Lifespan psychology: Theory and application to intellectual functioning. *Annual Review of Psychology, 50*, 471–507.

Beehr, T. A. (1986). The process of retirement: A review and recommendations for future investigation. *Personnel Psychology, 39*, 31–56.

Biemann, T., Zacher, H., & Feldman, D. C. (2012). Career patterns: A twenty-year panel study. *Journal of Vocational Behavior, 81*, 159–170.

Bijak, J., Kupiszewska, D., Kupiszewski, M., Saczuk, K., & Kicinger, A. (2007). Population and labour force projections for 27 European countries, 2002–2052: Impact of international migration on population ageing. *European Journal of Population, 23*, 1–31.

Blekesaune, M., & Solem, P. E. (2005). Working conditions and early retirement: A prospective study of retirement behavior. In M. Blekesaune & E. Verbye (Eds.), *Familieendring, helse og trygd. Fire ligitudinelle studier* (Rep. 22/03, pp. 68–87). Oslo, Norway: Norsk institutt for forskning orn oppvekst.

Borman, W. C., & Motowidlo, S. J. (1993). Expanding the criterion domain to include elements of contextual performance. In N. Schmitt & W. C. Borman (Eds.), *Personnel selection in organizations* (pp. 71–98). San Francisco, CA: Jossey-Bass.

Brandtstädter, J., & Greve, W. (1994). The aging self: Stabilizing and protective processes. *Developmental Review, 14*, 52–80.

Briscoe, J. P., & Hall, D. T. (2006). The interplay of boundaryless and protean careers: Combinations and implications. *Journal of Vocational Behavior, 69*, 4–18.

Brown, A., Bimrose, J., Barnes, S.-A., & Hughes, D. (2012). The role of career adaptabilities for mid-career changers. *Journal of Vocational Behavior, 80*, 754–761.

Bundesagentur für Arbeit. (2011). *Merkblatt 19. Entgeldsicherung für ältere Arbeitnehmer*. Available from www.arbeitsagentur.de

Centers, R., & Bugental, D. E. (1966). Intrinsic and extrinsic job motivations among different segments of the working population. *Journal of Applied Psychology, 50*, 1–5.

Cohan, S., & Wills, T. A. (1985). Stress, social support and the buffering hypothesis. *Psychological Bulletin, 98*, 310–357.

Cohen, J., Cohen, P., West, S. G., & Aiken, L. S. (2003). *Applied multiple regression/correlation analysis for the behavioral sciences* (3rd ed.). Mahwah, NJ: Lawrence Erlbaum Associates, Inc.

Cortina, J., Chen, G., & Dunlap, W. P. (2001). Testing interaction effects in LISREL: Examination and illustration of available procedures. *Organizational Research Methods, 4*, 230–258.

Dawson, J. F., & Richter, A. W. (2006). Probing three-way interactions in moderated multiple regression: Development and application of a slope difference test. *Journal of Applied Psychology, 91*, 917–926.

Defillipi, R. J., & Arthur, M. B. (2006). The boundaryless career: A competency-based perspective. *Journal of Organizational Behavior, 15*, 307–324.

Demerouti, E., Bakker, A. B., Nachreiner, F., & Schaufeli, W. B. (2001). The job demands-resources model of burnout. *Journal of Applied Psychology, 86*, 499–512.

Dries, N., van Acker, F., & Verbruggen, M. (2012). How boundaryless are the careers of high potentials, key experts and average performers? *Journal of Vocational Behavior, 81*, 271–279.

Ekerdt, D. J. (2004). Born to retire: The foreshortened lifecourse. *The Gerontologist, 43,* 3–9.

Elovainio, M., Forma, P., Kivimäki, M., Sinervo, T., Sutinen, R., & Laine, M. (2005). Job demands and job control as correlates of early retirement thoughts in Finnish social and health care employees. *Work and Stress, 19,* 84–92.

Eurostat. (2008). *The life of women and men in Europe: A statistical portrait.* Luxembourg: Eurostat Statistical Books, Office for Official Publications of the European Communities. Retrieved March 2012 from http://epp.eurostat.ec.europa.eu/cache/ITY_OFFPUB/KS-80-07-135/EN/KS-80-07-135-EN.PDF

Feldman, D. C. (1994). The decision to retire early: A review and conceptualization. *Academy of Management Review, 19,* 285–311.

Ferris, G. R., Arthur, M. M., Berkson, H. M., Kaplan, D. M., Harrell-Cook, G., & Frink, D. D. (1998). Towards a social context theory of the human resource management-organization effectiveness relationship. *Human Resources Management Review, 8,* 235–264.

Frerichs, F., Lindley, R., Aleksandrowicz, P., Baldauf, B., & Galloway, S. (2012). Active ageing in organisations: A case study approach. *International Journal of Manpower, 33,* 666–684.

Fried, Y. (1991). Meta-analytic comparison of the job diagnostic survey and job characteristic inventory as correlates of work satisfaction and job performance. *Journal of Applied Psychology, 76*(5), 690–697.

Fried, Y., & Ferris, G. R. (1987). The validity of the job characteristic model: A review and meta-analysis. *Personnel Psychology, 40,* 287–322.

Fugate, M., Kinicki, A. J., & Ashforth, B. E. (2004). Employability: A psycho-social construct, its dimensions, and applications. *Journal of Vocational Behavior, 65,* 14–38.

Grube, A., & Hertel, G. (2008). Altersbedingte Unterschiede in Arbeitsmotivation, Arbeitszufriedenheit und emotionalem Erleben während der Arbeit [Age-related differences in work motivation, job satisfaction and emotional experience during work]. *Wirtschaftspsychologie, 10,* 18–29.

Hackman, J. R., & Oldham, G. R. (1975). Development of the job diagnostic survey. *Journal of Applied Psychology, 60,* 159–170.

Hair, J. F., Black, W. C., Babin, B. J., Anderson, R. E., & Tatham, R., L. (2006). *Multivariate data analysis.* Englewood Cliffs, NJ: Prentice Hall.

Hall, D. T., & Mansfield, R. (1975). Relationship of age and seniority with career variables of engineers and scientists. *Journal of Applied Psychology, 60,* 201–210.

Harris, T. C., & Locke, E. A. (1974). Replication of white-collar-blue-collar differences in sources of satisfaction and dissatisfaction. *Journal of Applied Psychology, 59,* 369–370.

Hayward, M. D., Friedman, S., & Chen, H. (1998). Career trajectories and older men's retirement. *Journal of Gerontology, 53,* 91–103.

Heckhausen, J., & Schulz, R. (1995). A life span theory of control. *Psychological Review, 102,* 284–304.

Hedge, J. W., Borman, W. C., & Lammlein, S. E. (2006). *The aging workforce: Realities, myths, and implications for organizations.* Washington, DC: American Psychological Association.

Hershey, D. A., Henkens, K., & van Dalen, H. P. (2007). Mapping the minds of retirement planners: A cross-cultural perspective. *Journal of Cross-Cultural Psychology, 38,* 361–382.

Hess, N., & Jepsen, D. M. (2009). Career stage and generational differences in psychological contracts. *Career Development International, 14,* 261–283.

Hoffmann, S., & Müller, S. (2009). Consumer boycotts due to factory relocation. *Journal of Business Research, 62,* 239–247.

Hu, L., & Bentler, P. M. (1999). Cutoff criteria for fit indexes in covariance structure analysis: Conventional criteria versus new alternatives. *Structural Equation Modeling: A Multidisciplinary Journal, 6,* 1–55.

Ilmarinen, J. E. (2001). Aging workers. *Occupational and Environmental Medicine, 58,* 546–552.

Ilmarinen, J., & Tempel, J. (2002). *Arbeitsfähigkeit 2010—Was können wir tun, damit Sie gesund bleiben? [Workability 2010—What can we do to keep you healthy?].* Hamburg, Germany: VSA-Verlag.

Jacobs, J. A., Karen, D., & McClelland, K. (1991). The dynamics of young men's career aspirations. *Sociological Forum, 6,* 609–639.

Jenkins, R. (1991). Demographic aspects of stress. In C. L. Cooper & R. Payne (Eds.), *Personality and stress: Individual differences in the stress process* (pp. 107–132). New York, NY: Wiley.

Jepsen, D. A., & Dickson, G. L. (2003). Continuity in life-span career development: Career exploration as a precursor to career establishment. *Career Development Quarterly, 51,* 217–233.

Jöreskog, K. G., & Sörbom, D. (1982). Recent developments in structural equation modeling. *Journal of Marketing Research, 19,* 404–416.

Joulain, M., & Mullet, E. (2001). Estimating the "appropriate" age for retirement as a function of perceived occupational characteristics. *Work and Stress, 15,* 357–365.

Joulain, M., Mullet, E., Lecomte, C., & Prévost, R. (2000). Perception of "appropriate" age for retirement among young adults, middle-aged adults, and elderly people. *International Journal of Aging and Human Development, 50,* 73–84.

Kanfer, R., & Ackerman, P. L. (2004). Aging, adult development, and work motivation. *Academy of Management Review, 29,* 440–458.

Karasek, R. A. (1979). Job demands, job decision latitude, and mental strain: Implications for job redesign. *Administrative Science Quarterly, 24,* 285–308.

Kim, S., & Feldman, D. C. (2000). Working in retirement: The antecedents of bridge employment and its consequences for quality of life in retirement. *Academy of Management Journal, 43,* 1195–1210.

Koslovski, K., Ekerdt, D., & DeVincy, S. (2001). The role of job-related rewards in retirement planning. *Journal of Gerontology, 56B,* 160–169.

Kuester, S., Homburg, C., & Robertson, T. S. (1999). Retaliatory behavior to new product entry. *Journal of Marketing, 63,* 90–106.

Locke, E. A. (1973). Satisfiers and dissatisfiers among white-collar and blue-collar employees. *Journal of Applied Psychology, 58,* 67–76.

Loi, R., Hang-Yue, N., & Foley, S. (2006). Linking employees' justice perception to organizational commitment and intention to leave: The mediating role of perceived organizational support. *Journal of Occupational and Organizational Psychology, 79,* 101–120.

Mascher, U. (2010). Voraussetzungen für Rente mit 67 liegen nicht vor [Conditions for retirement age of 67 are not met]. *Sozialrecht und Praxis, 12,* 751–757.

Ng, T. W. H., & Feldman, D. C. (2009). Re-examining the relationship between age and voluntary turnover. *Journal of Vocational Behavior, 74,* 283–294.

Pelfrene, E., Vierick, P., Mak, R. P., DeSmets, P., Kornitzer, M., & DeBacker, D. (2001). Scale reliability of the Karasek "Job Demand-Control Support" model in the Belstress study. *Work and Stress, 15,* 297–313.

Phua, V. C., & McNally, J. W. (2008). Men planning for retirement: Changing meaning of pre-retirement planning. *Journal of Applied Gerontology, 27,* 588–608.

Purcell, P. (2005). *Older workers: Employment and retirement trends.* Washington, DC: Congressional Research Service, Senate Special Committee on Aging. Available at http://aging.senate.gov/crs/pension34.pdf

Roth, C., Wegge, J., & Schmidt, K.-H. (2007). Konsequenzen des demographischen Wandels für das Management von Humanressourcen [Consequences of demographic changes for the management of human resources]. *Zeitschrift für Personalpsychologie, 6,* 99–116.

Rüdiger, H. W. (2009). Ältere am Arbeitsplatz [Older people in the work place]. In S. Letzel & D. Nowak (Eds.), *Handbuch der Arbeitsmedizin* (B VI-2, pp. 1–20). Landsberg: Ecomed.

Salonen, P., Arola, H., Nygård, C. H., Huhtala, H., & Koivisto, A. M. (2003). Factors associated with premature departure from working life among ageing food industry employees. *Occupational Medicine, 53*, 65–68.

Sanderson, P. L., Todd, B. D., Holt, G. R., & Getty, C. J. M. (1995). Compensation, work status, and disability in low back pain patients. *SPINE, 20*, 554–556,

Schaufeli, W. B., & Bakker, A. B. (2004). Job demands, job resources, and their relationship with burnout and engagement: A multi-group study. *Journal of Organizational Behavior, 25*, 293–315.

Schmitt, N., Coyle, B. W., Rauschenberger, J., & White, J. K. (1979). Comparison of early retirees and non-retirees. *Personnel Psychology, 32*, 327–340.

Schreurs, B., van Emmerik, H., de Cuyper, N., Notelaers, G., & de Witte, H. (2011). Job demands-resources and early retirement intention: Differences between blue-collar and white-collar workers. *Economics and Industrial Democracy, 32*, 47–68.

Shultz, K. S., Morton, K. R., & Weckerle, J. R. (1998). The influence of push and pull factors on voluntary and involuntary early retirees' retirement decision and adjustment. *Journal of Vocational Behavior, 53*, 45–57.

Siegrist, J. (1996). Adverse health effects of high-effort/low-reword conditions. *Journal of Occupational Health Psychology, 1*, 27–41.

Siegrist, J., Wahrendorf, M., von dem Knesebeck, O., Jürges, H., & Börsch-Supan, A. (2006). Quality of work, well-being, and intended early retirement of older employees—baseline results from the SHARE Study. *European Journal of Public Health, 17*, 62–68.

Singh, R., & Greenhaus, J. H. (2004). The relation between career decision-making and person-job fit: A study of job changers. *Journal of Vocational Behavior, 64*, 198–221.

Statistisches Bundesamt. (2006). *Bevölkerung Deutschlands bis 2050: 11. koordinierte Bevölkerungsvorausberechnung [Population of Germany until 2050: 11th population prognosis]*. Wiesbaden, Germany: Author.

Stockes, R. G., & Maddox, G. L. (1967). Some social factors on retirement adaptation. *Journal of Gerontology, 22*, 329–333.

Sullivan, S. E., & Arthur, M. B. (2006). The evolution of the boundaryless career concept: Examining physical and psychological mobility. *Journal of Vocational Behavior, 1*, 19–29.

Super, D. E. (1957). *The psychology of careers*. New York, NY: Harper & Row.

Taylor, M. A., & Shore, L. M. (1995). Predictors of planned retirement age: An application of Beehr's model. *Psychology and Aging, 10*, 76–83.

Tett, R. P., & Meyer, J. P. (1993). Job satisfaction, organizational commitment, turnover intention, and turnover: Path analysis based on meta-analytic findings. *Personnel Psychology, 46*, 259–293.

Thoresen, G. J., Kaplan, S. A., Barsky, A. P., de Chermont, K., & Warren, C. R. (2003). The affective underpinnings of job perceptions and attitudes: A meta-analytic review and integration, *Psychological Bulletin, 129*, 914–945.

Toossi, M. (2007). Labor force projections to 2016: More workers in their golden years. *Monthly Labor Review, 130*, 33–52.

Tuomi, K., Huuhtanen, P., Nykyri, E., & Ilmarinen, J. (2001). Promotion of work ability, the quality of work and retirement. *Occupational Medicine, 51*, 316–324.

US Department of Labor. (2010). Record unemployment among older workers does not keep them out of the job market. *Issues in Labor Statistics, 10–04*, 1–3. Retrieved February 2012 from http://www.bls.gov/opub/ils/pdf/opbils81.pdf

Van der Heijde, C. M., & van der Heijden, B. I. J. M. (2006). A competence-based and multidimensional operationalization and measurement of employability, *Human Resource Management, 45*, 449–476.

Van der Heijden, B. (2002). Prerequisites to guarantee life-long employability. *Personnel Review, 31*, 44–61.

Walker, T. L., & Tracey, T. J. G. (2012). The role of future time perspective in career decision-making. *Journal of Vocational Behavior, 81*, 150–158.

Wang, M., & Shultz, K. S. (2010). Employee retirement: A review and recommendations for future investigation, *Journal of Management, 36*, 172–206.

Wang, M., Zhan, Y., Liu, S., & Shultz, K. (2008). Antecedents of bridge employment: A longitudinal investigation. *Journal of Applied Psychology, 93*, 818–830.

Warr, P. (1998). Age, work and mental health. In K. W. Schaie & C. Schooler (Eds.), *Impact of work on older adults* (pp. 252–296). New York, NY: Springer.

Watson, D., Clark, L. A., & Tellegen, A. (1988). Development and validation of brief measures of positive and negative affect: The PANAS scales. *Journal of Personality and Social Psychology, 54*, 1063–1070.

Weaver, C. N. (1975). Job preferences of white collar and blue collar workers. *Academy of Management Journal, 18*, 167–175.

Weis, J., Koch, U., Kruck, P., & Beck, A. (1994). Problems of vocational integration after cancer. *Clinical Rehabilitation, 8*, 219–225.

World Bank. (2011). *Population projection tables by country and group*. Retrieved February 2012 from www.worldbank.org

Zaniboni, S., Sarchielli, G., & Fraccaroli, F. (2010). How are psychosocial factors related to retirement intentions? *International Journal of Manpower, 31*, 271–285.

Domain specific effects of commitment on bridge employment decisions: The moderating role of economic stress

Yujie Zhan[1], Mo Wang[2], and Xiang Yao[3]

[1]School of Business and Economics, Wilfrid Laurier University, Waterloo, Ontario, Canada
[2]Department of Management, Warrington College of Business of Administration, University of Florida, Gainesville, USA
[3]Department of Psychology, Peking University, Beijing, China

Bridge employment is a labour force participation pattern increasingly observed in older workers. The present study applied the theory of planned behaviour and the principle of compatibility to predict two types of bridge employment decisions: career-based bridge employment and organization-based bridge employment. The study did this by examining the joint effect of work-related commitment variables and retirees' economic stress. Lagged data were collected from 164 Chinese retirees. Results of logistic regression analysis showed that career commitment and organizational commitment (i.e., affective and continuance commitment to the organization) had positive main effects in predicting career-based and organization-based bridge employment decisions respectively, supporting the principle of compatibility. In addition, these predictive effects were moderated by economic stress as a contextual constraint. The findings are discussed in terms of theoretical and practical implications for the bridge employment decision-making literature.

The ageing workforce is becoming a global challenge (Tyers & Shi, 2007). Demographic projections in multiple countries and regions, including but not limited to Europe (Eurostat, 2011), the United States (Vincent & Velkoff, 2010; Wheaton & Crimmins, 2012), and China (National Bureau of Statistics of China, 2011), have indicated a sizable increase in the number of people who will transition into retirement in the next several decades. Research has shown that 60–64% of older workers continue in some forms of paid work after retirement, and this percentage has been increasing in the past several years (Giandrea, Cahill, & Quinn, 2009). Paid work following retirement is commonly referred to as bridge employment, which is defined as the pattern of labour force participation exhibited by older workers as they leave their career jobs and move towards complete labour force withdrawal (Shultz, 2003).

As bridge employment becomes a popular option following official retirement, retirees who plan to stay longer in the workplace may face a variety of job options. However, studies predicting bridge employment intentions and decisions have largely focused on the predictions of bridge employment versus full retirement without specifying the types of bridge employment (e.g., Adams & Rau, 2004; Dendinger, Adams, & Jacobson, 2005; Loi & Shultz, 2007). Recent literature has categorized bridge employment into two types: career bridge employment (i.e., individuals accept bridge employment in the same industry/field as their career jobs) and bridge employment in a different field (Wang, Zhan, Liu, & Shultz, 2008). Following this categorization, empirical findings have demonstrated that the correlates of bridge employment vary as a function of the type of bridge jobs (e.g., Gobeski & Beehr, 2009; von

Bonsdorff, Shultz, Leskinen, & Tansky, 2009; Wang et al., 2008).

Compared to the study of career-based bridge employment decisions, a more practically important topic might be to understand bridge employment from the organization's perspective. Given the ageing trend of the workforce and organizations' mission to maintain critical talent and achieve successful knowledge transfer to younger employees, it is important for organizations to predict who among their retirees can be retained for bridge jobs (Shultz & Wang, 2011). However, this issue has been relatively understudied. To our knowledge, only two empirical studies categorized bridge employment based on the organizational domain (Jones & McIntosh, 2010; Kim & Feldman, 2000). Further, Kim and Feldman (2000) only focused on investigating outcomes rather than antecedents of bridge employment in the same versus different organizations, and Jones and McIntosh (2010) only examined the intentions rather than actual decisions of bridge employment as criteria. It is well-known that bridge employment intention does not necessarily translate into actual bridge employment decisions (Barnes-Farrell, 2003; Wang et al., 2008). Therefore, only studying bridge employment intention might constrain the implications for organizations' personnel planning given the importance to know not only who intend to pursue a bridge job but also who end up doing so. Thus, in order to better understand the antecedents of different types of bridge employment decisions, the current study examined predictors of actual bridge employment participation in both the career domain and the organizational domain.

Given the distinctive types of bridge employment decisions, we expect that attitudes towards different targets or content domains may contribute differently to one's bridge employment decisions regarding whether to stay in the same career field and whether to stay with the same organization. Over the past three decades, researchers (e.g., Fisher, 1980; Harrison, Newman, & Roth, 2006; Hulin, 1991) have argued that the association between job attitudes and job outcomes follows the principle of compatibility (Ajzen, 1991; Ajzen & Fishbein, 1977). According to this principle, when the attitudes and behaviours of interest are conceptualized and measured at the same level of generality, attitudes exhibit strong effects in predicting behaviours. Thus, the first purpose of this study is to apply the principle of compatibility and examine how attitudinal factors in different domains (i.e., career commitment and organizational commitment) may predict career-based and organization-based bridge employment decisions differently. Answering this research question also helps to address the research gap in that previous bridge employment research has largely focused on demographic and socioeconomic antecedents but not organization and job-related variables (Wang et al., 2008).

Another gap among studies predicting bridge employment decisions is the exclusive focus on predictive main effects of individual characteristics and/or work-related factors. Little attention has been paid to interactions between factors from different conceptual categories (Wang & Shultz, 2010). The only exception is the study by Gobeski and Beehr (2009). They conducted exploratory analyses and found that the interaction between local unemployment rates and work attachment predicted career-based bridge employment. Their findings provided preliminary evidence supporting that the strength of the link between work attitude and bridge employment decisions may vary depending on the contextual constraints experienced by the retirees. However, they did not provide a theory-based explanation for the interaction effect. Thus, the second purpose of this study is to apply the theory of planned behaviour to understand the interaction between work-related commitment and a contextual factor, economic stress, in predicting different types of bridge employment. We specifically focus on economic stress because financial needs are viewed as one of the most important concerns for retirees and are strongly related to one's postretirement activity and retirement satisfaction (Adams & Rau, 2011; Wang & Shultz, 2010). According to Barnes-Farrell (2003), the unavailability of sufficient financial resources functions as a constraining factor on a worker's ability to carry out a preferred path to retirement. In particular, financial well-being may override attitudinal factors in influencing bridge employment decision making.

In sum, the current study draws on the theory of planned behaviour to study the predictions of two different types of bridge employment behaviours simultaneously (i.e., career-based bridge employment and organization-based bridge employment decisions). First, the principle of compatibility is adopted to understand the domain-specific effects of career commitment and organizational commitment in predicting different types of bridge employment decisions. Second, this study makes an initial effort in testing how factors interactively affect retirees' bridge employment decisions (Figure 1). Time-lagged data from a Chinese sample were analysed to test our hypotheses.

THEORETICAL FRAMEWORK AND HYPOTHESES DEVELOPMENT

Bridge employment decisions

Retirement and bridge employment decisions are important life decisions for older adults. Applying a

Work Attitude   Bridge Employment Decisions

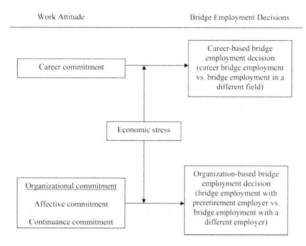

Figure 1. Hypothesized model.

decision-making perspective, different types of bridge employment decisions can be conceptualized as a motivated choice behaviour by retirees after weighing information regarding relevant work- and nonwork-related factors (Feldman, 1994). According to the model proposed by Shultz (2003), bridge employment is affected by (1) individual factors, such as demographic attributes, job-related efficacy and skills, attitudes towards and planning for retirement, and health; (2) contextual factors such as current and expected future economic conditions and job market conditions; and (3) organizational factors such as organizations' attitudes towards older workers. This decision-making conceptualization of bridge employment has been supported by many empirical studies. Surprisingly, the potential interactions among these factors are missing from prior research.

Following the decision-making perspective, the theory of planned behaviour (Ajzen, 1991) can be applied to understanding how individual attitudes and contextual constraints interactively impact bridge employment decisions. According to this theory, the performance of a given behaviour depends jointly on individual attitudes towards the behaviour (i.e., the favourable or unfavourable evaluation of the behaviour) and perceived behavioural control (i.e., perceived ease or difficulty of performing the behaviour of interest). In addition, the theory of planned behaviour suggests an interaction between attitude and perceived control in predicting behavioural outcomes, such that a favourable attitude can be expressed in an actual behaviour only if the person has the ability to choose or decide at will whether or not to perform the behaviour (Ajzen, 1991). Applying this reasoning to bridge employment decision making, it is expected that when an individual is limited by contextual constraints to choose preferred bridge employment type, his/her attitudinal preference is less able to predict the actual decision.

With the theory of planned behaviour as the theoretical framework, this study suggested that work-related attitude and economic stress would interactively impact individuals' decisions about career-based and organization-based bridge employment. Later, we review literature on work-related commitment and develop our hypotheses based on the principle of compatibility; we then propose economic stress as a constraining factor that might prevent people from following their own preferences in making bridge employment decisions.

Main effects of commitment and the principle of compatibility

According to the theory of planned behaviour, individual attitudes are one of the central determinants of behavioural intention and actual decisions and actions (Ajzen, 1991). Supporting this theory, work-related commitment, as an attitudinal construct, has been repeatedly shown to predict retirement intention and decisions (e.g., Gaillard & Desmette, 2008; Schmidt & Lee, 2008). Depending on different targets, work-related commitment can be specified as commitment towards different entities (Morrow, 1983). The current study focuses on the predictive effects of individuals' career commitment and two types of organizational commitment (i.e., affective and continuance commitment).

Career commitment. Career commitment refers to one's attitude towards one's occupation or profession (Blau, 1985). High levels of career commitment indicate a strong link between an employee and his/her chosen occupation or profession based on an affective reaction to that occupation or profession (Lee, Carswell, & Allen, 2000). In existing literature, "career" has been conceptualized in two different ways. Some studies conceptualize career as one's chosen field of work, and others conceptualize career as one's job trajectory over a lifetime, which may include a series of jobs, vocational choices, and other work-related activities from entry into the work force to complete work withdrawal (Lee et al., 2000; Meyer, Allen, & Smith, 1993). Although some researchers suggest that the term "career" should be avoided in research due to the possible ambiguous meaning (e.g., Lee et al., 2000; Meyer et al., 1993), we followed the original work by Blau (1985) and used "career" as a chosen field of work where an individual has spent a considerable duration of his/her lifetime. The main reason for this conceptualization is to use the term consistently with how "career" is usually defined in retirement and bridge employment literature (Feldman, 1994).

For retirees who are highly committed to their careers, they are likely to view their career as a "calling", which helps facilitate a broader sense of purpose of life (Duffy, Dik, & Steger, 2011). Thus, they may be willing to spend more time and invest more effort in the career that they identify themselves to. Consistently, prior studies have shown that career commitment was negatively related to career and job withdrawal intentions (e.g., Aryee & Tan, 1992). For older workers in particular, higher levels of career commitment may also result in strong motivation to pass professional skills and knowledge onto the next generation in one's professional field, which is referred to as generativity work motivation (Dendinger et al., 2005). The generativity motivation has been viewed as a unique component in defining the meaning of work for older adults (Mor-Barak, 1995). Retirees highly committed to their careers are more likely to be driven by the generativity motivation and take the opportunities of bridge employment in one's career field in order to promote the development of younger generations in the same career.

Organizational commitment. Organizational commitment is defined as the relative strength of an individual's identification with and involvement in a particular employing organization (Mowday, Steers, & Porter, 1979). Meyer and Allen (1991) clarified the distinctions among three types of organizational commitment: affective commitment, continuance commitment, and normative commitment. Specifically, affective commitment refers to employees' emotional orientation and attachment towards their organizations, continuance commitment refers to an awareness of the costs associated with leaving one's organization, and normative commitment refers to the perceived obligation to maintain employment in an organization. All three types of commitment predict employees' withdrawal cognition and turnover (Adams & Beehr, 1998; Meyer & Allen, 1991; Meyer, Stanley, Herscovitch, & Topolnytsky, 2002). However, normative commitment has not been as empirically differentiated as theoretically expected from affective commitment (Bergman, 2006; Solinger, van Olffen, & Roe, 2008). Therefore, the current study focused on examining affective and continuance commitment to the organization.

According to Solinger et al. (2008), affective commitment reflects an emotional attachment to an organization as a target. With a higher level of emotional attachment to and identification with the organization, retirees are likely to take bridge jobs in their preretirement organization simply because they enjoy working in their organizations and are willing to contribute to their organizations by increasing their work input (Wang & Zhan, 2012). Continuance commitment, on the other hand, is based on the perceived outcomes associated with leaving an organization, including the sacrifice of current income, familiar work environment, and social contacts, as well as the possible lack of alternate employment opportunities. For retirees with higher levels of continuance commitment, they tend to stay in their preretirement organization due to the potential costs and threats that may result from leaving their current organization and joining alternative organizations. In addition to the potential risks involved in finding alternative jobs, bridge employment in a different organization may lead to high work stress for older workers due to work role transition and social adaptation (Zhan, Wang, Liu, & Shultz, 2009).

Principle of compatibility. The construct of attitude is only meaningful when the attitudinal target, either an object or an issue, is clearly specified (Ajzen, 2001). When the measured attitude is matched in specificity or generality to the behaviour being predicted, a strong connection can be observed. This has been referred to as the "principle of compatibility" by Ajzen and Fishbein (1977). This principle has been well supported as an important component of the theory of planned behaviour (e.g., Harrison et al., 2006; Judge, Thoreson, Bono, & Patton, 2001).

Applying the principle of compatibility to the current research topic, we expect that career-based bridge employment decisions and organization-based bridge employment decisions may be better predicted by commitment in their compatible domains respectively. As supported by an empirical study (Jones & McIntosh, 2010), a stronger predictive effect was found for organizational commitment than career commitment in predicting retirees' intentions in staying with the same organization for their future retirement. Further, retirees with higher levels of career commitment may choose to stay in the same organization if their organization can facilitate their career-related goal pursuit or help them pass their professional knowledge onto younger workers. Hence, they may also choose to join an alternative organization when they find the alternative organization implements better career-related practices that can potentially satisfy their career-related goals (Chang, 1999). Therefore, we do not expect any significant cross-domain relationship between commitment variables and bridge employment decisions.

Hypothesis 1: Retirees with higher levels of career commitment are more likely to take career bridge employment than to take bridge employment in a different field.
Hypothesis 2: Retirees with higher levels of (a) affective commitment and (b) continuance commitment to their organization are more likely to take bridge employment in the same organization

117

than to take bridge employment in a different organization.

Moderating role of economic stress

Economic stress is defined as an evaluation of one's financial status, such as concerns and worries regarding one's current or projected financial situation (Probst, 2005; Voydanoff, 1990). In the current study, we hypothesized that economic stress might work as a constraining factor on people's postretirement employment decisions. According to the theory of planned behaviour (Ajzen, 1991), when one feels that a given behaviour is out of control (e.g., one does not have a choice to perform or not perform it), one is less likely to engage in this behaviour even though he/she may have a positive attitude towards the behaviour. In other words, perceived lack of control may constrain the association between attitude and corresponding behaviour.

In the current study, we expect that economic stress to constrain retirees' options regarding what type of bridge employment they take, thus moderating the predictive effects of career/organizational attitudes. Among many potential contextual constraints, economic stress is viewed as one of the most important concerns for retirees (Barnes-Farrell, 2003) and is highly relevant to one's retirement transition and adjustment (Adams & Rau, 2011; Wang & Shultz, 2010). In addition, economic stress has been identified as one of the job search constraints that may impact the effectiveness of job seeking activities (Adams & Rau, 2004; Wanberg, Kanfer, & Rotundo, 1999). Specifically, retirees who are not worried about their financial situations may perceive higher levels of autonomy in decision making and the bridge-job search process. Their bridge employment decision is more likely to reflect their attitudinal preferences. Thus, we expect a stronger association between career/organizational commitment and careerbased/organization-based bridge employment decisions. On the other hand, for retirees under financial pressure, they are less able to carry out a preferred path of action in bridge employment decision making (Barnes-Farrell, 2003). Therefore, the associations between commitment and bridge employment decisions are expected to be weaker.

Hypothesis 3: Economic stress moderates the relationship between career commitment and career-based bridge employment decisions. The predictive effect of career commitment is weaker for retirees with higher levels of economic stress than for retirees with lower levels of economic stress.

Hypothesis 4: Economic stress moderates the effects of (a) affective commitment and (b)

continuance commitment to one's organization in predicting organization-based bridge employment decisions. Specifically, the predictive effects of (a) affective commitment and (b) continuance commitment to one's organization are weaker for retirees with higher levels of economic stress than that for retirees with lower levels of economic stress.

METHOD

Sample

Data were collected from a sample of 164 highly educated retirees who retired from two organizations, a medical research institute and a postsecondary educational institution, located in Beijing, China. We chose to study well-educated retirees in order to adequately examine multiple types of bridge employment decisions. According to Wang et al. (2008), educated retirees are more likely to keep their working roles after official retirement. Consistently, the two organizations where the participants were sampled both have strong norms of bridge employment after official retirement, which provides an ideal research setting to study different types of bridge employment.

Data collections in these two organizations followed the same procedure. One month before their official retirement, participants received a letter from the human resources department of the institute, inviting them to participate in the current study and assuring confidentiality and voluntary participation. Among 244 retirees from these organizations, 164 agreed to participate in the current study and provided complete responses to the survey (response rate = 67.21%). The average age of the participants was 57.46 ($SD = 3.17$), and the average number of years of education was 13.72 ($SD = 2.33$). Among these participants, 73 (44.5%) were men. On average, these participants worked for 34.23 hours per week on their bridge jobs, with 90 of them (54.9%) working on a full-time basis (40 hours/week).

Procedure and measures

All participants were surveyed at two time points. The first survey was conducted right at the time of the official retirement for each participant. Participants were asked to report their demographic information, health condition, economic stress, career commitment, and organizational commitment. Participants' bridge employment status was measured in the second time of data collection, which occurred 1 month after official retirement. All surveys were conducted in Mandarin. A translation–back-translation procedure was followed to translate the English-based measures into Chinese (Brislin, 1980).

Control variables. Prior literature comparing bridge employment decision versus full retirement has shown that retirees who are younger, have received more years of education, have better health, and have no dependent children to take care of are more likely to engage in bridge employment than in full retirement (e.g., Kim & Feldman, 2000; Wang et al., 2008). In addition, female workers are usually expected to be less likely to take bridge employment because of their family-centred responsibilities and the lack of job opportunities available for women (Szinovacz, DeViney, & Davey, 2001). Given these findings, we measured participants' age, gender, years of education, number of dependent children, and self-report health condition at Time 1 and controlled their effects in data analyses. In addition, we also controlled for organizational membership.

Career commitment. Career commitment was measured by an eight-item scale developed by Blau (1985). Participants were asked to rate each item on a 5-point Likert scale (1 = "strongly disagree" to 5 = "strongly agree"). Sample items were "I like this vocation too well to give it up" and "if I could do it all over again, I would not choose to work in this profession" (reverse coded). The α reliability was .75.

Organizational commitment. Organizational commitment was measured by a scale developed by Meyer and Allen (1997). Participants were asked to rate each item on a 7-point Likert scale (1 = "strongly disagree" to 7 = "strongly agree"). Six items were used to measure affective commitment. A sample item was "I do not feel like part of the family at my organization" (reverse coded). Seven items were used to measure continuance commitment. A sample item was "too much of my life would be disrupted if I decided I wanted to leave my organization right now". The α reliability was .70 and .83 for affective and continuance commitment, respectively.

Economic stress. A five-item scale developed by Sinclair, Sears, Zajack, and Probst (2010) was used to measure economic stress. Participants were asked to rate each item on a 5-point Likert scale based on the financial status of their family (1 = "strongly disagree" to 5 = "strongly agree"). A sample item was "I feel pressured by my financial situation." The α reliability was .94.

Career-based bridge employment decisions. Career-based bridge employment decisions were measured by asking the participants to indicate whether they continued working in the same career field as their preretirement jobs. The response scale was dichotomous with 0 = "no" and 1 = "yes".

Organization-based bridge employment decisions. Organization-based bridge employment decisions were measured by asking the participants to indicate whether they continued working in their preretirement organization. The response scale was dichotomous with 0 = "no" and 1 = "yes".

Analytic strategy

Because the dependent variables (i.e., career vs. noncareer bridge employment and bridge employment in the same vs. different organizations) were categorical variables with two categories each, binary logistic regression analysis was used to test the hypotheses. Control variables were entered in the first step of the logistic regression. In the second step, work-related commitment variables in the *incompatible* domain with the outcome variable (i.e., organizational commitment in the model of predicting career vs. noncareer bridge employment, and career commitment in the model of predicting bridge employment in the same vs. different organizations) were entered to control for their respective effects. In the third step, commitment variables in the *compatible* domains with the outcome variables and economic stress were entered to test the main-effect hypotheses (i.e., Hypotheses 1–2). In the fourth step, interaction terms between domain-incompatible commitment and economic stress were entered. Finally, interaction terms between domain-compatible commitment and economic stress were entered into the logistic regression model (i.e., testing Hypotheses 3–4). Economic stress and commitment variables were centred before being entered into models in order to avoid the multicollinearity issue in testing the interaction effects.

RESULTS

Preliminary analysis

Means, standard deviations, and bivariate correlations among the current variables are presented in Table 1. Based on descriptive analysis, 135 (82.3%) retirees worked in their pre-retirement career field after retirement and 27 (16.5%) worked in a different career field for bridge employment; 99 (60.4%) retirees continued working in the same organizations as prior to retirement and 63 (38.4%) worked in a different organization for bridge employment.

Confirmatory factor analysis (CFA) was conducted to test the construct validity of the measures. Specifically, a four-factor model (i.e., economic stress, career commitment, affective commitment, and continuance commitment) was estimated using Mplus 6.11 (Muthén & Muthén, 2011), showing good fit to the current data, $\chi^2(293) = 414.20$, $p < .01$,

119

comparative fit index (CFI) = 0.94, Tucker-Lewis Index (TLI) = 0.93, root mean square error of approximation (RMSEA) = 0.05. In addition, all the scale items loaded significantly onto their corresponding latent factors (standardized factor loadings ranged from .21 to .96). Further, the correlations between the latent factors were weak (i.e., $|r|$ ranged from .10 to .23), demonstrating clear distinction among all the latent factors included in this model.

Considering the relatively small sample size, we tried to increase the ratio of the sample size to the number of parameters estimated by removing control variables that did not significantly relate to the criterion variables. A series of bivariate binary logistic regression analyses was conducted for each control variable. According to the results, education level was the only control variable that had a significant effect in predicting bridge employment decisions. Therefore, we only controlled for education level in multivariate logistic regression analyses.

Hypothesis testing in logistic regression

The results of multivariate logistic regressions for career-based bridge employment and organization-based bridge employment were presented in Tables 2 and 3, respectively. Specifically, Hypothesis 1 was supported (Step 3 in Table 2). After controlling for the effects of education level and organizational commitment, participants' career commitment was positively related to their likelihood of career versus noncareer bridge employment, $B = 0.92$, $p < .01$, odds ratio = 2.50, indicating that retirees who scored higher in career commitment were more likely to engage in career bridge employment instead of bridge employment in a different field. Regarding organization-based bridge employment, Hypotheses 2a and 2b were both supported. After controlling for the effects of education level and career commitment, participants' affective commitment, $B = 0.36$, $p < .05$, odds ratio = 1.43, and continuance commitment towards the organization, $B = 0.28$, $p < .05$, odds ratio = 1.32, were positively related to their likelihood of organization-based bridge employment. Specifically, retirees who scored higher in affective commitment and continuance commitment were more likely to engage in bridge employment in the same organization instead of bridge employment in a different organization (Step 3 in Table 3).

The hypothesized moderating effect of economic stress was tested in Step 5 of each model. Specifically, Hypothesis 3 was supported (Step 5 in Table 2). Economic stress significantly moderated the association between career commitment and one's career-based bridge employment decision, $B = -0.79$, $p < .05$, odds ratio = 0.45. The interaction was plotted in Figure 2. A simple slope test was conducted

TABLE 1
Means, standard deviations, and bivariate correlations

Variables	Mean	SD	1	2	3	4	5	6	7	8	9	10	11
1. Age	57.46	3.17											
2. Gender	0.55	0.50	-.13										
3. Years of education	13.72	2.33	.22**	-.17*									
4. Number of dependent children	0.42	0.69	-.14	.03	.06								
5. Health	3.36	0.62	-.03	-.02	-.11	.03							
6. Organizational membership	0.37	0.48	.00	-.64**	.16*	.20*	-.10						
7. Career commitment	3.23	0.61	.04	.01	.12	.04	.22**	-.07					
8. Affective commitment to organization	4.69	0.86	.09	-.10	.03	-.10	.07	.04	.26**				
9. Continuance commitment to organization	3.82	1.15	-.01	.18*	-.11	-.15	-.09	-.28**	-.04	.16*			
10. Economic stress	2.57	0.92	.03	.04	-.11	.01	-.25**	-.20*	-.23	-.08	.36**		
11. Career vs. noncareer bridge employment	0.83	0.37	-.05	.10	.05	.02	.03	-.12	.21	.07	.10	-.07	
12. Bridge employment in same vs. different organizations	0.61	0.49	-.03	-.04	.16*	.00	.06	.04	-.01	.16*	.11	-.07	.40**

$N = 164$. *$p < .05$, **$p < .01$.

TABLE 2

Logistic regression results for the prediction of career versus noncareer bridge employment

	Step 1			Step 2			Step 3			Step 4			Step 5		
	B	SE	OR	B	SE	OR	B	SE	OR	B	SE	OR	B	SE	OR
Intercept	0.77	1.27		0.65	1.28		1.07	1.33		1.02	1.33		0.68	1.35	
Years of education	0.06	0.09	1.06	0.07	0.09	1.08	0.05	0.10	1.05	0.06	0.10	1.06	0.08	0.10	1.09
Affective commitment to organization (ACOrg)				0.15	0.25	1.16	−0.05	0.26	0.95	−0.05	0.26	0.96	−0.08	0.27	0.92
Continuance commitment to organization (CCOrg)				0.22	0.19	1.24	0.30	0.21	1.35	0.30	0.21	1.35	0.32	0.21	1.38
Career commitment (CCar)							0.92	0.40	2.50**	0.91	0.40	2.49**	1.22	0.47	3.39**
Economic strain (ES)							−0.19	0.27	0.83	−0.21	0.27	0.81	−0.48	0.31	0.62
ACOrg × ES										−0.10	0.26	0.91	0.01	0.29	1.01
CCOrg × ES										−0.11	0.18	0.90	−0.02	0.19	0.99
CCar × ES													−0.79	0.44	0.45*
Change of χ²	0.46			2.00			7.29*			0.48			3.74*		
Change of df	1			2			2			2			1		
−2 log likelihood	145.53			143.52			136.24			135.76			132.02		
Cox and Snell R-square	.00			.02			.06			.06			.08		

N = 164. SE = standard error. OR = odds ratio. *p < .05, **p < .01.

TABLE 3

Logistic regression results for the prediction of bridge employment in same versus different organizations

	Step 1			Step 2			Step 3			Step 4			Step 5		
	B	SE	OR	B	SE	OR	B	SE	OR	B	SE	OR	B	SE	OR
Intercept	−1.55	1.01		−1.59	1.12		−1.72	1.05	*	−2.04	1.07	*	−2.10	1.08	*
Years of education	0.15	0.07	1.16**	0.15	0.07	1.16**	0.16	0.08	1.18**	0.18	0.08	1.20**	0.19	0.08	1.21**
Career commitment (CCar)				−0.09	0.27	0.92	−0.29	0.29	0.75	−0.23	0.31	0.80	−0.35	0.31	0.78
Affective commitment to organization (ACOrg)							0.36	0.21	1.43*	0.36	0.21	1.43*	0.38	0.21	1.46*
Continuance commitment to organization (CCOrg)							0.28	0.17	1.32*	0.29	0.17	1.33*	0.27	0.17	1.31
Economic strain (ES)							−0.27	0.20	0.76	−0.34	0.21	0.71	−0.37	0.22	0.69*
CCar × ES										−0.59	0.29	0.56**	−0.54	0.30	0.58**
ACOrg × ES													−0.36	0.22	0.69*
CCOrg × ES													−0.13	0.15	0.88
Change of χ²	4.18*			0.10			8.14*			4.60*			3.41		
Change of df	1			1			3			1			2		
−2 log likelihood	212.33			212.23			204.08			199.48			196.07		
Cox and Snell R-square	.03			.03			.07			.10			.12		

N = 164. SE = standard error. OR = odds ratio. *p < .05, **p < .01.

to further examine the effect of career commitment under different conditions of economic stress. According to the results, the predictive effect of career commitment was only significant for retirees with lower levels of economic stress, $B = 1.95$, $p < .01$, odds ratio $= 7.04$, and retirees with average levels of economic stress, $B = 1.22$, $p < .01$, odds ratio $= 3.39$, but it was not significant for retirees with higher levels of economic stress ($p > .05$). Therefore, for retirees with higher levels of economic stress, the predictive effect of their career commitment was weaker than retirees with lower levels of economic stress. In other words, retirees without financial pressure are more likely to make their career-based bridge employment decisions based on their career attitude.

Furthermore, Hypothesis 4a was supported (Step 5 in Table 3). Economic stress significantly moderated the association between affective commitment and the organization-based bridge employment decision, $B = -0.36$, $p < .05$, odds ratio $= 0.69$. The pattern of the interaction was plotted in Figure 3. We further tested the simple slopes and found that the effect of affective commitment was significant in predicting bridge employment in the same versus different organizations for retirees with lower levels, $B = 0.71$, $p < .01$, odds ratio $= 2.03$, or average levels of economic stress, $B = 0.38$, $p < .05$, odds ratio $= 1.46$, and it was not significant for retirees with higher levels of economic stress ($p > .05$). Again, high financial pressure was shown to restrain retirees from making their working decisions based on their attitude towards their organizations. However, the moderating effect of economic stress was not significant for continuance commitment. Hypothesis 4b was not supported.

DISCUSSION

The current study aimed to address two research questions. First, according to the principle of compatibility, we examined the domain specific effects of career commitment and organizational commitment in predicting retirees' career-based and organization-based bridge employment decisions. Second, based on the theory of planned behaviour, we tested retirees' economic stress as a constraining factor in moderating the predictive effects of commitment variables. Our hypotheses were largely supported by the current results.

Theoretical implications

First and foremost, this is one of the first studies that examined how different factors (i.e., individual attitudes and contextual constraints) could interactively influence retirees' bridge employment decisions. Given the complexity involved in this decision-making process, knowledge drawn from independent main effects of individual and contextual characteristics may limit our understanding of this process. By demonstrating the boundary role of economic stress, this study provided empirical evidence that supports the adoption of an interactive perspective to study bridge employment decision making. Specifically, the associations between work-related commitment and bridge employment decisions, which have been largely supported by existing literature, became weaker and not significant for retirees facing high economic stress. This finding is consistent with Barnes-Farrell's (2003) notion that retirees lacking financial resources to support their postretirement life tend to rely more on realistic factors than individual

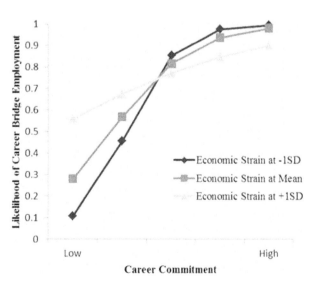

Figure 2. Moderating effect of economic stress on the association between career commitment and career-based bridge employment decisions.

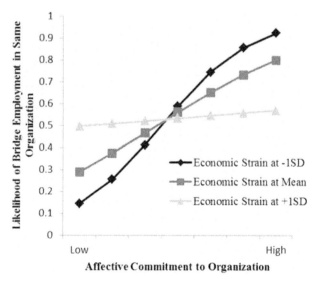

Figure 3. Moderating effects of economic stress on the associations between affective commitment to organization and organization-based bridge employment decisions.

preferences in making their retirement decisions in order to avoid unfavourable outcomes. Thus, realistic factors such as economic stress restrict retirees' opportunities in choosing from different types of bridge employment and reduce retirees' control on their bridge employment decision making. Further, supporting the theory of planned behaviour, our findings suggest that a favourable attitude towards certain types of bridge employment can be reflected in actual decisions only when retirees do not face financial constraints in making decisions. With high levels of contextual constraints, attitude becomes less relevant.

However, the boundary effect of economic stress was only significant in moderating the association between career commitment and career-based bridge employment decision making and the association between affective commitment to organization and organization-based bridge employment decision making. It was not significant when it came to continuance commitment (i.e., Hypothesis 4b). We believe that this is, at least partly, due to the conceptual difference between the two organizational commitment components. Specifically, affective commitment captures the emotional attachment of employees to their organization, whereas continuance commitment captures the realistic considerations related to staying or leaving an organization (Meyer, Allen, & Gellatly, 1990). Thus, the concept of continuance commitment might have partly accounted for one's subjective evaluation of the contextual constraints regarding the availability of alternative jobs and the sacrifice one might face if leaving the current employer. In other words, one's perceived control or contextual constraints may contribute to the formation of one's continuance commitment as an attitudinal construct. To contrast, affective commitment and career commitment are typically conceptualized as being more emotionally oriented (Lee et al., 2000) and less relying on the cognitive consideration of feasibility. This explanation was supported by the bivariate correlation coefficients in that economic stress was only significantly related to continuance commitment to the organization, $r = .36$, $p < .01$, but not related to the other two commitment constructs.

Second, the current study contributes to the bridge employment literature by examining multiple types of bridge employment simultaneously. Our current findings have important implications for the notion that retirement transition may take multiple pathways (Shultz & Wang, 2011; Szinovacz, 2003; Wang, 2007; Wang, Henkens, & van Solinge, 2011). These findings suggest that, in order to better explain these pathways, researchers must consider predictive factors from the perspective of compatibility. As such, previous studies using older workers' attitude

towards one's organization or organization-specific job characteristics to predict career-based bridge employment might underestimate the predictive effects (e.g., job characteristics such as skill variety, autonomy, and feedback are often organization specific, but not career specific; Gobeski & Beehr, 2009). The current findings encourage further research taking into account the domain-specific effects in testing predictors of different types of bridge employment intention or decision.

Third, the domain specific effects provide additional evidence for the principle of compatibility beyond existing literature. Prior studies that applied the compatibility principle often focused on the compatibility in terms of the level of specificity or generality (i.e., how broad an attitude and a behaviour are conceptualized). For instance, Harrison et al. (2006) demonstrated that a unified model in which the overall job attitude was associated with a higher order work behavioural construct worked better than a diversified model in which the overall job attitude was directly linked to several lower order work outcomes. The current study extends the principle of compatibility to the aspect of content domain or content level. Specifically, we differentiated career-based constructs and organization-based constructs, and significant main effects were only observed between constructs from compatible domains after controlling the effects from the incompatible domains. It should be noted that a few existing studies (e.g., Meyer et al., 1993) have shown that career commitment might function as a broader construct, which could contribute to the prediction of organizational domain outcomes above and beyond the effects of organizational commitment. However, the current findings did not replicate the independent effects of career and organizational commitment in predicting organization-based bridge employment decisions. A possible reason might be that career commitment only impacts organizational domain outcomes when organizations clearly show support to enhance employees' career-related pursuits (Chang, 1999). Future studies may continue to explore the conditions that may strengthen cross-domain associations.

Practical implications

The workforce is ageing. At the same time, many older workers will gravitate towards opportunities of continued employment after retirement. Organizations driven by the goal of knowledge retention may want to identify those employees who are most likely to be retained as valued assets to help maintain critical talent and achieve successful knowledge transfer to younger employees. Practically, the current study provides important implications to employers who would like to retain their retirees by explicitly differentiating career-based and organization-based bridge employment. First, employers are encouraged to pay attention to older employees' identification with the organization and try to improve their organizational commitment. Although employers should always aim to improve employees' organizational commitment, there is evidence suggesting that organizations often fail to pay attention to older workers' unique characteristics and needs when they develop policies and practices to promote the employee–organization relationship among older workers (Wang & Zhan, 2012). This is because older workers are typically expected to retire soon and to have increased continuance commitment (Allen & Meyer, 1983). This study provided evidence for the importance of nurturing older workers' organizational commitment. Specifically, improving older workers' organizational commitment is particularly important for organizations that need to retain their productive yet ageing workforce. Based on the employee–organization relationship perspective (Coyle-Shapiro & Conway, 2004), employers could promote older employees' perception of the employee–organization relationship by providing a supportive and flexible system for reemployed older workers, forming ageing-friendly norms, and providing training opportunities to help maintain the employability of older employees (Wang & Zhan, 2012). Further, by implementing career-related practices, an organization is likely to promote their employees' career commitment and organizational commitment (Chang, 1999).

Moreover, as suggested by the moderating role of economic stress, employers should be aware that commitment-promoting practices may work better for retirees or older employees who are free of financial constraints. For older employees who have high financial stress, employers may want to make an effort to help them relieve their financial stress by providing more tangible support rather than just psychosocial support.

Limitations and future directions

The generalizability of the findings may be limited by the current sample. Specifically, data was collected from a Chinese sample of highly educated retirees. As we described, similar to many Western countries, China also faces the trend of an ageing workforce (Chen & Liu, 2009), and bridge employment is becoming a more prevalent phenomenon for Chinese retirees, especially for the highly educated retirees (Xu & Bennington, 2008). Therefore, we feel that current retirees in research and postsecondary education occupations in China are appropriate for studying different types of bridge employment given the

strong norms of providing bridge jobs by organizations in these occupations as well as the autonomy retirees have in bridge employment participation. In terms of the cultural generalizability of career commitment, Noordin, Williams, and Zimmer (2002) compared career commitment of managers from collectivistic cultures and managers from individualistic cultures, and they found no significant difference in terms of their career identity and career planning commitment. Therefore, we do not expect different patterns of results across different cultures in terms of the effects of work-related commitment. Therefore, we believe this study contributed to extend our understanding of bridge employment from Western countries to China, the country on the earth with the most elderly people. Future research is encouraged to cross-validate the current findings by using samples from different countries and regions.

In addition, the current sample size was limited, especially the sample size for the category of bridge employment in a different career field ($n = 27$, 16.5%). Although the subsample size for noncareer bridge employment was much smaller than other categories, we believe that such distribution represented the bridge employment situation in general. For example, Wang et al.'s (2008) study reported that 10.2% of participants from a nationally representative sample of the United States engaged in bridge employment in a different career field. Nevertheless, the findings should be cross-validated by future research with larger sample sizes in each bridge employment category.

Another limitation of the current study regarded the different components of commitment. In this study, we treated organizational commitment as a multidimension construct (i.e., affective and continuance commitment) but measured career commitment as a single-dimension construct that mainly captured the affective component. Although most literature emphasizes the affective nature of career commitment (e.g., Blau, 1985; Duffy et al., 2011; Lee et al., 2000), career commitment has also been split into different components in some studies (e.g., Meyer et al., 1993). It is possible that one has to stay in one career field because he/she perceived low probability of finding a job in a different field and a lot of sacrifice in leaving his/her current career.

Last, the current study did not take subjective norms into account in explaining different types of bridge employment decisions. According to the theory of planned behaviour, subjective norms refer to the perceived social pressure to perform a given behaviour. We expected that subjective norms would play a less important role in the current study setting. As we described earlier, bridge employment is becoming a prevalent phenomenon for Chinese retirees, especially for the highly educated retirees

(Xu & Bennington, 2008). This is exactly the situation reflected by the sample of this study: In research and postsecondary education occupations, there are strong norms for organizations to provide bridge jobs and for retirees to prolong employment life by taking bridge jobs. Therefore, we believe that such occupational norms serve as an important part of subjective norms (e.g., colleagues' attitudes) favouring bridge employment. Also, given the overall occupational norms, people (e.g., retirees' families and friends) not working in those occupations may also share the understanding and have high acceptance towards others taking bridge employment in those occupations. Therefore, subjective norms were not examined as a predictor in the current study. Nevertheless, we believe that there is still variance in perceived subjective norms for different individual retirees depending on their families' and friends' attitudes towards and experiences with bridge employment, which could be an interesting question to explore in future studies.

Finally, the current study may shed light on some new directions for future research on bridge employment. In particular, researchers are encouraged to further examine the moderating effects of contextual and organizational factors. According to Shultz's (2003) model of bridge employment, bridge employment decisions are determined by individual attributes, contextual factors, and organizational factors. According to the theory of planned behaviour, in addition to one's financial situation, the effects of individual attitudes may also be moderated by contextual constraints driven by family conditions, organizations' policy and attitude towards older workers, and job market conditions. When facing strong contextual demands, retirees' bridge employment decisions become more complicated and cannot be well explained by personal preferences. Therefore, beyond examining the effects of job or retirement attitudes, an interactive approach should be considered to better understand bridge employment decisions embedded in social contexts. In addition, the current study only focused on individuals' attachment to the career and organization as motivational predictors of different types of bridge employment. Future research may take a broader theoretical perspective to better understand this decision-making process. For example, bridge employment decisions might be influenced by one's links to other people, teams, and groups in an organization or an occupation (Mitchell, Holtom, Lee, Sablynski, & Erez, 2001). Also, some retirees may set different goals for postretirement life in other domains than work (Jex & Grosch, 2012), which may impact their choice of bridge employment. Future researchers are encouraged to explore the other motivational aspects in the bridge employment decision-making process.

REFERENCES

Adams, G. A., & Beehr, T. A. (1998). Turnover and retirement: A comparison of their similarities and differences. *Personnel Psychology, 51*, 643–665.

Adams, G., & Rau, B. (2004). Job seeking among retirees seeking bridge employment. *Personnel Psychology, 57*, 719–744.

Adams, G., & Rau, B., (2011). Putting off tomorrow to do what you want today: Planning for retirement. *The American Psychologist, 66*, 180–192.

Ajzen, I., (1991). The theory of planned behavior. *Organizational Behavior and Human Decision Processes, 50*, 179–211.

Ajzen, I., (2001). Nature and operation of attitudes. *Annual Review of Psychology, 52*, 27–58.

Ajzen, I., & Fishbein, M., (1977). Attitude–behavior relations: A theoretical analysis and review of empirical research. *Psychological Bulletin, 84*, 888–918.

Allen, N. J., & Meyer, J. P., (1983). Organizational commitment: Evidence of career stage effects? *Journal of Business Research, 26*, 49–61.

Aryee, S., & Tan, K., (1992). Antecedents and outcomes of career commitment. *Journal of Vocational Behavior, 40*, 288–305.

Barnes-Farrell, J. L., (2003). Beyond health and wealth: Attitudinal and other influences on retirement decision-making. In G. A. Adams & T. A. Beehr (Eds.), *Retirement: Reasons, processes, and results* (pp. 159–187). New York, NY: Springer.

Bergman, M. E., (2006). The relationship between affective and normative commitment: Review and research agenda. *Journal of Organizational Behavior, 27*, 645–663.

Blau, G. J., (1985). The measurement and prediction of career commitment. *Journal of Occupational Psychology, 58*, 277–288.

Brislin, R. W., (1980). Translation and content analysis of oral and written materials. In H. C. Triandis & J. W. Berry (Eds.), *Handbook of cross-cultural psychology* (Vol. 2, pp. 389–444). Boston, MA: Allyn & Bacon.

Chang, E., (1999). Career commitment as a complex moderator of organizational commitment and turnover intention. *Human Relations, 52*, 1257–1278.

Chen, F., & Liu, G., (2009). Population aging in China. In P. Uhlenberg (Ed.), *International handbook of population aging* (pp. 157–172). New York, NY: Springer.

Coyle-Shapiro, J. A.-M., & Conway, N., (2004). The employment relationship through the lens of social exchange. In J. A.-M. Coyle-Shapiro, L. M. Shore, M. S. Taylor, & L. E. Tetrick (Eds.), *The employment relationship: Examining psychological and contextual perspectives* (pp. 5–28). Oxford: Oxford University Press.

Dendinger, V. M., Adams, G. A., & Jacobson, J. D., (2005). Reasons for working and their relationship to retirement attitudes, job satisfaction and occupational self-efficacy of bridge employees. *International Journal of Aging and Human Development, 61*, 21–35.

Duffy, R. D., Dik, B. J., & Steger, M. F., (2011). Calling and work-related outcomes: Career commitment as a mediator. *Journal of Vocational Behavior, 78*, 210–218.

Eurostat. (2011). The greying of the baby boomers: A century-long view of ageing in European populations. *Statistics in Focus*, No. 23/2011.

Feldman, D. C., (1994). The decision to retire early: A review and conceptualization. *Academy of Management Review, 19*, 285–311.

Fisher, C. D., (1980). On the dubious wisdom of expecting job satisfaction to correlate with performance. *Academy of Management Review, 5*, 607–612.

Gaillard, M., & Desmette, D., (2008). Intergroup predictors of older workers' attitudes towards work and early exit. *European Journal of Work and Organizational Psychology, 17*, 450–481.

Giandrea, M. D., Cahill, K. E., & Quinn, J. F., (2009). Bridge jobs: A comparison across cohorts. *Research on Aging, 31,* 549–576.

Gobeski, K. T., & Beehr, T. A., (2009). How retirees work: Predictors of different types of bridge employment. *Journal of Organizational Behavior, 30,* 401–425.

Harrison, D. A., Newman, D. A., & Roth, P. L., (2006). How important are job attitudes? Meta-analytic comparisons of integrative behavioral outcomes and time sequences. *Academy of Management Journal, 40,* 305–325.

Hulin, C. L., (1991). Adaptation, persistence, and commitment in organizations. In M. D. Dunnette & L. M. Hough (Eds.), *Handbook of industrial and organizational psychology* (Vol. 2, 2nd ed., pp. 445–505). Palo Alto, CA: Consulting Psychologists Press.

Jex, S. M., & Grosch, J., (2012). Retirement decision making. In M. Wang (Eds.), *The Oxford handbook of retirement* (pp. 267–279). Oxford: Oxford University Press.

Jones, D. A., & McIntosh, B. R., (2010). Organizational and occupational commitment in relation to bridge employment and retirement intentions. *Journal of Vocational Behavior, 77,* 290–303.

Judge, T. A., Thoreson, C. J., Bono, J. E., & Patton, G. K., (2001). The job satisfaction-job performance relationship: A qualitative and quantitative review. *Psychological Bulletin, 127,* 376–407.

Kim, S., & Feldman, D. C., (2000). Working in retirement: The antecedents of bridge employment and its consequences for quality of life in retirement. *Academy of Management Review, 43,* 1195–1210.

Lee, K., Carswell, J. J., & Allen, N. J., (2000). A meta-analytic review of occupational commitment: Relations with person- and work-related variables. *Journal of Applied Psychology, 85,* 799–811.

Loi, J., & Shultz, K., (2007). Why older adults seek employment: Differing motivations among subgroups. *Journal of Applied Gerontology, 26,* 274–289.

Meyer, J., & Allen, N., (1997). *Commitment in the workplace.* Thousand Oaks, CA: Sage.

Meyer, J. P., & Allen, N. J., (1991). A three-component conceptualization of organizational commitment. *Human Resource Management Review, 1,* 61–89.

Meyer, J. P., Allen, N. J., & Gellatly, I. R., (1990). Affective and continuance commitment to the organizational Evaluation evaluation of measures and analysis of concurrent and time-lagged relations. *Journal of Applied Psychology, 75,* 710–720.

Meyer, J. P., Allen, N. J., & Smith, C. A., (1993). Commitment to organizations and occupations: Extension and test of a three-component conceptualization. *Journal of Applied Psychology, 78,* 538–551.

Meyer, J. P., Stanley, D. J., Herscovitch, L., & Topolnytsky, L., (2002). Affective, continuance, and normative commitment to the organization: A meta-analysis of antecedents, correlates, and consequences. *Journal of Vocational Behavior, 61,* 20–52.

Mitchell, T. R., Holtom, B. C., Lee, T. W., Sablynski, C. J., & Erez, M., (2001). Why people stay: Using job embeddedness to predict voluntary turnover. *Academy of Management Journal, 44,* 1102–1121.

Mor-Barak, M. E., (1995). The meaning of work for older adults seeking employment: The generativity factor. *International Journal of Aging and Human Development, 41,* 325–344.

Morrow, P. C., (1983). Concept redundancy in organizational research: The case of work commitment. *Academy of Management Review, 8,* 486–500.

Mowday, R. T., Steers, R. M., & Porter, L. W., (1979). The measurement of organizational commitment. *Journal of Vocational Behavior, 14,* 224–247.

Muthén, L. K., & Muthén, B. O., (2011). *Mplus user's guide* [Computer software manual]. Los Angeles, CA: Muthén & Muthén.

National Bureau of Statistics of China. (2011, April). *Press release on major figures of the 2010 National Population Census.* Reported on http://www.stats.gov.cn/was40/gjtjj_en_detail.jsp?searchword=census&channelid=9528&record=5

Noordin, F., Williams, T., & Zimmer, C., (2002). Career commitment in collectivist and individualist cultures: A comparative study. *International Journal of Human Resource Management, 13,* 35–54.

Probst, T. M., (2005). Economic stressors. In J. Barling, K. Kelloway, & M. Frone (Eds.), *Handbook of work stress* (pp. 267–297). Thousand Oaks, CA: Sage.

Schmidt, J. A., & Lee, K., (2008). Voluntary retirement and organizational turnover intentions: The differential associations with work and non-work commitment constructs. *Journal of Business and Psychology, 22,* 297–309.

Shultz, K. S., (2003). Bridge employment: Work after retirement. In G. A. Adams & T. A. Beehr, *Retirement: Reasons, processes, and results* (pp. 215–241). New York, NY: Springer.

Shultz, K. S., & Wang, M., (2011). Psychological perspectives on the changing nature of retirement. *The American Psychologist, 66,* 170–179.

Sinclair, R. R., Sears, L. E., Zajack, M., & Probst, T., (2010). A multilevel model of economic stress and employee well-being. In J. Houdmont & S. Leka (Eds.), *Contemporary occupational health psychology: Global perspectives on research and practice* (pp. 1–20). New York, NY: Wiley.

Solinger, O. N., van Olffen, W., & Roe, R. A., (2008). Beyond the three-component model of organizational commitment. *Journal of Applied Psychology, 93,* 70–83.

Szinovacz, M. E., (2003). Contexts and pathways: Retirement as institution, process, and experience. In G. A. Adams & T. A. Beehr (Eds.), *Retirement: Reasons, processes, and results* (pp. 6–52). New York, NY: Springer.

Szinovacz, M. E., DeViney, S., & Davey, A., (2001). Influences of family obligations and relationships on retirement variations by gender, race, and marital status. *Journals of Gerontology: Series B: Psychological Sciences and Social Sciences, 56B,* 20–27.

Tyers, R., & Shi, Q., (2007). Demographic change and policy responses: Implications for the global economy. *World Economy, 30,* 537–566.

Vincent, G. K., & Velkoff, V. A., (2010, May). *The next four decades, the older population in the United States: 2010 to 2050* (Current Population Reports P25-1138). Washington, DC: US. Census Bureau.

von Bonsdorff, M. E., Shultz, K. S., Leskinen, E., & Tansky, J., (2009). The choice between retirement and bridge employment: A continuity theory and life course perspective. *International Journal of Aging and Human Development, 69,* 79–100.

Voydanoff, P., (1990). Economic distress and family relations: A review of the eighties. *Journal of Marriage and the Family, 52,* 1099–1115.

Wanberg, C. R., Kanfer, R., & Rotundo, M., (1999). Unemployed individuals: Motives, job-search competencies, and job-search constraints as predictors of job seeking and reemployment. *Journal of Applied Psychology, 84,* 897–910.

Wang, M., (2007). Profiling retirees in the retirement transition and adjustment process: Examining the longitudinal change patterns of retirees' psychological well-being. *Journal of Applied Psychology, 92,* 455–474.

Wang, M., Henkens, K., & van Solinge, H., (2011). Retirement adjustment: A review of theoretical and empirical advancements. *The American Psychologist, 66,* 204–213.

Wang, M., & Shultz, K., (2010). Employee retirement: A review and recommendations for future investigation. *Journal of Management, 36,* 172–206.

Wang, M., & Zhan, Y., (2012). Employee-organization relationship in older workers. In L. M. Shore, J. A.-M. Coyle-Shapiro, & L. Tetrick (Eds.), *The employee-organization relationship: Applications for the 21st century* (pp. 427–454). New York, NY: Psychology Press.

Wang, M., Zhan, Y., Liu, S., & Shultz, K. S., (2008). Antecedents of bridge employment: A longitudinal investigation. *Journal of Applied Psychology, 93*, 818–830.

Wheaton, F., & Crimmins, E. M., (2012). The demography of aging and retirement. In M. Wang (Ed.), *The Oxford handbook of retirement* (pp. 22–41). Oxford: Oxford University Press.

Xu, L., & Bennington, L. (2008). Xiagang and re-employment policies in Shanghai. *Management Research News, 31*, 976–986.

Zhan, Y., Wang, M., Liu, S., & Shultz, K. S., (2009). Bridge employment and retirees' health: A longitudinal investigation. *Journal of Occupational Health Psychology, 14*, 374–389.

Index

www.routledge.com/9780415520140

Related titles from Routledge

Work and Family Policy
International Comparative Perspectives
Stephen Sweet

Numerous challenges exist in respect to integrating work and family institutions and there is remarkable cross-national variation in the ways that societies respond to these concerns with policy. This volume examines these concerns by focusing on cross-national variation in structural/cultural arrangements. Consistent support is found in respect to the prospects of expanding resources for working families both in the opportunity to provide care, as well as to remain integrated in the workforce. However, the studies in this volume offer qualifiers, explaining why some effects are not as strong as might be hoped and why effects are sometimes restricted to particular classifications of workers or families. It is apparent that, when different societies implement similar policies, they do not necessarily do so with the same intended outcomes, and usage is mediated by how policies are received by employers and workers. The chapters in this book speak to the merits of international comparative analysis in identifying the strategies, challenges and benefits of providing resources to workers and their families.

This book was originally published as a special issue of *Community, Work & Family*.

June 2012: 246 x 174: 152pp
Hb: 978-0-415-52014-0
£85 / $145

For more information and to order a copy visit
www.routledge.com/9780415520140

Available from all good bookshops